The Hell
of the English

The Hell
of the English
Bankruptcy and the Victorian Novel

Barbara Weiss

Lewisburg
Bucknell University Press
London and Toronto: Associated University Presses

Associated University Presses
440 Forsgate Drive
Cranbury, NJ 08512

Associated University Presses
25 Sicilian Avenue
London WC1A 2QH, England

Associated University Presses
2133 Royal Windsor Drive
Unit 1
Mississauga, Ontario
Canada L5J 1K5

The paper used in this publication meets the
requirements of the American National
Standard for Permanence of Paper for Printed
Library Materials Z39.48-1984.

Certain passages, pages 141–45 and 151–52, originally appeared in the author's "Secret Pockets and Secret Breasts: *Little Dorrit* and the Commercial Scandals of the Fifties," *Dickens Studies Annual: Essays on Victorian Fiction* 10:67–76, copyright 1982 by AMS Press, Inc., New York.

Library of Congress Cataloging-in-Publication Data

Weiss, Barbara.
   The hell of the English.

   Bibliography: p.
   Includes index.
   1. English fiction—19th century—History and
criticism.   2. Bankruptcy in literature.   3. Debt in
literature.   4. Economics in literature.   5. Ethics
in literature.   6. Middle classes in literature.
7. Capitalists and financiers in literature.
I. Title.
PR878.B35W45   1986   823'.8'09355   85-48057
ISBN 0-8387-5099-0 (alk. paper)

For Robert, Stephanie,
and Karen.
And for Ruth and Mickey.

Contents

Acknowledgments

I wish to express my gratitude to Martin Meisel of Columbia University, in whose seminar the idea for this book originated and whose suggestions and comments have been invaluable. I am also grateful to John Rosenberg of Columbia for his advice and encouragement. I am indebted as well to the suggestions of Karl Kroeber and the late Stephen Koss of Columbia, and also of Kevin Dougherty of Manhattanville College. Peter Mathias and W. J. Reader in England graciously answered my inquiries and provided some suggestions that were extremely helpful in the research of this book, and Katharine Turok of Associated University Presses was invaluable in smoothing over the rough edges. And, finally, my thanks to the Tate Gallery, London, the Bodleian Library at Oxford, and the Trustees of the British Museum for the use of the photographs in this book.

The Hell
of the English

1

Introduction: The Hell of the English

> The word Hell . . . generally signifies the Infinite Terror,
> the thing a man *is* infinitely afraid of, and shudders and
> shrinks from, struggling with his whole soul to escape from
> it . . . but the Hells of men and Peoples differ notably . . .
> what is it that the modern English soul does, in very truth,
> dread infinitely, and contemplate with entire despair? . . .
> With hesitation, with astonishment, I pronounce it to be:
> the terror of "Not Succeeding"; of not making money, fame,
> or some other figure in the world—chiefly of not making
> money! Is not that a somewhat singular Hell?
>
> Thomas Carlyle, *Past and Present*

In the early and middle years of Queen Victoria's reign, the process of
industrialization had advanced with such dizzying speed that a tumult of
change appeared to be remaking the traditional English world. Whether or
not such change was beneficial was a subject of bitter debate. Such relatively
new phenomena as industrial poverty, urban slums, and the breakdown of
traditional economic morality seemed to many to be an exorbitant price to
pay for industrial progress. In the acrimony over what came to be called
"the Condition of England" no voice was more vociferous or more ominous
than that of Thomas Carlyle, who had the greatest moral and philosophical
influence upon his generation of novelists. Throughout the forties and
fifties, Carlyle thundered that the new industrial wealth of England had
brought only discontent. "All is grown acrid, divisive, threatening dissolution," he charged, "and the huge tumultuous Life of Society is galvanic,
devil-ridden, too truly possessed by a devil."[1] The devil that had taken
possession of England was Mammon, and his sign was what Carlyle called
the "cash-nexus," the reduction of all relationships between men to the level
of cash payment. In this world governed by Mammon and his values,

13

failure to possess money was the thing most dreaded in the innermost soul; according to the "Gospel of Mammonism" the Hell of the English soul was the failure to possess money.

It is small wonder, then, that in the Victorian novel which was emerging at this time as a great new popular and artistic force, economic struggle would become a major theme. With the triumph of realism, nineteenth-century art began to concern itself with humble subjects and the prosaic life of the work-a-day world. For the bourgeois hero of the Victorian novel, earning a living was often the first order of business, and his most trivial economic successes and failures became for the first time acceptable as the material from which literature could be made. Nor is it surprising that the subject of failure should suddenly loom so large in the Victorian novel, for indeed economic failure was a stark fact of life in the Victorian economy. The upheavals of the bewildering new kind of economy had created great opportunities for those who possessed both courage and luck, but industrial capitalism took a heavy toll on those who could not adapt to the new conditions, or on those who had tried their hand and failed. Bravely the Victorians built a Crystal Palace as a monument to their progress and prosperity, and indeed the benefits of industrialism were substantial, but at the same time the swelling Bankruptcy Lists of the *Gazette* were a dark troubling underside to the apparent prosperity of the era. With the prospect of financial ruin all too vivid, then, what more appropriate Hell for the English soul, than the fear of not making money, or, once in possession of money, the dread of losing it.

In dealing with a subject as voluminous as the role of economic failure in the Victorian novel, it has of course been necessary to establish some boundaries. Potentially the ways of failing in the nineteenth-century economy were many and varied; this study will concentrate on only one aspect of such failures. In choosing bankruptcy as a topic, I have been influenced by its dramatic qualities as it is represented in popular fiction and in the imagination of Victorian culture. Bankruptcy is the most spectacular form of economic failure in Victorian society. It is sudden, catastrophic, and final—an acute crisis as opposed, for example, to insolvency, which tends to be a chronic and tedious condition. By focusing on episodes of bankruptcy I have eliminated a whole range of economic failures, including the aristocrat fallen on hard times (until 1861, bankruptcy by definition applied only to "trading" classes), the marginal workers of the lower middle class who hovered on the threshold of debtors' prison, and the very lowest rungs of the nineteenth-century society—the agricultural poor dependent upon the uncertain charity of a parish, and the urban poor described by Mayhew as living in wretched slums or sleeping at night under the bridges of the Thames. I have chosen, instead, to deal with those characters of the middle class who, having possessed a substantial number of assets, suddenly find themselves facing the economic disaster of poverty and the moral dilemma of being unable to meet their financial obligations.

This peculiarly middle-class nightmare of bankruptcy, which surfaces so frequently in the novels of the period, seems to have been a special manifestation of the very universal Victorian fear of poverty and failure—a fear that appears to have had a compelling foundation in reality. Chapter 2 and the Appendix will deal with the statistics of bankruptcy in the early and middle Victorian years; but for the average Victorian there could scarcely have been any need to dwell upon published statistics. Economic failure could hardly fail to touch in one way or another the lives of almost every member of society, if not personally, then through family and acquaintances; the incidence of episodes of economic failure in the lives of Victorian writers alone is staggering. The tragic spectacle of Sir Walter Scott's last wretched years was ominously present for the Victorians, but perhaps more typical of the nineteenth-century writer was a history of early struggle and failure. The story of Dickens's early life—his father's incarceration in debtors' prison and the young Charles's child labor—is too familiar to require recounting here,[2] but the struggles of other artists are perhaps less known.

Thackeray, for example, saw his entire fortune, and that of his stepfather, lost in the failure of a great Indian agency house in 1834; the incident is almost certainly the inspiration for Colonel Newcome's disaster with the Bundelcund Bank in *The Newcomes*. The author lived for more than a decade after in a chronic condition of insolvency. Anthony Trollope had even more painful recollections of such an episode. In 1834 his father was forced to flee to Ostend to avoid his creditors, and Trollope returned home from seeing him off to find in progress that most dreaded of disasters, "the bailiff in the house." Other writers were scarred by similar brushes with bankruptcy and failure. Macaulay struggled to repay the enormous debts left by his father; Tennyson lost his small legacy in the bankruptcy of an unscrupulous business partner.

The experience of bankruptcy was thus only too common an occurrence to the Victorians. Chapter 2 will discuss some of the causes of what seemed to be an enormous rise in bankruptcy during the Victorian years, and the reasons for the great moral stigma attached to it. Throughout the period, the outrage stirred by the issue complicated the attempts of the Victorians to deal with the legal problems of bankruptcy. The great emotional impact of bankruptcy, moreover, would clearly be demonstrated in the frequency with which the fear of financial ruin surfaces in Victorian popular art.

And nowhere does the specter of losing one's fortune occur more obsessively than in that most middle-class of art forms, the popular Victorian novel. The preeminence of money in the Victorian imagination in fact ensures a literature haunted by the fear of bankruptcy. As John Vernon has pointed out, the very idea of money "contains its own lack as a nightmare always ready to surface,"[3] and so it is with the novels examined in this study: Charles Dickens's *Dombey and Son* (1848); Charlotte Brontë's *Shirley* (1849); Elizabeth Gaskell's *North and South* (1855); William Makepeace Thackeray's *The Newcomes* (1855); Dickens's *Little Dorrit* (1857); George Eliot's *The Mill on the Floss* (1860); and Anthony Trollope's *The Way We Live Now* (1875).

All of these novels were published in the early or middle years of Victoria's reign amid the rapidly changing economic conditions that characterized those years. Each has as its focal point an episode involving bankruptcy or the threat of bankruptcy. In selecting these novels, it should be noted, I have not always adhered to a strict legal definition of bankruptcy. In *The Mill on the Floss* George Eliot describes the reaction of Tom Tulliver to the news of his father's loss of fortune: he is faced with "the much dreaded blow of finding that his father must be a bankrupt after all; at least, the creditors must be asked to take less than their due, *which to Tom's untechnical mind was the same thing as bankruptcy*"[4] [emphasis added]. It is in this "untechnical" sense that most of the novels included in this study are novels about bankruptcy. Legally, bankruptcy requires the commission of certain "acts of bankruptcy" (such as suffering one's goods and chattel to be attached) that are followed by a series of legal proceedings extremely complicated and subject to frequent changes during the Victorian period.

Though the legal implications of bankruptcy, discussed in chapter 2, are important to understanding its troubling presence in the national consciousness, in most cases the novels themselves are not concerned with legal detail. Only Mr. Newcome in Thackeray's *The Newcomes* is actually pictured in Bankruptcy Court. Mr. Dombey, in *Dombey and Son,* and Mr. Sedley, in Thackeray's *Vanity Fair,* commit formal acts of bankruptcy, but the ensuing process is not described. Mr. Tulliver in *The Mill on the Floss* does not legally go bankrupt at all; his son is apparently able to come to a private arrangement with the creditors and eventually repays all of his father's debts. Both Mr. Merdle in *Little Dorrit* and Mr. Melmotte in *The Way We Live Now* commit suicide when faced with imminent bankruptcy. (During most of the Victorian period the estate of a deceased bankrupt would have gone into Chancery rather than Bankruptcy Court.) But in each of these cases the character who loses his money seems to think of himself as "a bankrupt" and is regarded as such by other characters. In the popular (and highly untechnical) imagination, any man who had lost his money and could not repay his debts had suffered the stigma and disgrace of bankruptcy.

With the Victorian emphasis upon literary verisimilitude, it was to be expected that episodes of bankruptcy would crop up frequently in the novel. To an even greater extent than other popular artists of the time, the major Victorian novelists began to examine the issue of bankruptcy for its moral ramifications, its impact upon individual personality, upon family life, social relationships, and the welfare of the community. In fact, so deeply does the idea of bankruptcy permeate the novels discussed in this study, that all may be considered, in various ways and to varying degrees, to be "novels of bankruptcy"; that is, the image of bankruptcy has influenced not only the plot, but the language, theme, symbolism, and structure of the novels in question.

In discussing the emergence of bankruptcy as a literary theme and metaphor, it is important to emphasize the inherently dramatic nature of the event itself that uniquely qualifies it for literary purposes. The idea of bankruptcy, after all, implies a catastrophic downfall, a reversal of fortune such as those that have always figured prominently in literature and legends. In a sense many of the novels under consideration here could be regarded as reworkings of the old mythic parables of Fortune's Wheel, and the legends of the downfalls of heroes. Indeed, the idea figures prominently in most of these novels.

The cover design of *Dombey and Son*, for example, planned by Dickens when only a few of the early numbers had been written, offers allegorical scenes at the foot of the design that are meant expressly to illustrate the turning of the Wheel of Fortune. A hopeful youth sets out on one side to seek his fortune with the sun rising before him, as a sturdy Mr. Dombey lightly balances his wealth; on the other side, amid an evening sky, and scenes of shipwreck and storm, the old and battered figure of Dombey is almost crushed by the weight of falling money bags. In the central figures, as well, the allegory is clearly drawn, with Mr. Dombey's fortunes rising from the left upon precariously balanced ledgers, climaxing in the center with Dombey enthroned upon a cash-box, and collapsing on the right in a disintegrating house of cards.[5] The idea of the turning of Fortune's Wheel is also made explicit in Trollope's *The Way We Live Now*, when the ever-hopeful Lady Carbury entitles her novel *The Wheel of Fortune*.

But in one way or another almost all of the novels discussed in these pages offer some kind of variation upon an archetypal pattern of prosperity followed by catastrophe. As in the ancient myths, we are introduced to the protagonist at the height of his prosperity (or just slightly previous to the height) and are told of the deeds he has accomplished to achieve his lofty position. The core of the story is usually some rash act by the hero, some provocation of the gods, or simply some mysterious working out of his destiny by the fates, which sends him plunging from the height of his good fortune. Such tragic falls from happiness to despair, from prosperity to adversity, and from power to impotence, have long been the stuff of which literature is made.

The old mythic patterns take on a new resonance, however, when set against the unique economic conditions of the nineteenth century. In the world of Victorian capitalism the individual suddenly became vulnerable as never before to the vicissitudes of the economy. In this harsh new reality it was probably inevitable that in literary reworkings of the myth of the hero's

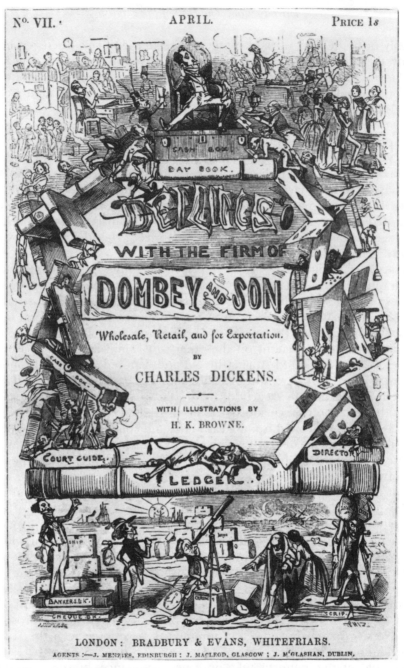

Cover design for *Dombey and Son*. Arch AA. d105 T/P (no. 7 April) Bodleian Library, Oxford, England.

fall, a loss of money would be the *peripeteia* around which the fortunes of the hero revolve. Thus novel after novel portrays the archetypal rise and fall in terms of financial prosperity, with bankruptcy or the threat of bankruptcy as the climax toward which the novel builds and from which it descends; and all of the novels to be discussed within these pages are thus novels of bankruptcy in the sense that, whatever other themes and motifs they may contain, they are designed from the very beginning to lead us to the downfall of the protagonist through the specific agency of bankruptcy.

In an age in which the underlying certainties of man's existence were slipping away with alarming rapidity, a novel focused in this way upon an episode of bankruptcy can not help but suggest something of mutability and change, something of the uncertain condition of man's existence. We have been used to thinking of the nineteenth century as an age of "materialism," but in fact the material quality of life in these novels turns out to be an illusion. Just as money is moving from a solid foundation of land or gold to a mere abstraction of paper, so the solid middle-class reality that money can buy proves in these novels to be unreliable. The dense material comfort of bourgeois lives can evaporate in the same way that money does, leaving behind (as in the Tullivers' parlor after their goods have been auctioned) only the outlines of where the material objects once stood. The Tullivers' dilemma demonstrates the great paradox of the age that prides itself on its increasing mastery of the material world—only to find the material taking its revenge upon the human spirit.

This triumph of the material world that is everywhere apparent in the Victorian novel was later described by Georg Simmel as "objectivism," "the power inherent in things, especially mechanical things, and processes, and systems, all brought, in Simmel's view, to a high peak of development in the capitalist system."[6] Marx, too, contended that human relationships in the nineteenth century had come to be dominated by the pursuit of monetary gains as an end to itself, alienating the individual from the community and enslaving him to an impersonal and merciless economy. Marx's theories are nowhere more relevant to a study of the Victorian novels of bankruptcy than in his theory of "crises," for it is in crisis that the relationship of the individual to the system is most dramatically tested. Marx predicted that the internal contradictions of the capitalist system would lead to periodically recurring crises and depressions, crises caused not by the mistakes committed by individual capitalists, but by the inevitable results of the normal activity of capital. The capitalist himself would become, in Marx's view, a victim of forces well beyond his own power to control.

The prevailing economic theory of the Victorian years would of course run counter to Marx. Failure was considered by the Victorians to be the result of inefficiency or even lack of virtue on the part of the individual, and the novelists of the period for the most part did not directly challenge that view. But the public rhetoric in many ways did not match the underlying economic realities of the age. The Victorian legislators would discover when they attempted to enact bankruptcy reform (described in chapter 2) that despite all the public outrage vented on bankrupts, it would in the end be necessary to make some provision for the alarmingly numerous failures of capitalism. Similarly, the novelists, while paying lip service to the moral stigma of bankruptcy, would come increasingly to sympathize with the hapless individual crushed by an implacable economic system.

Thus in many of these novels, the economic vulnerability of the individual, devastating enough on its own terms, in turn implies the even more terrifying peril of the human soul threatened by a harsh and incomprehensible world. Bankruptcy emerges as the perfect structural metaphor for the vulnerability of the individual in *The Mill on the Floss* and other novels of the time. The specific working out of the theme could vary, of course, from author to author, or even within the work of one author, from novel to novel. In the early years of the Victorian period there is certainly an admiration for the energy of the industrial revolution as well as a distrust of its consequences. Such early heroes as Robert Moore in *Shirley* and Mr. Thornton in *North and South* are allowed to emerge from the spiritual purgatory of bankruptcy with their souls freed from the stain of the "cash-nexus." Guided by a new moral imperative, they return to the challenge of the industrial marketplace determined to harness its formidable energies. But later economic developments of the Victorian period, particularly the appearance of limited liability and the development of the corporation, along with what seemed to be an increase in corruption and speculation, seem to have darkened the novelists' outlook. Increasingly, Victorian writers would have agreed with Marx that economic crises (public or individual in nature) "put on its trial, each time more threateningly, the existence of the entire bourgeois society."[7]

This grim perception on the part of Dickens, Thackeray, and Trollope, would emerge, of course, out of Christian rather than Marxist theology. But as the years of the Victorian era progressed, bringing always new economic vicissitudes and an ever-stronger grip of materialism, the novelists' vision of a world threatened by social dislocation came to resemble strikingly Marx's concept of alienation.

Increasingly the novelists saw bankruptcy as a symptom of social disintegration, of a world that was losing its sustaining ties of community, stability, and order. The themes of alienation and breakdown of community were of course not unique to the Victorians or to the novel. They were present in the writings of Coleridge, Southey, Carlyle, and Ruskin in England, and Chateaubriand, Balzac, Stendhal, Nietzsche, and Wagner on the Continent.[8] But the Victorian novelists were able through the specific image of bankruptcy to depict with great vividness the possibilities for social dissolution and apocalypse inherent in nineteenth-century industrialism and portrayed so dramatically in such later works as *Little Dorrit* and *The Way We Live Now.*

It is interesting to note of these latter two novels that the fate of their financiers is not only bankruptcy but *suicide*, especially in the light of Emile Durkheim's theories concerning the increase of suicide in "anomic" societies. On the surface, of course, the deaths of Dickens's Merdle and Trollope's Melmotte are simply a stage convention, the necessity for the villain to pay for his crimes at the end of the melodrama. But as Durkheim observed in *Suicide*, "The victim's acts which at first seem to express only his personal temperament are really the supplement and prolongation of a social condition they express externally."[9]

Durkheim had noted that suicide rates were rising among the non-religious and the followers of nonauthoritarian religions, among the non-agricultural, and among the urban industrial workers, and concluded that the increase of suicide was due to the growth of individualism and the resulting loss of ties to the community. But Durkheim also clearly saw that this sense of dislocation had at its basis an economic cause. Suicide rates increased in times of economic depression, he found, but also in times of marked economic prosperity; each had a disruptive effect upon the customary values and traditions of life. Wealth, Durkheim wrote, "deceives us into believing that we depend upon ourselves alone. Reducing the resistance we encounter from objects, it suggests the possibility of unlimited success against them. The less limited one feels, the more intolerable all limitations appear."[10] When a crisis occurs, the individual is thrown back upon himself and suffers from "anomie"; that is, his needs cannot be met by his means. What is true of an individual, moreover, is equally true of the capitalist society as a whole. When the division of labor has outstripped the development of moral regulation, when one class has to coerce the other into labor, the economy is in a state of "anomie" that will inevitably lead to crisis.[11]

Durkheim contended that economic crisis went hand in hand with a broader social dislocation. The material improvement of life led, not to greater contentment and harmony, but to greater disillusionment as social needs and expectations rapidly exceeded social means. Urbanism and industrialism had fragmented the social bonds that normally tied men to one another. The rising rate of suicide, in Durkheim's words, marked "the relaxation of social bonds, a sort of collective asthenia, or social malaise . . . a state of crisis and perturbation not to be prolonged with impunity."[12]

The social dislocation portrayed by Dickens in *Little Dorrit* and by Trollope in *The Way We Live Now* is strikingly similar to Simmel's, Marx's, and Durkheim's vision although, again, it is naturally expressed in language and images more Christian than sociological. The Victorian era is portrayed in the pages of these novels as existing in a state of moral crisis and social disintegration. And a bankruptcy that shakes society to its foundations is the perfect representation of this shattered structure. What Simmel described as "objectivism," what Marx called "alienation," what Durkheim termed "anomie," the Victorian writers portrayed metaphorically in their novels as "bankruptcy"—a great social and spiritual void or apocalypse lurking ominously beneath the seeming prosperity of the Victorian years and threatening to engulf society with its dislocations and contradictions.

The development of the metaphor of bankruptcy is a fascinating history of the Victorian literary imagination in the era in which the modern form of corporate capitalism was beginning to emerge. The novels about bankruptcy discussed in the following pages could perhaps only have been written at such a transitional moment of history. Certainly there are no novels of bankruptcy being written today; it is difficult to imagine a major contemporary work of fiction that would rise and fall with the business fortunes of its characters. It may well be that the coming of limited liability and the modern corporation have changed our perceptions about the role of the individual in economic enterprise; the modern novel, one suspects, would be far more likely to portray economic activity in terms of murky corporate maneuvers than to focus upon the precarious efforts of the individual man or woman of business. Perhaps we are more at home with the perils of industrial capitalism, or more fatalistic about them. Or perhaps we are simply more cynical about ambition, success, and the value of "getting on" in the world. We have constructed more elaborate hells for ourselves than that of economic failure; that which we dread infinitely has become more complex than bankruptcy. But the world that so bewildered the Victorians is the forerunner of our own—indeed, their very Hell foreshadows ours, and it is therefore instructive to examine through the pages of the great novels of the period the Victorians' struggle to understand their world and its emerging terrors.

2

The Reality of Bankruptcy

The great fear of economic failure that appears to have haunted the imagination of the Victorians was solidly grounded in reality. There is little doubt that the emergence of industrialization greatly increased the amount of risk involved in economic activity, and many factors combined to make the threat of failure both more likely and more terrifying than ever before. Moreover, the extremely high rate of bankruptcy was not only a troubling economic question but a deeply painful dilemma of public morality as well. Throughout the Victorian era, the question of what to do about appalling statistics of bankruptcy provoked the most bitter debate concerning the proper moral attitude toward bankruptcy, and the proper legal measures to be adopted. Indeed the recurring controversies of the bankruptcy question seem to have brought to light some of the most painful and contradictory problems inherent in this era of phenomenal industrial progress.

THE HIGH INCIDENCE OF FAILURE

As Peter Mathias has pointed out, the state in England played only a very minor role in industrialization. Unlike Russia after the revolution, or some modern nations that have attempted to industrialize abruptly, the government of England neither encouraged nor financed industrial development.[1] Individual entrepreneurs bore the cost of industrialization with almost no help from government revenues, and with no form of social services or support in the case of failure. Furthermore, the practice of unlimited liability, which ensured that a man was responsible for the debts of an enterprise in which he had a share "to his last shilling and his last acre," meant that the failure of a business could be ruinous. While many profited from the whirlwind of economic growth that seized England in the eighteenth and nineteenth centuries, many of the would-be entrepreneurs fell victim to the very conditions that had spurred their ambition. As small mills became huge factories, and modest partnerships turned into large stockholding companies, many traditional, family-managed enterprises were devoured in the process,[2] while newer enterprises often turned out to be too weak to withstand the vicissitudes of nineteenth-century capitalism. H. Heaton has stated that for many men, "while death and taxes alone were inevitable, bankruptcy was probable."[3]

The incidence of bankruptcy rose and fell during the eighteenth and nineteenth centuries, but just how many individuals were actually plunged into ruin is not an easy matter to assess. Historians have tended to examine in great detail the broad trends of capital and production, without overmuch concern for the fate of the individual capitalist. And even among those writers who address the question of personal bankruptcy, there is some disagreement. E. J. Hobsbawm, for example, has stated that "the very horror of bankruptcy is itself a symptom of its comparative rarity." (His statistics, however, relate primarily to the very late years of the Victorian age, and to the Edwardian years.)[4] Most commentators are in general agreement that there was overall a sharp increase in bankruptcy from the middle of the eighteenth century to the later Victorian period. Bankruptcy tended to be less severe during periods of prosperity, and to rise with every depression or commercial crisis.[5] Often, however, bankruptcy was extremely high during boom periods as well, in part because the weakest enterprises were not able to compete for resources and markets at such times, and in part because boom periods tended by their nature to encourage marginal projects predestined for failure.[6] Even the strongest enterprises found themselves vulnerable to the fluctuations of the economy caused by external circumstances such as the outbreak of war, crop failures, depressions in foreign trade, the availability of credit, and panics in the money market.

Industrialization and technological changes involved risks of an altogether new kind. The costs of manufacture that had previously been variable—raw material and labor—would increasingly have to be sunk into fixed plant. The flexibility of the older system had given the entrepreneur certain options; in time of depression he had been able to halt production at little cost, biding his time until conditions were more favorable. Now, according to David Landes, "he was to be a prisoner of his investment."[7] Nor was manufacturing the only form of business affected by the need for a larger outlay of capital. In his *Sketches by Boz* Dickens noted the process by which shopkeepers were forced by the presence of competition into a ruinous expansion:

> Six or eight years ago, the epidemic began to display itself among the linen-drapers and haberdashers. The primary symptoms were an inordinate love of plate-glass, and a passion for gaslights and gilding. The

disease gradually progressed, and at last attained a fearful height. Quiet dusty shops in different parts of town were pulled down . . . doors knocked into windows; a dozen squares of glass into one; one shopman into a dozen; and there is no knowing what would have been done, if it had not been fortunately discovered, just in time, that the Commissioners of Bankruptcy were as competent to decide such cases as the Commissioners of Lunacy, and that a little confinement and gentle examination did wonders.[8]

Dickens's tone in this sketch is highly satirical; in later years his works would exhibit greater sympathy for the victims of economic expansion and the "disease" of speculation.

The nineteenth-century entrepreneur was nowhere so vulnerable as in the waves of speculation that repeatedly seized the Victorian public. (Chapter 7 will deal with this phenomenon in greater detail.) The railway mania of the 1840s was only the first of a series of booms in which thousands invested money in precarious "bubble" ventures, only to see their savings wiped out during the ensuing panic. According to Leland Jenks, the railway revolution was not financed out of accumulated wealth, but chiefly by people who had invested beyond their means: "They carried consols to the bank, to secure loans to make initial payments upon railway shares, and pledged those shares anew to start the purchase of more. And it was a characteristic of the railway banker and broker to pyramid loans in this fashion."[9] When the collapse of the railway shares finally occurred in 1847, concurrently with agricultural failures, it undermined the entire economy. More than twenty major, long-established firms failed in one month, including that of a former governor of the Bank of England. The enormity of the situation was noted in Parliament when Disraeli, addressing the House of Commons on 30 August 1848 spoke of "a commercial crisis, perhaps of unprecedented severity. There were uprootings of commercial dynasties in England not less striking than the fall of those political houses of which we have lately heard so much. Day after day, gentlemen whom we had lived with in this house, and whom we had respected and regarded, merchants of the highest European reputation, were during that crisis rudely torn, . . . from these benches, if not with disgrace and dishonour, yet with circumstances of pitiable vicissitudes seldom equalled."[10]

The panic of 1847–48 was prophetic of the excesses of speculation and the consequent crises that were periodically to shake the Victorian economy. These recurring waves of panic and failure were produced in part because the credit system of the period was extremely vulnerable. The investment required for industrial development was financed primarily by a system of credit that served as quasi-capital. Banks customarily allowed revolving credit, or even standing overdrafts, which became, in effect, short-term loans.[11] In addition to such loans, a national network of easily available credit evolved through the use of bills of exchange. The commercial bill was a promise of future payment based usually upon dock-warrants or warehouse receipts. It could be passed on from one creditor to another, each one endorsing it, and thus by the forties the bill of exchange had become a sort of substitute currency among ordinary business men. Jenks estimates that in 1840 the leading London banks alone paid bills of exchange amounting to more than one billion pounds.[12] By the middle of the century the circulation of bills was far greater than the circulation of all bank notes.[13]

An even less secure form of credit was the accommodation bill. Unlike the bill of exchange, which at least had its origin in a commercial transaction, with an accommodation bill the acceptor received no collateral at all for what was basically a promissory note. Because of the enormous circulation of such bills, the most powerful institutions in the money market were the bill-brokers, who purchased bills from those anxious for immediate funds and sold them to bankers and other creditors. Overend, Gurney and Company was the largest of these firms, a sort of gigantic, respectable usurer, doing about 64 million pounds in business each year,[14] and its failure in the panic of 1866 sent shock waves throughout the financial community. The dangers of using commercial bills as currency became quite apparent during such crises, for the failure of one or two large acceptors of bills would force creditors to call in other bills, and thus set up a domino effect, in which many businesses would fail. In addition, there were many country traders and country banks that depended upon London houses, and that used London bills in their transactions; thus a fluctuation in the London money market could set off "a chain reaction of failures" throughout England.[15]

Thus there were many factors that made economic survival a precarious affair in the Victorian period and resulted in an enormous rise in personal bankruptcy. Exact statistics, however, are not easy to come by, and are often contradictory, or influenced by external circumstances such as changes in the bankruptcy law. (For a more detailed discussion of the difficulties in establishing accurate statistics for nineteenth-century bankruptcies, see the Appendix.) In spite of the difficulty of interpreting such flawed statistics, however, it seems apparent that cases of bankruptcy increased tremendously during the early years of industrialization. (Although these were also years of population growth, the percentage of increase in bankruptcy far outstripped the growth of population.)[16] The figures seem to indicate a major increase in bankruptcy during the eighteenth century (the figures rise from 200 bankruptcies a year in the 1730s to about 1,000 a year by the first quarter of the nineteenth century) and a pretty steady rate of bankruptcy for the first fifty years of the nineteenth century (between 1,000 and 1,500 bankruptcies a year). (See Appendix, Tables 1, 2, and 3.) During the same period the number of insolvent debtors (that is, debtors not involved with trade, or those who owed sums too small to be handled in Bankruptcy

Court) rose from 1,000 a year to 5,000 a year, and then fell again in the 1840s as laws were passed to relieve the insolvent debtor.

What the statistics do not show is the enormous increase in private arrangements (in which creditors accepted a settlement of less than twenty shillings in the pound) such as liquidation, inspectorships, and compositions with creditors, all of which were handled outside the machinery of Bankruptcy Court in the first half of the century. There is no way to gauge the numbers of such arrangements with any certainty, but appearing before a Parliamentary Commission in 1851, William Hawes, a prominent manufacturer influential in the creation of new bankruptcy laws, testified that deeds of composition and assignment amounted to *ten times* the number of official bankruptcies.[17] (See Appendix, Table 4.)

A slight drop in the statistics may be noted after 1849, when a new reform bill made the process of bankruptcy somewhat more difficult. During the 1850s, however, the number of official bankruptcies seems to have risen to its former level, slightly over 1,000 a year. (See Appendix, Table 5.) The Reform Act of 1861 did away with the Insolvent Debtors' Court, and brought all insolvents under the same machinery as bankrupts. It also allowed for the formal registration of previously private arrangements. The statistics for the first year after the new law show that there was a giant leap to 9,663 bankruptcies (a figure that would include all of those who would previously have been insolvent debtors) and 2,651 arrangements, compositions, and deeds of inspectorship, making a total of 12,304 failures that came within the jurisdiction of Bankruptcy Court (see Appendix, Table 6). These figures continued to rise throughout the sixties until 1869, when a total of 15,064 people took refuge in bankruptcy proceedings or some arrangement within the purview of the court. Another new law in 1869 created a separate machinery for dealing with debtors whose assets were too small even to pay the costs of adjudication, and thus reduced the figures by about two-thirds, but throughout the seventies the figures again rose until they had almost doubled. (See Appendix, Table 7.)

Thus even the most cursory look at the statistics of bankruptcy, flawed as such statistics may be by confusion, error, and changes in the laws, will show that bankruptcy had increased, and continued to increase alarmingly in the early and middle years of Queen Victoria's reign. Such statistics, however, do not reveal the whole picture. Statistics from the Court of Bankruptcy measure personal bankruptcy only, and do not reflect the bankruptcies of partnerships, or the winding-up of joint-stock companies, both of which would be handled by other procedures. Neither do they include many occupations that were not classified as "traders," and therefore until 1861 came under the jurisdiction of the laws for insolvent debtors rather than bankruptcy laws. The high incidence of failure among farmers, for example, would not appear at all in bankruptcy statistics. In addition, the statistics ignore the large number of failures in which the creditors

declined to spend the time, effort, and money necessary to bring the
bankrupt to court, believing that there would not be enough assets to make
such an effort worthwhile. There can never be an accurate measure of such
failures, but many commentators have testified to their belief that such
instances were extremely common.

What is important for the purposes of this study is to establish not the
exact number of failures in the Victorian economy, but rather the perceptions of the Victorians themselves concerning these failures. There is every
evidence that contemporary Victorians viewed bankruptcy as a problem of
such alarming proportions that it seemed to them to be undermining the
prosperity and stability of their country. As early as 1819 the *Pamphleteer* was
declaring with indignation that insolvency had become "as familiar as if it
were necessarily a branch of commerce, and inseparably connected with
the intercourse of engagements of mercantile pursuits."[18] In 1831 a tradesman named Thomas Foster published "A Letter Addressed to the Right
Hon. The Earl Gray, First Lord of His Majesty's Treasury On the Subject of
Our Commercial Laws In So Far As They Relate to Bankrupts and Insolvents," in which he states "That the affairs of these realms are and have
been for some time in an unhealthy state . . ."[19] Foster claims that the
commercial distress is due to the bad debts and habits of speculation, made
worse by permissive bankruptcy laws, which

> fixed an intolerable burthen upon and paralysed the industry and exer-
> tions of the Nation; undermining and destroying the integrity and virtue
> of the people. This burthen, I calculate, is now become more, in its
> amount, than the interest of the National Debt—much more ruinous to
> this commercial Empire than the whole of the national expenditure;—
> nay, than that added to the poor-rates and tithes—grievous as the three
> together may be found.[20]

By the 1840s, Parliamentary commissions had estimated the annual loss
by insolvency at about £50,000,000, and the *Westminster Review* refers in
1846 to "this gigantic sum" which (along with permissive laws which encourage insolvency) have "robbed the middle classes of their due and fair rate of
profit."[21] *Banker's Magazine* accepts the same estimate of annual loss in 1849
and claims that such debt creates a hidden cost for the nation: "This sum is
mainly lost, spent, or squandered by the careless, improvident, and reckless
tradesman. It is all repaid to those merchants, manufacturers, and traders
who first bear the loss by the consumer. It forms a given percentage added
to the cost of every article produced, and is paid by the prudent, the
careful, and the industrious classes."[22] In the same year the *Times* of
London also spoke of this hidden cost of bankruptcy: "the amount of
indirect taxation levied upon the public . . . is about equal to the amount of
indirect taxation demanded annually by the Chancellor of the Exchequer.
Every head of a family in the three kingdoms contributes as his quota to the

bankrupt interest pretty nearly as much as he pays to the Customs, Excise, Stamps, etc."[23] In Parliament, ominous proclamations about the terrifying proportions of the bankruptcy problem were heard regularly. Speaking in 1864, one gentleman declared that "the transactions governed by the Bankrupt Act, had attained an amount so marvelous as scarcely to be measured by figures . . ." and that the annual loss to insolvency was "a sum approaching the yearly expenditure of the nation."[24] In spite of the constant attention of Parliamentary commissions, and constant changes in bankruptcy law, the problem of huge sums of money lost in bankruptcy seems to have remained unabated throughout the middle of the Victorian years. As late as 1879, *Fraser's Magazine* was still complaining of this "prodigious loss to the community every year."[25]

BANKRUPTCY AS A PROBLEM OF MORALITY

The perplexity and anger of Victorian commentators concerning the problem of bankruptcy, however, cannot be explained merely by the size of such monetary losses. Debates among Victorians concerning what actions to take about bankruptcy reform reveal some of the most dramatic contradictions that lay beneath the apparent surface of Victorian unity and prosperity. Jerome Buckley has described some of the common perceptions about Victorians: they were "crass materialists, wholly absorbed in the present . . . but they were also excessively religious, lamentably idealistic, nostalgic for the past, and ready to forgo present delights for the vision of the world beyond. . . . they were besides, at once sentimental humanitarians and hard-boiled proponents of free enterprise."[26] Nowhere do our received notions of Victorian character ring as true as in the confusion and contradictions of the Victorian debate over bankruptcy reform, in which moral condemnation and self-righteousness on the one hand were opposed by a combination of earnest reformism and hard-headed pragmatism. The problem of bankruptcy was deeply disturbing to the Victorian sensibility precisely because it unearthed such painful contradictions.

There is no denying the sincerity of the Victorians' moral outrage toward bankruptcy. In order to appreciate the depth of such outrage, it is necessary to understand the way in which widespread bankruptcy challenged the Victorians' most cherished ideas about economic virtue. Such ideas were firmly entrenched in the period, having been established by the new priorities created by the industrial revolution. It is beyond the scope of this study to enter into the long-standing disputes concerning the cause-and-effect relationship between Protestanism and the rise of capitalism. It is sufficient for our purposes to note that the growth of a market economy clearly went hand in hand with the evolution of a moral and religious ethos that stressed such virtues as hard work, thrift, and accumulation of wealth as intrinsic goods to be sought for their own sake.[27] The necessity for urging such virtues as thrift and hard work upon a population undergoing industrialization is clear. Mathias states that "On the part of the business man they gave the chance for ploughing back profits in investment for expansion, for the working family they brought the chance of security for bad times. The lack of either quality could ruin a family as easily as a business. Both attitudes were significant of a period when the state did very little to help either industrial progress or its social casualties."[28]

Thus the new demands of an industrial economy fostered a set of economic virtues that would favor economic growth and stability. (And the implied corollary was clear: if virtue and hard work led to success, then failure was necessarily caused by a lack of virtue.) The need for such prudential virtues as thrift and hard work can be seen clearly in Hogarth's eighteenth-century series of prints chronicling the lives of the idle apprentice and the industrious apprentice. The moral of this series was not lost upon the popular writers of the Victorian period. Dickens, for example, based *David Copperfield* upon the contrasting fates of the industrious David and the idle Steerforth.[29] (As noted by J. R. Harvey, David "wins, not once but twice, the industrious apprentice's traditional reward, his master's daughter's hand.")[30]

The gospel of work, which would seem to be negated by widespread bankruptcy, was proclaimed insistently throughout the period. One of its earliest and most eloquent proponents in the Victorian era was Carlyle, who wrote in *Past and Present,* "Genuine WORK alone, what thou workest faithfully, that is eternal."[31] No one had a greater influence on his generation than Carlyle, particularly among the writers of his time, and no dogma of his was more universally accepted than this insistence that work alone ennobled the soul. (Mrs. Gaskell, for example, often quoted Carlyle's *Sartor Resartus* on the value of work.)[32] Nonconformist and evangelical doctrine were quick to espouse this philosophy, perceiving that such virtues as energy, prudence, and thrift would be of prime importance for the survival and success of all classes in an industrial economy. The bourgeois virtues were preached in Sunday schools and pulpits, and were adopted for working-class audiences by Chartist orators and newspapers, trade unions, and friendly societies.[33]

Of all the enthusiasts for the gospel of work, none was more successful or more representative than Samuel Smiles, whose book *Self-Help* sold nearly a quarter of a million copies in the nineteenth century. *Self-Help* was not published until 1859, but in fact it reflected a wave of "success" literature which had been popular on both sides of the Atlantic for many years.[34] The book consisted of a series of capsule biographies designed to inspire the reader with the belief that industry and prudence would invariably lead to success. Smiles took his examples from a wide range of luminaries in the arts, the sciences, and the military, but his quintessential subjects are those men such as Josiah Wedgewood who rose to eminence in industry. Smiles's championship of the economic virtues of energy and frugality is expanded upon in a later work, *Thrift* (1875), in which he begins the first chapter with an epigraph from Carlyle: "Not what I have, but what I do, is my kingdom." It should be noted here that Smiles's emphasis was not upon accumulation of money for its own sake, or for the sake of ostentatious display—indeed, he preached vigorously against greed and selfishness; rather, as implied by the quotation from Carlyle, Smiles regards success in business as a badge of meritorious character that would contribute to the general social good. ("Every thrifty person may be regarded as a public benefactor, and every thriftless person as a public enemy.")[35]

This emphasis, however, upon success as a reward for virtue seems by implication to suggest that failure must in turn be due to moral inadequacies and does much to explain the great moral stigma which was associated with bankruptcy. In his preface to the 1866 edition of *Self-Help*, Smiles defended his neglect of the subject of failure: "As for failure, per se, . . . readers do not care to know about the general who lost his battles, . . . the merchant who could not keep out of the *Gazette*."[36] In his chapter on "Men of Business," Smiles is quite explicit about the moral implication of an economic failure: "Those who fail in life are, however, very apt to assume a tone of injured innocence, and conclude too hastily that everybody excepting themselves has had a hand in their personal misfortune . . . It will often be found that men who are constantly lamenting their luck are in some way or other reaping the consequences of their own neglect, mismanagement, improvidence, or want of application."[37] Smiles expanded upon this wisdom in *Thrift*:

Industry enables the poorest man to achieve honour, if not distinction.(19)

Competence and comfort lie within the reach of most people. (23)

There is no reason why the highly paid workman of today may not save a store of capital. It is merely a matter of self-denial and private economy . . . it depends upon the workman himself whether he will save his capital or waste it. (24)

Comparatively few people can be rich, but most have it in their power to acquire by industry and economy, sufficient to meet their personal wants. . . . It is not, however, the want of opportunity, but the want of will, that stands in the way of economy. . . . The majority prefer the enjoyment of pleasure to the practice of self-denial. With the mass of men the animal is paramount. (27)

The implications of such a message are clear. If every man can succeed by self-help, by industry, frugality, and the subjugation of his "animal" nature, then clearly failure and poverty become moral weaknesses. In the confusions and uncertainties of bewildering new economic conditions, Smiles's philosophy must have been a welcome haven of simplicity, as well as a clear challenge to ambition.

One of the most interesting aspects of Smiles's writing is his insistence upon the commercial aspect of the idea of "honour." Like many of his contemporaries, Smiles links the economic virtues of his own age with an older code of chivalric and aristocratic virtues. The system of credit so vital to ordinary business functions is, according to the author, "based upon the principles of honour," and the trust with which merchants confide in distant agents, "often consigning vast wealth to persons, recommended only by their character . . . is probably the finest act of homage which men can render to one another."[38]

This attempt to ennoble economic dealings by linking them with earlier forms of chivalry is characteristically Victorian. In her novel *Marian Withers* (1851) Geraldine Jewsbury writes approvingly of a character threatened with ruin: "Credit meant to the cotton manufacturer what the idea of honour did to the aristocrat; no old Castilian noble ever felt more jealous of the honour of his house than did John Withers of his commercial credit."[39] In the same year that *Marian Withers* appeared, the *Economist* ran a series of leading articles which celebrated the moral progress of the Victorian era. It claimed, among other reasons for congratulation, that the "tone of morality" had improved in the last generation; as proof it cited the fact that "debt, which used to be considered as an indispensable characteristic of the man of fashion, is now almost everywhere scouted as disreputable. . . ."[40]

In an older time, men proved their honor by fighting duels; by the time of Queen Victoria, at least among those men of business who valued mercantile honor and respectability, the "gentleman" seems to have been one who paid his debts. Thus in many of the novels that will be discussed in this study, the hero feels obligated by his personal sense of honor to make enormous sacrifices to repay his debts, or even those of his father. Respectable men of business like Dickens's Mr. Dombey and Arthur Clennam and Thackeray's Colonel Newcome willingly beggar themselves in order to return to their creditors as many shillings in the pound as possible.

By such stringent standards of commercial honor, one of the true Victorian heroes was Sir Walter Scott. Smiles recounts the story of Scott's bankruptcy as one of his examples of commercial honor in *Thrift:* "Though the debts had been contracted by others, he had made himself legally responsible for them; and strong in his principle of integrity, he determined, if he could, to pay them off to the last farthing."[41] Although his creditors were willing to accept a composition (that is, to take less than twenty shillings in the pound), Scott felt "what every sensitive nature must feel, that poverty is a much lighter burden to bear than debt."[42] Smiles portrays Scott in his last years, exhausted and partially paralyzed by his burdens, but compelled by the principles of honor to keep working.

The tale of Scott's wretched end was an all too familiar one to his age. Because the Bubble Act of 1720 had forbidden the formation of corporations except by express Parliamentary charter, most businesses before the 1850s operated under the principle of *un*limited liability; that is, any investment in an enterprise, even of a small amount, made the investor responsible to the full extent of his own assets for the debts of a company. Thus the failure of a company could be the ruin of its shareholders, no matter how small their part in its capital or its daily operation.[43] The rule of unlimited liability, with its guarantee that each man would be responsible for the debts of his enterprise "to the last shilling and the last acre," was commonly considered to be the very cornerstone of English commerce, but it presented some grave handicaps in the raising of investment capital, and by the 1850s there was a determined effort to change the law. The debate over limited liability (or limited partnerships in which an investor would be liable only to the extent of his original investment) was vociferously argued in Parliament and in contemporary journals. It was declared that limited liability would endanger the reputation of British merchants because they would no longer be expected to stand behind their engagements.[44] Great fear was expressed in Parliament that limited liability would impair the credit of the country. It was claimed that "the principle of unlimited liability was founded upon an unalterable rule of national justice, viz., that a man who shared in the profits of a concern should bear its losses."[45] Another speaker insisted that "what was necessary in this country was, that the man with the money should be responsible for the character of the business, and they ought never to do away with that which fixed in the right quarter the amount of censure which, to a certain degree attached to the man that failed in business."[46]

One of the great fears concerning limited liability was that it would allow the unchecked growth of stock companies, and consequently encourage speculation. This is a subject that will be examined in some detail in chapter 7, which will deal with economic developments in the middle years of the Victorian period. For the moment it will be sufficient to note that every discussion of debt and bankruptcy in the nineteenth century includes a condemnation of reckless overtrading and speculation. To speculate necessarily involved the risk of capital that one could not guarantee could be repaid, and therefore such an act was considered to be the first step on the road to bankruptcy, and a misdemeanor equal to bankruptcy itself. The *Westminster Review* preached sternly to that effect: "No man is justified in speculating beyond the limit of his ability easily to bear the loss. If a man . . . involve the property of his neighbors, he becomes an offender, and is punishment worthy."[47]

In Parliament, in leading newspapers and journals, Victorians urged the strictest standards of commercial morality. To pass more lenient laws of bankruptcy, "to destroy trade and commerce, by making it lawful to willingly break the most solemn engagements, was to subvert no small part of the national morality."[48] Honor in commercial dealings was considered the foundation of England's greatness as a trading nation, and this concept of honor was severely threatened by the scandal of bankruptcy. The bankrupt who had accepted money which did not belong to him and which he was not able to repay, was often compared to a thief, with the proviso that "the act of theft is completed at once, not so the debt. . . ."[49] A parliamentary speaker declared that bankrupts "were no better than thieves, and should be treated accordingly."[50] In an editorial in 1840, the *Times* declared that "*Prima facie* the man who fails to pay a debt due from him is not to be regarded as blameless. He has, at all events broken a promise . . . there is a just presumption of misconduct. To that extent default is fault."[51] The editorial reports the testimony of witnesses before the Parliamentary Commission of 1840. J. H. Elliott, for example, is reported to have stated unequivocally that:

> The causes which produce insolvency are negligence, extravagance, speculation, and dishonesty . . . it thus appears that the *unfortunate* insolvents, if by that term be understood persons who become so by causes beyond their own control are so few as hardly to bear any assignable proportion to the whole body of debtors.
> Another officer states: "Many insolvencies are produced by tradesmen's indolence. They keep no books, or at least imperfect ones, which they never balance; they never take stock, they employ servants, if their trade be extensive, whom they are too indolent to supervise; and then become insolvent.[52]

(The same portion of testimony is also reported and endorsed by John Stuart Mill in his *Principles of Political Economy*.)[53]

In addition to this unfortunate propensity to carelessness and indolence, the bankrupt was often accused of exhibiting deliberate dishonesty. The ways of defrauding one's creditors were apparently numerous: one could declare bankruptcy with the deliberate intention of evading debts; one could make a gift of all of one's assets to a son-in-law or some other confederate and then declare bankruptcy; one could conspire with one creditor to defraud the others, etc. Contemporary accounts suggest that such stratagems were frequently used, and popular opinion on the subject was correspondingly savage. A *Times* editorial written in the same year as the one quoted above, declares that "we fear in each year's list of bankrupts there is a considerable proportion of persons who have incurred their debts and wasted their assets with the specific intention of coming to the Bankruptcy Court and starting afresh . . ."[54] A generation later one member of Parliament declared that "under the existing state of things a premium was held out to fraud and dishonesty, and many men who, having behaved in a most reckless way, became bankrupts, lifted up their heads in the world a few months after, in a manner perfectly scandalous."[55]

THE TERRIBLE STIGMA OF BANKRUPTCY

It is clear from such statements that bankruptcy was considered a shameful condition, worthy of the harshest language. Members of Parliament state that "we are all aware that a great stigma attaches to the name of bankrupt,"[56] or refer to "the opprobium and stigma of having gone through the Bankruptcy Court."[57] A mercantile witness before the Select Committee of the House of Lords investigating bankruptcy in 1852–53 testified that "bankruptcy itself conveys a stigma in the mercantile world, that when a man has ever been a bankrupt he is looked upon as a grade lower than if it had never occurred. . . ."[58] An earlier commission in 1840 heard evidence that the growth of trust deeds was due to the desire to avoid "the obnoxious name of bankruptcy." Several witnesses before this commission testified that merchants could be induced to come to Bankruptcy Court sooner (that is, while they still had some assets to divide), "if some milder term could be found than that of a bankrupt."[59] It was thought that renaming the Court of Bankruptcy might lessen the stigma; among the suggestions were Court of Commerce, Court of Adjustment, and Court of Distribution. At least one mercantile witness, however, was decidedly in favor of retaining the old name:

MR. THOMAS JAMES: I think the terror of the Court of Bankruptcy desirable, because I think it induces parties to make such a composition with their creditors as shall save them the disgrace of a Court of Bankruptcy.
CHAIRMAN: You would retain it as a screw?
MR. JAMES: Yes, as a moral screw.[60]

In part, this "terror" on the part of respectable businessmen at the name of "bankrupt" may be explained by the criminal origins of the laws of bankruptcy. The statutes passed by Henry VIII in 1542, which established the principles of later bankruptcy law, were penal laws aimed solely at fraudulent traders. These early bankrupts were treated as criminal offenders, and commissioners were given the power to summon them for examination, to confiscate their property, and to punish fraud.[61] There was no consideration given to relieving the bankrupt from his distress; the purpose of the law was to take control of the property of the bankrupt on behalf of the creditors,[62] and the bankrupt remained forever liable for his debts. For almost two hundred years these harsh laws remained in effect, and were strengthened by additional statutes, such as those passed under James I, which condemned those bankrupts who lied under oath, or concealed property, to be pilloried and to have an ear chopped off.[63]

The criminal origins of bankruptcy law were very likely one reason for the social disgrace that attached to it. Another reason may have been the class distinctions that associated bankruptcy with "trade" and commerce.

From its very origin, bankruptcy law was restricted to those involved in trade, although the definition of trade proved somewhat troublesome. Theoretically, the bankrupt possessed several advantages over the insolvent debtor; since modern bankruptcy laws entitled him to a certificate of discharge, the bankrupt could be freed from future liability for his debts, and was more likely to avoid the ignominy of imprisonment than the insolvent debtor.

Nevertheless, there remained a strong feeling among the landed classes that bankruptcy was a harsh set of laws designed purely for those who had soiled their hands with trade and ought therefore to be held responsible for a strict accounting of their financial dealings. Lord Brougham, the great authority on bankruptcy law, defended the distinction between trader and nontrader: "Men were divided into classes, and they thought they enjoyed or were entitled to certain immunities. Members of both Houses of Parliament, lawyers, judges, physicians, the clergy, and country gentlemen are secure in contracting debts that they are not liable to be summoned before a Commissioner of Bankruptcy Court and directed to deliver up their property in fourteen days."[64]

When it was finally decided in 1861 to sweep away the traditional distinctions between insolvency and bankruptcy, a hue and cry ensued, in which "private gentlemen" expressed a great distaste for being brought within laws designed for the trading classes. In Parliament a speaker found it objectionable that the holder of mortgaged property should be subjected to "the screw of threatening to make such a person a bankrupt, to send him to prison, to seize everything belonging to him, even his most private papers, and to drag his wife into a court, which they had just heard was unfit for any one to enter."[65] Sir George Bowyer warned ominously, "Let people consider what it was to be brought under the saws and harrows of the bankruptcy law. To a person of high rank, the very fact of being a bankrupt was a slur and a stain, and a thing which, in the history of a family, looked very ugly."[66] The *Times* gave its qualified approval to changes in the law, but the fears of the nontrading classes seemed entirely reasonable to the *Times:* "Quiet folk, who have nothing to do with money or articles of merchandise, and who know money only as a regular income which they earn, receive, and spend, were afraid of being caught up and drawn into a terrible machinery, the rapid action of which was only necessary to seize the fleeting assets of men whose business it is to deal with large sums of money as jugglers deal with balls and knives, making them move rapidly before our eyes for a certain time, and then mysteriously disappear altogether."[67] This last bit of satire, with its suggested association of trade with fraud and chicanery, is typical of the protests of the time, and suggests that the social disgrace of bankruptcy had much to do with traditional class distinctions and the inferior status of "trade."

THE DEMAND FOR HARSH LEGISLATION

The connotations of inferior social class and criminal origin that clung to the idea of bankruptcy thus seem to have deepened even further the moral repugnance with which the Victorians regarded it. Widespread bankruptcy threatened their most cherished concept of themselves as a virtuous and therefore justifiably prosperous people. It is understandable, then, that public opinion would call frequently for harsh laws which would discourage traders from resorting to bankruptcy, and such, indeed, is the case. Throughout the century political and business leaders complained vociferously that bankruptcy laws were far too lenient, and pleaded with the legislature to make them more severe. In his letter to Earl Grey in 1831, Thomas Foster begged the Lord of the Treasury to "let the laws be corrected, so as to make men answerable for their actions . . . let indolence and improvidence and folly and vice of every kind be exposed and execrated as they deserve."[68] In Parliament, member after member deplored the laxity of the government in abolishing arrest on mesne process (that is, after the filing of a creditor's claim, but before the claim had been proved), claiming that the fear of arrest was absolutely essential in forcing men to pay their bills.[69]

The Commissioners for Inquiring into Bankruptcy and Insolvency in 1840 circulated a questionnaire concerning attitudes toward bankruptcy among leading solicitors and business men. The returns showed opinion quite divided on most topics, with one exception. Respondents replied overwhelmingly (65 to 2) that they believed that imprisonment for debt was effective in inducing debtors to pay debts.[70] John Stuart Mill heartily deplored the relaxation of laws for imprisonment for debt: "Imprisonment at the discretion of a creditor was really a powerful engine for extracting from the debtor any property which he had concealed. . . ." Mill urged the most severe bankruptcy laws possible. "It is the business of law to prevent wrongdoing, and not simply to patch up the consequences of it when it has been committed. The law is bound to take care that insolvency should not be a good pecuniary speculation. . . ."[71] The *Westminster Review* likewise called for laws that would enforce the strictest commercial morality and discourage insolvency. "Insolvency and bankruptcy laws," it was claimed, "are the poor-laws of the middle class" because "they repress the vices that create and encourage poverty, these vices being idleness and sensual indulgence."[72]

In the sixties the debates over reforming bankruptcy laws revived the old charge that the legislature had been too lenient with bankrupts. One member declared in the House of Commons "that House would, he thought, be only performing one of its clearest duties by doing something to correct the lax commercial morality of the present age."[73] Another deplored the fact that "previous legislation had dealt too compassionately with the debtor, it was that that had done so much commercial harm."[74] As late as 1879, similar complaints were still being voiced. *The Fortnightly Review* insisted that the law was failing to instill "a wholesome horror of the disgrace of bankruptcy" because "the vicious weakness and laxity of the bankruptcy laws are rapidly expelling the honesty and putting an end to the sentiment of disgrace,"[75] while *Fraser's Magazine* was insisting that "a harder bankruptcy law would . . . serve as a check on reckless trading."[76]

THE PRAGMATIC REALITIES OF BANKRUPTCY

In the light of such demands for harsh treatment of bankrupts, one might expect that the Victorian period would have produced some exceedingly severe laws on bankruptcy and insolvency. In fact, quite the opposite is true. Although the process was tedious and uneven, there is a clearly discernible trend in nineteenth-century legislation toward more lenient treatment of debtors. In the course of the Victorian period much was done to ameliorate the condition of bankrupts and insolvents, and to "decriminalize" the entire procedure, leaving it more or less a private affair between debtor and creditor, with as little punitive governmental interference as possible. In order to comprehend the reasons for this surprising trend of bankruptcy legislation, it is necessary to examine the way in which the economic realities of bankruptcy undermined the public rhetoric about it. In a great many ways, the actual facts about bankruptcy did not match the public perceptions about it, and these underlying contradictions were constantly surfacing to force the Victorians to reappraise their traditional attitudes.

From the very beginning of the century it was clear that the public rhetoric about the disgrace and stigma of bankruptcy was qualified by the fact that many bankrupts apparently had little difficulty in starting over again in business. This is not to suggest, however, that public rhetoric about bankruptcy was hypocritical. The shame of going bankrupt was probably felt deeply by the more respectable class of tradesman. There is evidence to suggest, however, that private business arrangements were conducted on a much more pragmatic level than the public debates. In his 1831 letter Foster gives case histories of merchants who have declared bankruptcy and then emerged from it unscathed to rise in business again. In parliamentary debate in 1861 the attorney general declared that some men had become bankrupt five or six times. "They rose from the ground as often as they fell with new vigour, new means and new prosperity."[77] Later in a similar debate, Alderman Lusk claimed that "Much scandal arose from the fact that so many persons became bankrupts and again set up immediately in business."[78] It was estimated in 1878 that one out of every sixteen solicitors had once been bankrupt, and some had survived several bankruptcies.[79]

The scandal of bankrupts who failed more than once was not ignored by Victorians; in fact, it formed the basis of one of the most persistent stereotypes of disputes about bankruptcy—the bankrupt as an audacious scoundrel. Horror stories are recounted in parliamentary debates about notorious blackguards, such as the gentleman who kept a carriage for his mother in town, kept one woman at Brighton, and another one (with whom he had two children) at Hampstead, then went bankrupt, and was currently carrying on his business once again.[80] One member declared that "he could not conceive any state of society more discreditable or more distressing than that in which they might see a man who had been bankrupt three or four times, a daring and unscrupulous speculator, riding in his carriage while his unfortunate creditors were ruined."[81]

The image of the bankrupt as a rich wastrel recurs often in such debates, and certainly there must have been many such cases. A careful examination, however, of the *London Gazette* and other sources that identify bankrupts by their occupation, reveals a far different picture. The "Bankruptcy Analysis" of the *British Almanac* of 1847, for example, enumerates bankrupts who seem to encompass a full range of mercantile occupations. For every manufacturer, ship owner, broker, or merchant listed, there is a baker, shoemaker, bricklayer, druggist, linen draper, butcher, lodging-house keeper, pawnbroker, tailor, or cheesemonger.[82] Bankruptcy listings in the *Times,* reprinted from the *Gazette,* seem to bear out the same conclusion, that the typical bankrupt was as likely to be a lower-middle-class shopkeeper as a manipulator of high finance, and would hardly fit the stereotype of the cynical scoundrel who took advantage of Bankruptcy Court.[83] The cheesemonger who failed, whatever his private morality, was hardly likely to have been riding in a carriage, either before his bankruptcy or after it.

In fact, there are indications that most bankruptcies involved relatively small sums. A commission in 1854 headed by Walpole heard evidence from Edward Goulburn, a commissioner of bankruptcy, that most of the bankruptcies in which large assets were involved were settled by private arrangements, as the "mercantile aristocracy" was reluctant to enter what it considered to be a "shopkeepers' court."[84] The tendency of Bankruptcy Court to be cluttered with cases involving few or no assets was greatly increased after 1861, when the new law placed all insolvents, traders or nontraders, under the jurisdiction of one court. *The Gazette of Bankruptcy,* an official document published briefly from 1861 to 1863, shows that a substantial number of bankrupts were in relatively low status occupations. There are still bankrupt merchants and manufacturers (and now an occasional clerk in Holy Orders, lieutenant in 2d Battalion Foot, baronet, and a lorn "gentleman"), but by far the greatest number of bankrupts occupy relatively unexalted positions such as poulterer, apothecary, engraver, stone mason, carpenter, dealer in pigs, hosier, tanner, glazier; there is even a "Tripe-dresser."[85]

In Parliament it was claimed that 85 percent of all bankruptcies involved estates which did not exceed £1000 in value, many being as low as £300.[86] By the middle of the nineteenth century it was clear, therefore, that bankruptcy had become a necessary refuge for those marginal entrepreneurs who were unable to survive the vicissitudes of a capitalist economy.

LEGAL REFORMS

Thus the Victorians were forced by the economic realities of the new industrial economy to make some provision for those who failed. The process of reform was a slow and uncertain one, often set back by opposition from the mercantile community and by public outrage over large numbers of bankruptcies. But the overall pattern of bankruptcy reform in the nineteenth century (influenced by the growth of humanitarian sentiments in evangelical religion, and perhaps by Benthamite thought) was toward ameliorating the plight of the victims of capitalism.[87] The most visible indication of the Victorians' changing attitudes toward economic failure was the abolition of imprisonment for debt. Due to the efforts of Lord Brougham, arrest for debt on mesne process was abolished in 1838. Although the mercantile interest in Parliament continued to demand the reinstitution of this power of arrest for many years, there was a growing recognition that imprisonment for debt served no interest, least of all the creditors', and further restrictions were gradually placed on imprisonment until 1869 when it was formally abolished. A less dramatic but equally important development was the growth of official control of the bankruptcy process, so that the debtor was no longer dependent upon the mercy of his creditors.

The process of bankruptcy reform was slow and tortuous, often beset by conflicting interests, and by the contradictions between traditional morality and economic necessity. In theory, nothing should have been simpler than to construct a set of just and rational bankruptcy laws. The principle of bankruptcy was never in doubt: that all property of the bankrupt should be confiscated to be distributed rateably among his creditors. The tortured history of bankruptcy legislation, however, demonstrates the problems of translating moral and legal theories into practice.[88] Often conflicting interests were involved: justice for the creditor vs. mercy for the debtor; moral outrage over bankruptcy vs. recognition of economic realities; idealism vs. pragmatism. On the other hand, many of the controversies over bankruptcy laws were simply concerned with legal machinery, such as the number and nature of the assignees, registrars, etc. In the mechanics of bankruptcy proceedings the pendulum swung back and forth during the Victorian years between allowing the creditors full control (which often led to confusion and corruption), and a more official system in which assignees of the court investigated cases and took charge of the assets—a system that was less corrupt, but more time-consuming and expensive, often absorbing the entire assets of an estate in costs.

With so many legal and economic complications to consider, it was small wonder that bankruptcy legislation was something of a politician's nightmare. The Victorians had inherited a cumbersome and contradictory mass of statutes. In 1814, when Earl Stanhope presented a petition in the House of Lords calling for a consolidation of the law, he declared that "The noble and learned lord on the woolsack [Lord Eldon] was stated to have said that he had read the Bankrupt Laws 72,000 times, and did not understand them yet." (The Lord Chancellor denied this—but conceded that Earl Stanhope did not understand them.)[89] In the ensuing years, bankruptcy legislation was discussed again and again. Major reform bills were passed in 1825, 1831, 1842, 1849, 1861, and 1869, and in the years between there were royal commissions, select committees, and public petitions. Scarcely a session of Parliament went by without a thick blue book on the subject of bankruptcy law. The *Times* declared in 1847, "the law is in a continual state of transition. It is always being pieced and botched, and mended. . . . We confess to an absolute dread and abhorrence of any additional legislation on this subject."[90] Twenty years later, the *Times* was still wearily editorializing, "We have had many Bankruptcy Bills, and they have all been treated in the same manner. Each measure has been hailed as an improvement on its predecessor, and after a lapse of a few months the law has commonly been pronounced to be as bad as ever."[91] And a debater in Parliament declared in 1867 that "there was no department of the law or its administration which was in a more unsettled and unsatisfactory state than the law of bankruptcy. Within the last thirty or forty years they had three or four new systems and schemes. One after another of these had proved failures."[92] In spite of the good intentions of its legislators, Victorian society seemed incapable of producing a satisfactory law about bankruptcy, and indeed the subject has remained troublesome down to the present era.

We have already seen that the origin of the bankruptcy laws was in certain criminal statutes passed in the sixteenth century. These were designed in the interest of the creditor and contained severe penalties for the fraudulent bankrupt. The debtor was not discharged from his debts even after bankruptcy, but remained legally liable for them. Very early, the principle was established that only traders could be bankrupt.[93] The law continued in its severity for about two centuries, and then the growth of capitalism forced the legislators to recognize that those who traded might be faced with certain unique problems under the newly competitive economic conditions. In recognition of the fact that merchants and other traders were more liable to be ruined by a stroke of misfortune than, for example, the "gentleman debtor," a statute in 1705 for the first time granted the bankrupt a "discharge" from his debts. Thus it was recognized even in the earliest years of economic growth that capitalism would claim a certain number of victims each year, and that the economic welfare of the entire community could best be served by allowing such traders to re-establish themselves as productive members of the economy.

Before 1831, the district of London alone had seventy different commissioners of bankruptcy (referred to as the "Septuagint"). As there was hardly any qualification necessary for appointment, these commissioners were not particularly competent, and there was little uniformity in their decisions.[94] Hearings were held in a room in the Guildhall sometimes used as an auxiliary kitchen.[95] Many cases were heard simultaneously in a noisy, chaotic atmosphere; in Parliament it was declared that "the Guildhall on a busy day could be compared to nothing but a cock-fight."[96] The creditors had a great deal of power during this period because they appointed their own assignees to handle the bankrupt's assets, and because the bankrupt could only obtain his discharge on the consent of four-fifths of his creditors.[97] This situation seems to have led to a very high degree of corruption on the part of debtors, creditors, and assignees alike.[98] One commissioner stated that the majority of commissions of bankruptcy might be considered conspiracies between the bankrupt and the petitioning creditor to defraud all the rest.[99] In addition, the system was inefficient and led to costly delays and frequently to further litigation. A prominent advocate of bankruptcy reform, Basil Montagu, mentioned in Parliament a well-known case which lasted for many years, and "when it was at length decided, the barren sentence was all that could be obtained; the assignees, creditors, and all parties had disappeared:—some were dead, the rest could not be found; not a single party interested could be discovered, and there was not one single farthing to be divided, the whole proceeds of the estate having evaporated in litigation."[100] The futility of litigation in Chancery Court will be recollected by every reader of Dickens's *Bleak House;* apparently the same prolonged and costly agony was likely to entrap the principals of a proceeding in Bankruptcy Court.

This state of affairs was universally deplored, and in 1831 Lord Brougham's reforms swept away the sinecures of the seventy commissioners, and replaced them with six commissioners who constituted a Court of Bankruptcy for London. (In 1842 this system was extended to the country districts.) The creditors' assignees were replaced with official assignees appointed by the court. Upon taking office, these assignees found that £2,000,000 which ought to have been distributed to creditors under the old system was still in the hands of London bankers, and managed to distribute this sum in a relatively short time.[101] On the other hand, the cost of this official staff was great, and had to be borne largely by the estates of the bankrupts. Reforms in the 1840s removed the power of the creditors to veto the bankrupt's discharge, and left the power of granting a certificate of discharge entirely to the discretion of the Bankruptcy Court.[102] The trader was also allowed under certain conditions to make himself a bankrupt, in order to extricate himself from his debts.

At the same time, efforts were also being made to ameliorate the conditions of the insolvent debtor who did not qualify as a bankrupt. The bankrupt, as was mentioned before, had to prove that his occupation could be classified as "trader," and also had to owe at least £100 to the petitioning creditor—thus many insolvent debtors were actually traders who owed sums too small to qualify them as bankrupts. The insolvent debtor could obtain no discharge from his debts, and was always liable to arrest for them. A bill in 1826 first enabled a debtor actually in prison to surrender his property and in exchange to obtain his release from prison, although he was still liable for his debts. A Court for the Relief of Insolvent Debtors was set up in 1842 to speed their release. By this time conditions in debtors' prisons had been given much harsh publicity, and the average stay in such a prison had been reduced to a very brief period. Further restrictions were placed on imprisonment in the succeeding years, and by the middle of the nineteenth century, imprisonment for debt had been all but eliminated.[103]

Thus by the 1840s the Victorians had more or less accepted the principle that debt was not necessarily a crime to be revenged upon the body of the debtor. There was still a strong segment of opinion, however, calling for harsher treatment of debtors, particularly among the mercantile community. A growing number of petitions in the late 1840s complained that the laws now failed to protect the creditor at all.[104] Even Lord Brougham, one of the leading reformers, admitted before a select committee that the laws had gone a little too far in favor of the debtor[105] and thus the law passed in 1849 was designed in reaction to the previous leniency. A debtor was no longer allowed to become bankrupt voluntarily unless he could pay his creditors dividends of at least five shillings in a pound, a provision that cut down the annual number of official bankruptcies. The law also made provisions for regulating private arrangements, such as liquidations, compositions, and inspectorships. Evidence heard before the commission of 1840 proved that these arrangements now outnumbered official bankruptcies,[106] and the Act of 1849 provided that all such arrangements would now be registered with the court.

But the major innovation of this act was a unique system of classifying the bankrupt's certificate of discharge into moral categories according to the amount of fault involved. The suggestion for such a system had originated in the mercantile community, which had long demanded some way of distinguishing between those bankrupts who were fraudulent, those who were improvident, and those who were merely unfortunate. Actually, a kind of moral judgment already existed in the unofficial comments of the judge in granting the certificate. Such remarks were quite customary, and Thackeray used such an incident in *The Newcomes,* in his portrayal of Colonel Newcome's passage through Bankruptcy Court: "The judge made a very feeling speech to the Colonel when he came up for his certificate. He passed very different comments on the conduct of the Manager of the Bank, when that person appeared for examination."[107]

Under the law of 1849, the certificate would now become an official instrument of such judicial praise or blame. A first-class certificate would be awarded in cases where bankruptcy was caused wholly by unavoidable misfortune, a second-class in cases where the cause was partially due to misfortune (that is, the bankrupt may have been careless or reckless, but not dishonest), and a third-class in cases not due in any way to misfortune, but rather to the dishonesty of the trader. For the first time in bankruptcy proceedings, the judge would be empowered to examine carefully not only the conduct of the bankrupt during the proceedings (that is, whether he made accurate statements, cooperated in producing records, etc.) but also his entire course of business prior to the bankruptcy, and to make judgments upon the bankrupt's honesty.

Although the merchant community was overwhelmingly in favor of such a system, which would reinforce the moral stigma of the fraudulent bankruptcy, only a few years after the Act of 1849 a great deal of dissatisfaction was being expressed about the practical operation of such a system.[108] Testimony before parliamentary commissions showed that there was little uniformity between the various commissioners of bankruptcy in granting certificates. Commissioner Evans complained that "there is no moral, legal, or commercial standard on which to base a decision as to the classes of certificate," and testified that there was much disagreement among the commissioners.[109] In Parliament the lord chancellor complained that in one hundred cases, one commissioner had given thirteen first-class certificates, whereas another had given sixty.[110] Most cases proved to be too complicated for a quick judgment on the morality of the bankrupt, or the exact degree of fault involved in his failure.

In addition, it proved very difficult to define imprudence and recklessness at a time when so many business ventures seemed to exhibit similar attributes with great success. Lord Brougham pointed out that "in a commercial country" it was difficult to ascertain "where enterprise ends and reckless trading begins."[111] The attorney general put the problem before Parliament: "Bankruptcy is a strange admixture of civil and criminal law. You have got a criminal jurisdiction of a most singular character, because it is a jurisdiction which treats the bankrupt as a criminal without at the same time giving any definition of his offense. Nothing more, in fact, is given [in the statute] than a mere description of moral misconduct, extravagance, recklessness, and a general want of prudence."[112] Such qualities as lack of prudence in fact only became offenses if they led to failures and could thus be judged only in the result.

In addition to the difficulties of judging such offenses, evidence began to accumulate that the system of classifying certificates was not effective in improving morality. Bankrupts did not seem to have more difficulty obtaining credit with a third-class certificate than with a first,[113] and many bankrupts seemed indifferent as to which class they received. Sir G. Stephens, a barrister, testified before Walpole's commission in 1854: "A court of law cannot be converted into a school of morality, except so far as its punishments are substantial. The bankrupt is either a knave or he is not. If he is a knave, he cares for nothing but his 'white washing.' If he is an honest man, he merits no punishment."[114] The disgrace of a third-class certificate could thus weigh heavily only upon the man who by definition did not merit it.

The Reform Act of 1861 repealed the system of classification of certificates, and the Victorians never again attempted such a specific means of legislating morality in bankruptcy. More and more the legislators began to believe that fraud in bankruptcy should be punished by the regular criminal courts, while the Bankruptcy Court should exist solely to provide the most efficient means of distributing the assets of a debtor. The Act of 1861 was the beginning of modern bankruptcy codes in that it abolished the basic distinction that had existed so long between trader and nontrader, making all debtors liable to bankruptcy, and consequently doing away with the Court for the Relief of Insolvent Debtors.[115] The principle was therefore established that all debtors, of whatever description, could by surrendering their property for distribution among their creditors, absolve themselves of liability and earn the right to reestablish themselves. Debtors were allowed greater freedom to become bankrupt voluntarily, but more stringent powers were given to the judge to refuse the discharge or even sentence to prison if there was evidence of fraud. The act also greatly facilitated the opportunities for settlement by private arrangements.

Not many years had passed before new committees were being appointed to consider the unsatisfactory condition of the bankruptcy system set up in 1861. The Select Committee of 1864 reported that the new procedure was costly and inefficient, and "fruitful in negligence and malversation." The system "is found to work so disadvantageously for creditors, that few willingly avail themselves of it."[116] The figures of the committee showed that while bankruptcies under the workings of the new act had increased eightfold, the number of assets distributed to creditors had actually shrunk by half.[117] The committee further reported that "the experience of the last forty years points . . . to the renunciation of the attempt to collect and distribute the assets of an insolvent . . . by any other agency than that of the creditors themselves."[118] The "officialdom" that

had resulted in a large and costly staff of bankruptcy officials was pronounced a failure, and the committee recommended instead the least
possible interference of the court, retaining only the right of appeal to
secure just distribution of assets and to punish fraud. It was generally
accepted that almost all bankruptcies would be settled by trust deeds in
which the court would have no other function but to officially record the
procedure.

Thus the Act of 1869 reversed the nineteenth-century trend toward
giving more power to officials of the court, and entrusted the management
of bankruptcy to the creditors in the belief that self-interest would inspire
efficiency.[119] The official assignees were replaced by assignees appointed
by the creditors, and voluntary arrangements were further facilitated.

Unfortunately, this system seems to have worked no better than its many
predecessors, and before long angry denunciations in Parliament were
once again deploring the scandalous state of the bankruptcy laws. Leaving
the administration of bankruptcy to the creditors had failed because the
creditors were not an organized body. Often they had conflicting interests,
and few had either the time or the inclination to attend frequent meetings
or to pursue complicated investigations. More often than not, the creditors
would simply write off their debts, a situation that understandably led to a
great rise in corruption, and a corresponding decrease in the amount of
assets divided. By 1879, *Fraser's Magazine,* among others, was pronouncing
the Act of 1869 "a most humiliating and disastrous failure."[120]

The Act of 1883 pursued a radical change in policy that in some ways
hearkened back to earlier policies of more control by the court, strict
investigations, and an emphasis on commercial morality. Bankruptcy came
under the jurisdiction of the Board of Trade, which appointed official
receivers to act as trustees and make recommendations as to discharge. The
trustee would also report on any scheme of composition, which now had to
obtain the sanction of the court. With a few modifications, this system
survived into the twentieth century.

The long and seemingly ill-starred history of nineteenth-century bankruptcy legislation is testimony to the complexity of the issues involved. With
every good intention, Victorian legislators seem to have found it impossible
to reconcile the opposing interests of society in dealing with bankruptcy.
Nevertheless, over the course of the Victorian years, certain broad legal
principles seem to have emerged. Bankruptcy by the 1880s was no longer
treated as a criminal offense, nor was the bankrupt thrown upon the mercy
of his creditors. Instead, by yielding up his property for distribution, every
man could earn the right to reestablish himself in the economic community.
Thus in spite of the fact that public rhetoric continued to denounce bankruptcy as an outrage against morality, and in spite of the fact that the public
demand for harsh treatment of bankrupts was apparently louder than the
voices calling for reform, the condition of the bankrupt was materially

improved by the end of the nineteenth century. In spite of their deeply felt moral convictions about the shame of bankruptcy, the Victorians had been forced by economic necessity to adopt a more humane and pragmatic attitude toward the failures of the capitalist economy.

It is small wonder, then, that the subject of bankruptcy was distasteful. By its very nature, it challenged the most cherished ideals of the period. The capitalist system was supposed to reward the virtuous, the prudent, the energetic, the thrifty; the prosperity of England was therefore proof of the national righteousness. Widespread economic failure, on the other hand, was a reality which simply could not be ignored. Bankruptcy was a glaring defect in the otherwise gilded surface of Victorian prosperity, a defect that suggested the possibility of a void beneath, and the specter of this ugly reality seems to have haunted the Victorian imagination. The next chapter will trace the way in which bankruptcy seems to have become a cultural obsession, the common nightmare of Victorian art and literature.

3

The Specter of Bankruptcy in Popular Art

The fear of losing one's money seems to have been a universal theme of Victorian literature, painting, drama, and popular culture. As Thackeray wrote in *Vanity Fair* about the bankruptcy of Mr. Sedley, "If success is rare and slow, everybody knows how quick and easy ruin is." There seems to have been a grim fascination for the Victorians in contemplating the spectacle of threatened poverty from the comparative safety of a theater balcony or a parlor reading chair. As one commentator observed about the steady stream of broken bankrupts upon the Victorian stage: "the rich like to imagine themselves poor, the poor like to imagine themselves dispossessed."[1]

Many Victorians indeed seem to have derived a kind of perverse enjoyment from experiencing vicariously the dreadful disgrace of bankruptcy. The previous chapter has already described the frequency with which editorials and crusading articles about bankruptcy reform appeared in the newspapers and periodicals of the day. The bankruptcy lists from *The London Gazette* were reprinted faithfully by the *Times* and other journals each day; and the bankruptcy of a long-established house, a respected merchant, or a well-known member of parliament was sure to be given prominent coverage in the same publications. The public seems to have been avid for news of such spectacular downfalls. Dickens capitalized on such interest in more than one of his novels and also exploited this public obsession with bankruptcy in his capacity as the editor of *All The Year Round*. He published a series of articles in 1867 chronicling the history of a respectable commercial traveler fallen on hard times through the "sponging-house," the debtors' jail at Whitecross Street, and finally Bankruptcy Court,[2] and followed this by an indignant article the following year on the unequal treatment given to wealthy bankrupts.[3]

When the pages of the daily papers and journals reflected such a preoccupation with bankruptcy, it is small wonder that the more imaginative forms of Victorian culture reveal a similar obsession. In its popular fiction, in its melodrama, and even in its paintings, the Victorian audience seemed never to tire of contemplating the threat of bankruptcy that might plunge a man into disgrace, and destroy the comfort and security of his family. Indeed, in the iconography of the Victorian popular imagination, the domestic hearth holds the highest place as the repository of all that the Victorians considered most sacred, and it is precisely this domestic haven which is most threatened by the horrors of bankruptcy as it is portrayed in Victorian art. This chapter will explore the way in which bankruptcy emerges in various forms of the Victorian imagination as the specter that threatens the tranquillity of the sacred domestic circle, and thus becomes a kind of universal nightmare for its time; the heartrending dislocations of bankruptcy which we will later examine in the Victorian novel were written within the context of a popular art obsessed with the idea of economic failure.

VICTORIAN PAINTING

In an age in which all forms of art were becoming more strongly representational, it was not surprising that a mundane matter such as the loss of money began to make its way into Victorian painting. Although critical opinion continued to stress the "higher" art of historical or religious subjects, among the popular audience the new "narrative" style in which a story or anecdote was conveyed in contemporary dress and setting gained great favor. Such artists as Sir David Wilkie and William Powell Frith proved to be so popular with the general public that a railing had to be placed before their works at the Royal Academy Exhibit to protect the paintings from the crowds.[4] The narrative painting usually conveyed some moral import; according to Raymond Lister, the narrative pictures "provided the bourgeois with his parables."[5] In the moral universe of such paintings, the cult of domesticity is one of the strongest influences, and among the most popular of the narrative genre were those pictures that emphasized the threat to the domestic circle by such evils as adultery, liquor, or economic profligacy. Augustus Egg's *Past and Present* (1858), for example, portrayed the downfall of an unfaithful wife, the desolation of the bereft family, and the subsequent career of the outcast woman.[6]

In adapting certain moral themes as the fit subjects for art, Victorian painters could not fail to be influenced by their eighteenth-century predecessor, Hogarth, and many of the narrative painters attempted a Hogarthian series of pictures that illustrated a moral virtue or told a cautionary tale of vice. For example, Cruikshank's series, "The Bottle," was issued in 1847 as a set of glyphographic plates, with text by Charles Mackay, illustrating the perils of alcohol and was followed by a sequel in 1848 entitled "The Drunkard's Children."

Like other temperance propaganda, "The Bottle" portrays the drama of alcoholism primarily through its domestic and economic ramifications. In plate 1 the husband induces the wife to take her first drop of liquor amid a convivial family scene: the table is laden with an inviting array, a cheerful fire warms the hearth in the lower righthand foreground, the room is comfortably furnished, and the children cluster around their parents. By the second plate the husband has lost his job, and they are pawning their clothes to supply money for drink; the room is less comfortably furnished, and the table no longer suggests plentiful abundance. Plate 3 pictures an "execution" in which the bailiffs strip the walls of their remaining ornaments, and plate 4 reveals the infant of the family dead, the room now barren and its hearth cold and empty. In the fifth and sixth plates violent quarrels break out, and the husband kills his wife "with the instrument of all their misery." In the final plate, according to Mackay's text, "The bottle has done its work—it has destroyed the infant and the mother, it has brought the son and daughter to vice and to the streets, and has left the father a hopeless maniac." The last plate portrays the drunkard huddled before a grated fire in a cell with barred windows. The position of the hearth in this institutional cell is in the lower righthand foreground, precisely the same as that of the hearth in the scenes of the drunkard's home; the unchanging position of the symbolic hearth contrasts strongly with the rapid disappearance of all other decorative objects, and with the deterioration of the family group.[7] Such strongly narrative and representational works as Egg's and Cruikshank's depend for their impact on certain emotional values implied in the portrayal of the intact domestic circle in the first scene, and its subsequent destruction; it is interesting that in the Cruikshank series the family's downfall is portrayed in economic terms, as well as moral and emotional ones.

Many narrative paintings of the period indeed attest to the dread of poverty and the destructive impact that it could have upon family life. Collinson's *Answering the Emigrant's Letter* (1850), for example, portrays the dislocation of family members forced by poverty to emigrate,[8] while earlier in Sir David Wilkie's *Distraining for Rent* (1814) a rural family faces economic disaster—a bailiff and his clerk confront an anguished farmer while the poor man's wife and children look on despairingly.[9]

It is clear from such paintings that the fear of poverty and the fear of the destruction of the domestic hearth were inextricably intertwined, and several narrative paintings portrayed in heartrending terms the family circle shattered by economic recklessness in the form of either gambling or stock speculation. Of the two, gambling was the more conventional subject, perhaps because there still clung to the world of painting enough of a desire for "high" subjects to render it more desirable to paint aristocratic characters than mercantile ones (who no doubt seemed "low" without being picturesque).

In Robert Braithwaite Martineau's *The Last Day in the Old Home* (1862), an old family seat is being sold up to pay for gambling debts. The heir to the estate is the familiar figure of the rake who has gambled his way through his family's fortune. In the foreground of the picture he and his young son carelessly toast the future with upraised glasses, surrounded by the tokens of his passon for racing. Beyond the open door behind those figures, one can see the auctioneer's men stripping the house of its furnishings in preparation for a sale, while in the main room all of the paintings and objets d'art have already been ticketed for the auctioneer's lot. As with most Victorian images of bankruptcy and ruin, there is great stress upon the devastation of the family, particularly upon the helpless females who are so dependent economically upon their men. Opposed to the recklessly optimistic heir is his weeping mother, who sits at a desk on the left side of the picture handing her keys to the auctioneer's agent. Linking the two groups at the center of the painting are the distraught wife who stretches an arm

Robert Braithwaite Martineau's *The Last Day in the Old Home* **(1862). Tate Gallery, London.**

pleadingly to her disregarding husband and son, and a female child who gazes with solemn sympathy at her grandmother.

This emphasis upon the suffering of the wife, mother, and daughter gives great poignancy to this pictorial parable of the evils of gambling, and a similar story is recorded in a later series of paintings by Frith, *The Road to Ruin* (1878). Like Martineau, Frith depicted in this immensely popular work an aristocratic young man who shatters his vulnerable family with his passion for gambling. In the first painting of this series (which has been referred to as a "Victorian version of 'The Rake's Progress' "),[10] the young profligate is shown gambling through the night with his college chums. The second picture shows the young man surrounded by avaricious touts at the Royal Enclosure at Ascot. The third and central painting contains the essence of Frith's solemn moral—the betrayal of the family. In this scene the bailiff and his men have entered the hero's home, as the retiring servants exchange surprised glances. The husband leans against the mantelpiece calmly surveying the bailiff with defiance and contempt, but the wife has half-risen from her chair, alarm apparent in every feature of her face and body, and the bailiff's man stares with pity at the wife and children. The fourth painting continues the inevitable downfall; in a shabbily furnished room abroad, the wife pleads with the landlady to be patient, while the husband, who has been trying to earn a living by writing, sits in discourage-ment at his desk. There is a new baby present, to add to the financial burdens, and the older boy and girl are now thinner and perhaps ill. In the final scene, alone in a wretched garret, the husband prepares to commit suicide with a pistol that lies ready on the table. Only a woman's hatbox, a few old toys, and an empty cradle remain as pathetic emblems of the family he has destroyed with his economic recklessness.[11]

Although Frith's *The Road to Ruin* and Martineau's *The Last Day in the Old Home* deal with some of the peripheral implications of bankruptcy in nineteenth-century art, essentially they hark back to earlier images. They portray wealth as property, land, old homes, and valuable possessions, and "ruin" as the consequence mainly of such rakish vices as gambling and horse racing. Very few paintings of the Victorian period actually portrayed the confusing new economic realities of the mercantile world; a notable exception was a later series of narrative paintings by Frith entitled *The Race for Wealth* (1880), which follows the career of an audacious swindler similar to Dickens's Mr. Merdle (*Little Dorrit*) or Trollope's Mr. Melmotte (*The Way We Live Now*), and may indeed have been based upon Trollope's villain.[12] The first painting of the speculator and his victims is entitled "The Spider's Office." It pictures the victims flocking to the office of the financier who stands arrogantly in their midst, ignoring their curious stares and servile bows. The second painting shows "The Spider at Home" entertaining his intended victims at an elegant reception. Like the fictional speculators of Dickens and Trollope, he is assuming a grand manner that perhaps is at

Drawing for William Powell Frith's "The Spider's Office" from his series *The Race for Wealth* (1880). Trustees of The British Museum.

Drawing for "The Spider at Home" from Frith's series *The Race for Wealth* (1880). Trustees of The British Museum.

Drawing for "The Victims" from Frith's series *The Race for Wealth* (1880). Trustees of The British Museum.

Drawing for "Judgement—The Old Bailey" from Frith's series *The Race for Wealth* (1880). Trustees of The British Museum.

Drawing for "Retribution" from Frith's series *The Race for Wealth* (1880). Trustees of The British Museum.

odds with his true origins and upbringing. (The young lady directly behind him may be laughing behind her fan as she gazes at him.) The speculator points with pride to one of his expensive paintings, using his sumptuous surroundings to arouse the confidence of his prospective clients.

The third picture, "The Victims," portrays the consequences to these clients. A woman of eminently respectable circumstances reads from the *Times* the news of the swindler's unmasking to a family assembled at the breakfast table, as the servant turns discreetly aside. The father, a clergyman, listens with horror and dejection as he realizes the imprudence of his financial dealings, while the two grown daughters stand clutching each other, figures of mute worry and concern. (The scene echoes other nineteenth-century images of women as the victims of men's financial recklessness.) The fourth painting, "Judgement—The Old Bailey," shows the swindler on trial in central criminal court, his face impassive. In the foreground the lawyers in robes and powdered wigs talk among themselves, while on all sides the spectators stare in curiosity and excitement. As the clergyman testifies to the sordid circumstances in which he has become enmeshed, a few obvious victims in the crowd, a widow and her young son among them, register their despair. "Retribution," the last painting, shows the swindler in prison, distinguishable from the other inmates even in his prison garb by his arrogant stance. Among the many paintings of the Victorian period that convey the dread of sudden poverty and its catastrophic effect upon the domestic life, *The Race for Wealth* is almost unique in its willingness to visualize the sordid and unpicturesque realities of entrepreneurial capitalism.

VICTORIAN MELODRAMA

In the early and middle Victorian years the stage was unquestionably a more "popular" medium than was painting, and it attracted a far larger and far less affluent audience. The stage, correspondingly, was less inhibited in portraying such "low" subjects as the desperate need for economic security, the precariousness of low-status occupations such as farming and factory labor, and the uncertain vicissitudes of the City world of finance and industry. The melodrama of this period attests to the overwhelming dread of poverty which apparently haunted the Victorian imagination; the air of many Victorian plays is heavy with the threat of "ruin," and a great variety of much-persecuted characters bemoan their fear of the "workhouse." Such dramas are most typically presented in rural settings. In John Baldwin Buckstone's *Luke the Labourer* (1826), for example, the heroine's father, described as a "decayed farmer," bemoans his fate: "but what are hopes to me—am I not ruined? —No farm, no land! Blight, distemper, misfortune have swept all away and I am now a bereft and comfortless old man"(1.2).[13]

Although such plays seemingly ignore the industrial world, the class resentments stirred by the advent of capitalism are nevertheless clearly conveyed. The villain in such rural melodramas as *Luke the Labourer* is usually one of the gentry, generally the local squire, or his agents, and his power over the lives of the older characters is clearly economic. Douglas Jerrold's melodrama *The Rent Day* (1832) was suggested by two paintings of Sir David Wilkie, *The Rent Day* (1807) and *Distraining for Rent* (1814). (In act 2 of Jerrold's play the scene and furniture are copied from Wilkie's paintings, and at the end of the act, as the bailiffs take over the heroine's home, the stage directions instruct the actors to freeze in a tableau "as to represent Wilkie's picture of *Distraining for Rent.*")[14] As is usually the case in melodrama, the farmer's ruin in Jerrold's *The Rent Day* has been the result of forces beyond his control—harvests have failed, flocks have died. The steward and the bailiff, agents of the local squire, who take inventory of his beloved possessions with a totally businesslike indifference ("one toasting-fork, one bird-cage, one baby's rattle") convey the inhumanity of those who have economic power over the dispossessed.[15]

Nor was the industrial world completely ignored by Victorian melodrama. "Factory plays" such as R. B. Peake's *The Climbing Boy,* Jerrold's *The Factory Girl,* and John Walker's *The Factory Lad* were domestic dramas that showed the threat to the tranquillity of the home inherent in the new industrial world which was bringing about mechanization, inhuman working conditions, low wages, and unemployment.[16] For the audience of these melodramas, which was primarily lower-class, the factory owners as well as the aristocratic landowner were the rich tyrants who oppressed the downtrodden but noble heroes of the stage.

Even when the threatened "ruin" fails to materialize, an air of economic insecurity seems to hang over many of the characters of Victorian drama. Like the comedies of the eighteenth century, Victorian plays are filled with men in debt, who flee from their endlessly pursuing creditors and constantly fear the bailiff at the door. In Dion Boucicault's *London Assurance* (1841), for example, Charles, the son of Sir Harcourt Courtly, is beset by "duns" and makes his escape to the country upon being informed that "Mr. Solomon Isaacs is in the hall, and swears he will remain until he has arrested you . . ."(1.2).[17] Charles's friend Dazzle is a young dandy with a more nonchalant attitude toward his creditors. He proclaims that "Nature made me a gentleman—that is, I live on the best that can be procured for credit. . . . I'm an epidemic on the trade of a tailor" (act 5). He is severely contradicted, however, by Sir Harcourt in the last speech of the play: "The title of gentleman . . . should be engrossed by Truth—stamped with Honour . . . and enrolled in every true young English heart" (5). (It is significant that also in act 5 Solomon Isaac gets paid; Sir Harcourt Courtly's son could not be a true gentleman if he refused to honor his debts.)

The economic insecurity of the bewildering world of Victorian industrialism is often conveyed by a stock character, the "good old man," often the father of the heroine, who is forever tottering on the brink of ruin. According to Jerome K. Jerome's description of "the good old man" in *Stage-Land* (1899): "anything he is mixed up in seems to go wrong. If he is manager or director of a bank, smash it goes before even one act is over. His particular firm is always on the verge of bankruptcy. . . . If we lived in Stage-Land, and were asked to join any financial scheme, our first question would be: 'Is the good old man in it? If so, that would decide us.' "[18] The bankruptcy of the heroine's father became one of the stock situations of popular drama; thus the ruin of Amelia Sedley's father in Thackeray's *Vanity Fair* and the ruin of Maggie Tulliver's father in Eliot's *The Mill on the Floss* are in the tradition of a standard cliché of the stage.

In the world of the Victorian drama, then, bankruptcy, or equally catastrophic rural poverty seems to lurk around every corner, and the bailiff seems to be forever threatening at the door. The scene of an "execution" with the bailiffs brutally stripping a family of its most beloved possessions was a common one on the stage (as it would be one of the standard scenes of the novels of bankruptcy to be discussed in the next chapter). Such emotionally charged scenes are indicative of the strong connection between the fear of poverty and the fear of the destruction of the family circle that were so strongly linked in Victorian narrative paintings. Indeed, Victorian melodrama displays an even greater obsession than Victorian painting with the theme of the betrayal of the family by such vices as adultery, drink, gambling, or imprudent speculation.

Temperance dramas, in particular, portray the grim consequences of drink almost entirely in terms of the ensuing economic catastrophe that destroys the family. T. P. Taylor's *The Bottle*, written in 1848, illustrates Cruikshank's series of that title, in which a worker corrupted by drink loses all his money and allows his child to die of starvation. In John Allen's *The Fruits of the Wine Cup* (1858), the old protagonist loses his business because of alcoholism and ends in debtors' prison, while playwright James Mac-Closky in *The Fatal Glass, or The Curse of Drink* (1872) generously bestows a warning vision upon his hero—in which the hero becomes a drunken pauper, his child dies of starvation, and his wife dies in the snow outside the poorhouse door—that causes him to reform in time and thus to avert disaster.[19]

The vulnerability of the family is obviously the key element in the Victorian dread of economic catastrophe; chapter 5 will deal with this theme as it occurs in the works of the great novelists—for example, in the disharmony that bankruptcy produces in the Tulliver family in *The Mill on the Floss*. The artistic obsession with bankruptcy and other financial disasters which could threaten the family with destruction is clear evidence of the fact that, in a world in which women were economically dependent upon men, the possession of money played an enormous role in the relationships between the sexes. Occasionally the Victorian melodrama portrays the equation of money and sexual dominance with startling bluntness. In a play by Dion Boucicault, *Mercy Dodd; or Presumptive Evidence* (1869) the hero, Matthew Dodd, informs his sweetheart that his bankruptcy has made him unable to marry her: "I have tried the battle of life, and I cannot hold my own with my fellow men. I have no right to own a woman until I have won a home for her. My wife must not pity me as you do—she must respect me" (1.2).[20] Economic success and sexual pride of ownership are firmly linked in this statement, and make it abundantly clear that the ramifications of bankruptcy for men went far beyond the financial loss.

For women, the consequences could be equally dire. The woman who was not protected economically by a man clearly found herself sexually vulnerable as well; thus in countless melodramas the villain assaults the virtue of the innocent heroine by means of economic threat. The hoariest plots of the Victorian stage were those in which the villain eliminated the heroine's male protector (husband, brother, father, lover) with some elaborate device, sometimes falsely accusing him of a crime, but often manipulating events to ruin him economically, and then demanded the heroine's sexual favors as she was about to be evicted for lack of rent money. (Most often, in fact, the lecherous villain is himself the landlord.)

One of the classic examples of this genre was *Luke the Labourer* (1826) in which the lecherous village squire attempted to corrupt the heroine by ruining her father. Douglas Jerrold's *Black Ey'd Susan* (1829) achieved enormous popularity a few years later by having *two* evil villains assaulting the purity of the heroine.[21] In act 1 the heroine is told that her sailor husband is dead, and that she must marry the villain, or her evil-hearted uncle (who is also her landlord) will seize for long arrears of rent the property of the old woman with whom Susan lives. In the very first moments of the play there is already a bailiff in possession of this home. By the second act, Susan's husband William has returned home to rescue her, and her virtue is now being tried by William's captain (who is also his economic superior).

Even an aristocratic background seems to offer women no protection against this kind of sexual vulnerability. In Tom Taylor's *Our American Cousin* (1858) a dishonest agent has ruined Sir Edward Trenchard and now holds his mortgage, demanding the hand of Sir Edward's daughter.[22] One of the evil villains of Boucicault's *The Colleen Bawn* (1860), on the other hand, is an older man who desires to marry the hero's mother.[23] Once again he is a corrupt agent who holds the mortgage on the family property, and his intended victim protests ineffectually but truthfully: "You hold ruin over our heads" (1.1). So standard was this situation that by the time W. S. Foote's *Bitter Cold* (1865) pictured a murderous, lecherous squire evicting the heroine from her home on a cold Christmas eve, even the dialogue had become a thundering cliché, generations old:

Mary Manners, tomorrow the rent of this farm becomes due. See that you are prepared to pay it! The wife of an assassin has no claim upon a landlord's indulgence, and you have but one claim upon mine. Be prepared either with the money or your consent to my proposals, or by Heaven, I hurl you forth helpless, friendless upon the world—to beg, to starve!(Pp.150–51)[24]

The hero can usually be depended upon to emerge from the villain's machinations unscathed and in time to protect the heroine from the fate worse than death. The happy ending, however, merely serves to emphasize the helplessness of the female; the economic protector of the female (he who comes up with the money for rent) is considered by all to be entitled to her sexual favors.

In countless such scenes, the threat of bankruptcy or poverty is the fulcrum upon which the plot turns; it is rare, however, for an actual bankruptcy to materialize. When bankruptcy actually takes place upon the Victorian stage it is likely to be a first-act phenomenon. Bankruptcy is sometimes described as having already occurred before act 1, or else it takes place within moments of the raising of the curtain. These actual bankruptcies (as opposed to the theoretical ones, which are the weapons of villains) are usually used to establish the fortunes of the heroine, the bankruptcy of her father being one of the persecutions a heroine is naturally liable to, or else to establish clearly the honor or dishonor of a character. In *Mercy Dodd; or Presumptive Evidence* Matthew Dodd learns of the failure of a brewery company, of which he is a director, in the first moments of act 1, and he discovers that there is a warrant for him and the other directors on charges of misconduct. Matthew responds: "I do not know how far the errors of these men may involve me in their ruin—but surely it cannot involve me in their shame" (1.1). [25] In fact, his innocence is quickly established, the charges are promptly dismissed, and the failure of the company has nothing to do with the plot—it serves only to bring the detective Brassey onto the scene, and to firmly establish the honorable conduct of Matthew Dodd.

In a similar fashion, bankruptcy was used to establish the honor of a character in a much earlier play, George Coleman's *John Bull, or The Englishman's Fireside* (1803).[26] John Thornberry is an honorable old tradesman who has lent a friend the whole profit of his trade to save him from sinking. The friend has walked off with the money, leaving Thornberry a bankrupt. By the second act we are told that the bailiffs have arrived down below, but Thornberry remains unbowed in his idealized mercantile honor:

I began with a little; I made that little great by industry; I never cringed to a customer to get him into my books, that I might hamper him with an overcharged bill for long credit; I earned my fair profits; I paid my fair way; I break by the treachery of a friend; and my first dividend will be seventeen shillings in the pound. I wish every tradesman in England may clap his hand on his heart to say as much when he asks a creditor to sign his certificate . . . I can face my creditors like an honest man. (2.3)

Such a speech not only establishes Thornberry as an honest merchant and gentleman, but makes him a very unique bankrupt indeed. (As was mentioned in chapter 2, only a small proportion of all bankrupts ever paid more than a few shillings in the pound.) A similar use of bankruptcy to establish honorable character may be found in Isaac Pocock's *The Miller and His Men* (1813).[27] In act 1 the curtain rises on Kelmar, the bankrupt miller, who says:

What! more sacks, more grist to the mill! Early and late the miller thrives, he that was my tenant is now my landlord; this hovel, that once sheltered him, is now the only dwelling of bankrupt, broken-hearted Kelmar— well, I strove my best against misfortunes, and thanks to heaven, have fallen respected, even by my enemies.(1.1)

Kelmar, like John Thornberry, has been ruined by a villain rather than by his own improvidence. The arbitrary nature of such downfalls may well have appealed to an audience that had come to suspect with a growing sense of unease its lack of control over its own economic fate. Equally appealing was the certainty that by the final curtain the Kelmars and the Thornberrys would surely be restored to their rightful place. A bourgeois audience haunted always by an underlying fear of failure was certain to be reassured by the happy ending of melodrama that proved in play after play that providence would not fail to right the wrongs of the virtuous.

The bankruptcies of such good old men as Kelmar the miller and John Thornberry were not often the focus of the drama, but instead remained peripheral incidents designed to set other events in motion. Toward the middle of the century, however (the precise date seems to be in dispute among authorities), the upper middle classes apparently returned to the theater, thus reclaiming it once again as "respectable" entertainment. With a new audience, a new range of themes began to appear in Victorian drama. For the first time plays appeared that were set in the City, and that concerned themselves with such new subjects as commercial ambitions, intrigues of high finance and speculation, the promise of power and wealth, and the sudden bankruptcies that could plunge the unwary, the unscrupulous, or the unlucky from riches to sudden poverty. Such themes had long been common on the French stage from which enterprising English directors often borrowed material. The French money-play dates back to the days of Molière, and nineteenth-century French drama was filled with speculators, confidence men, and swindlers trying to make a spectacular *coup de Bourse*.[28]

Now such English writers as Dion Boucicault and Tom Taylor seized upon these new themes, sensing the drama inherent in the effect that commercial life was beginning to have upon the individual character and upon domestic life.[29] As early as 1847, Boucicault's comedy, *The School for Scheming*, featured Mr. Macdunnum, the audacious creator of a phony joint-stock company, "The Railway Scheme Assurance Co."[30] Speaking of the current boom in stock enterprises (1847 was, of course, the height of the Railway Mania), Macdunnum boasts that it is an age "when England's aristocracy are ennobling her enterprises, making speculation fashionable." His practical friend Mrs. Singleheart replies ironically, "and England's merchants enriching her Gazette, making bankruptcy respectable" (1.2). As the play progresses, Macdunnum is reported to have made a fortune and become a "great capitalist." By act 5, of course, we discover him a ruined man and properly chastened.

Even more audacious is the swindler Affable Hawk, the hero of *The Game of Speculation*, translated by G. H. Lewes in 1851 from Balzac's *Mercadet*.[31] Hawk is a man who chooses to live by the precarious chances of speculation. His servant observes, "Every day a new speculation; every day a new committee formed! Wood pavement—quilted pavement—salt marshes—railways—waterworks—and yet always in debt!" (1.1). Unlike the good old men and befuddled heroes of other dramas who seem always to suffer bankruptcy through some other agency than their own, Affable Hawk deliberately courts ruin by his defiance of his creditors, although he is apparently reformed in the last act by a rather improbable turn of events. A more hardened swindler is the speculator Bloodgood of Boucicault's *The Poor of New York* (1857), which was also produced as *The Streets of London* (1864). A financial panic and the corrupt manipulation of the evil Bloodgood result in the dire poverty of the hero's family, who end up begging in the snow-covered streets.[32]

Several of the dramas of Tom Taylor explore the dramatic possibilities of the commercial world. *Still Waters Run Deep* (1855)[33] contrasts the gentle husband Mildmay with the flashy speculator Captain Hawksly, who dazzles Mildmay's wife and in-laws with his Inexplosible Galvanic Boats that are run on a new secret "motive principle." The turning point of the drama occurs when Mildmay proves himself to be a competent and honorable man of business by unmasking Hawksly as a corrupt swindler. Another of Taylor's speculators turns out to have redeeming qualities. Reuben Goldsched in *Payable on Demand* (1859) thrives on daring speculation not merely out of greed, but out of a sense of adventure and power.[34] He buys shares recklessly in a falling market ("Today, master of millions—tomorrow, on the verge of beggary"), and risks every penny of his fortune in an elaborate speculation that depends for its success on his being able to receive news of Napoleon's abdication by carrier pigeon before anyone else has heard of it. Coolly he assesses his prospects: either "Victory and a million" or "Bankruptcy and the Gazette." Like Lewes's Affable Hawk, Goldsched is redeemed in a somewhat arbitrary manner by good fortune and his own integrity.

The theme of speculation and commercial dishonesty also enters Taylor's *The Settling Day* (1865), in which another bold speculator offers the hero Markland a directorship in his new company which proposes to drain the Thames River ("to decompose the water of one of our noble metropolitan rivers by powerful voltaic action") to convert its hydrogen into heating for homes.[35] Markland, the model of an honorable English financier, refuses such a scheme, but discovers to his horror that his partner in his own bank has taken advantage of Markland's year-long honeymoon to use the clients' funds for speculative purposes. (The plot mirrors actual banking scandals which will be discussed at length in chapter 7, in a description of later Victorian commercial problems.) The consequent failure that threatens the company becomes a test of integrity; Markland wants to make the facts known to the world, while his dishonest partner wishes to deceive by covering up the truth.

Unable to face the dishonor and shame of such a scandalous bankruptcy, Markland considers suicide as he thinks of the scorn that will be heaped upon him: "Markland, the fraudulent banker, the appropriator of his clients' securities, will be the nine day wonder of the police reports, the mark of the finger of public scorn" (4.1). Markland is as innocent and passive a hero as any of the other characters of Victorian melodrama who are brought to the brink of bankruptcy by forces beyond their control, but *The Settling Day* is a serious examination of the morality of the commercial world, and is one of the few Victorian dramas to make the threatened bankruptcy the central focus of the play.

POPULAR FICTION

A vast new audience of readers led to the creation of a virtual flood of sentimental and sensational popular fiction during the Victorian years. Although the primary intention of such works was simply to entertain its audience with an engrossing story, there seems to have clung to the activity of reading certain earlier notions about reading as a means of "improvement."[36] Thus many authors claimed that their purpose was to educate their readers (especially the impressionable young females who were the novels' primary audience), to inculcate certain prudential virtues, and to warn of the pitfalls of certain dangerous vices. At the very least this desire for a high "moral" tone ensured that in popular fiction, as in melodrama, the wicked were always certain to be punished, and the virtuous, after much suffering, were sure to be rewarded.

As in Victorian painting and melodrama, the world of Victorian popular fiction is filled with economic insecurity. The characters are habitually concerned with money, debt, and sudden financial loss.[37] There are a truly remarkable number of heroines whose fathers suffer bankruptcy; Margaret Dalziel comments that "When our credibility is strained by following over and over again the fortunes of the beautiful girl whose father has lost all in financial speculation and committed suicide, leaving his penniless family to contend with a cruel world, we must remember that this was a period of financial instability, when fortunes were won and lost with a speed and frequency we can hardly realize."[38] As in painting and melodrama, bankruptcy was seldom at the center of the stage; the popular sentimental novel did not begin to examine the world of finance and industry until at least the middle of the century.[39] As J. M. S. Tomkins observes, "It is indeed singular how slowly the prevailing interests of the day, as they are reflected in the magazines, make their way into the novel . . . such important aspects of society as trade . . . are hardly to be found."[40]

Even as late as the 1860s, it is instructive to note that Geraldine Jewsbury, who was an influential reader for several publishers (it was she who urged Bentley to publish *East Lynne*) was warning against novels that dealt with the commercial problems of a merchant, on the grounds that the readers of the influential circulating libraries such as Mudie's would not want to read about the troubles which they (or some member of their family) might face in real life. One particular novel, which she found otherwise "clear, vivid, and truthful" she advised Bentley not to publish on just such grounds. She wrote to Bentley: "Will fashionable fine ladies and gentlemen read of the painful anxieties of a broken merchant? Will ordinary female readers care to read of the gradations of business speculation? . . . Would men of business care to *read* what they have to face . . . six days in every week?"[41] (One recalls the protests of Samuel Smiles that "readers do not care to know about the general who lost his battles . . . the merchant who could not keep out of the *Gazette*.")

Bankruptcy, then, is seldom considered in the popular sentimental novel for its own intrinsic interest, but rather for its effect upon the domestic hearth. As in other forms of Victorian art, there is great interest in the popular fiction of the day in all of the vices which might constitute a threat to family life. J. M. S. Tomkins has described the typical novel of "gaming":

> The apprehensive wife, raking together the sacred embers of her hearth, sees her infatuated husband scatter them once more, and draws her children to her in the cold wind of misfortune. From the moment when she is told that she is no longer the mistress of these splendid apartments, through the arrival of the bailiff . . . the novelist's eye is turned on her. It is not gaming that is studied, but the effects of gaming on the domestic circle.[42]

As in painting and drama, in popular fiction the family is forever being threatened with economic downfall.

Bankruptcy is merely one of the most frequent of the disasters that beset the much-persecuted heroine who lives at the heart of the sentimental novel. One such suffering maiden, for example, was the heroine of *Ellen Maynard; or The Death Wail of the Hawkshaws* (serialized in *The Family Herald* in 1857). A gently-reared orphan, beautiful and virtuous, is reduced to sudden poverty and forced to begin life as a governess.[43] Ellen Maynard and her sisters in suffering were the staples of the popular sentimental novel, which portrayed a feminine world of domestic problems and was created by female authors for female readers. From this feminine perspective the world of business seems remote and mysterious; as Dalziel observes, "Her father's or her husband's business was something of which the heroine remained completely and contentedly ignorant. Again and again total financial ruin overwhelms a gently nurtured woman and she is left penniless, without having had the faintest warning of such possibility."[44] J. M. S. Tomkins confirms this phenomenon: "Man is seen in his domestic aspect as father, husband, son or lover; if a merchant, we never accompany him to his counting house. . . ."[45] Such a limited feminine perspective emphasizes, of course, the complete economic dependence of women; bankruptcy is viewed as a terrifying catastrophe from a distant and mysterious economic life felt only in its shattering reverberations in the feminine world of the home.

Thus in the sentimental popular fiction of the day, as well as in Victorian painting and drama, bankruptcy is seldom an event that occupies the center of the stage. It is a threat that hangs heavy in the air, a specter that haunts both characters and audience, or a disaster that creates sympathy for the protagonist and sets the plot in motion. Although Victorian imagination seems to have been permeated with an ever-present fear of economic disaster, it is only in a few rare exceptions that a painting, drama, or sentimental novel will focus primarily upon an event of bankruptcy as possessing intrinsic interest in and of itself. It was left instead to the major novelists of the day to fully utilize the experience of bankruptcy, and to examine not only its effect upon the domestic hearth, but also its implications for the character of the individual, and its meaning in a wider social context as well. With surprising consistency, the great novelists of the early and middle Victorian years chose to explore the dramatic possibilities inherent in the act of bankruptcy; Dickens, Thackeray, Brontë, Gaskell, Eliot, and Trollope all wrote at least one major novel in which an episode of bankruptcy is the central focus of plot, character development, and metaphorical implications. The remainder of this study, then, will be devoted to examining those novels in which the great writers of the Victorian period confronted the specter of bankruptcy and wrestled with its contradictions to extract some kind of meaningful protrait of their age.

4

The Major Novelists' View of Bankruptcy

The reality of bankruptcy was clearly an unpleasant one for the Victorians, and chapter 2 and 3 have described the persistence with which it refused to be ignored, swelling the lists of the daily newspapers, plaguing the debates of parliamentary committees, and haunting the imagination in painting, drama, and fiction. The subject was indeed so painful that many critics—such as Geraldine Jewsbury—considered it inappropriate for a mass audience. (The feeling is perhaps best expressed by that arbiter of public taste, Mr. Podsnap, who dismisses bankruptcy as "an odious subject, an offensive subject," and sweeps it away as one of the many crude realities of life not fit for public mention.)

As we have seen, most of the artists of the Victorian period concurred in the feeling that the public would not care to examine too thoroughly an experience that they might well have to undergo in reality some day, and thus Victorian art is filled with paintings, dramas, and fictions that exhibit a fear of economic disaster amounting almost to paranoia, and yet with rare exceptions manage to avoid lingering upon the unpleasant details of the experience of bankruptcy. The major novelists, however, were more concerned with creating a realistic and truthful portrait of their age, and were more skillful at doing so. At a time in which the pages of the daily newspaper attested to the overwhelming concern of the Victorians with the stubborn challenge of bankruptcy, the demands of verisimilitude alone ensured that the great novelists would be forced to dwell upon this painful reality with greater emphasis than it had yet been given in any other form of art.

A number of important novels of the early and middle Victorian years are built around an episode of bankruptcy: Dickens's *Dombey and Son* (1848) and *Little Dorrit* (1857), Thackeray's *The Newcomes* (1855), which was anticipated by the episode of Mr. Sedley's bankruptcy in *Vanity Fair* (1848),

Brontë's *Shirley* (1849), Gaskell's *North and South* (1855), Eliot's *The Mill on the Floss* (1860) with a further consideration of bankruptcy in the episode of Lydgate's ruin in *Middlemarch* (1872), and Trollope's *The Way We Live Now* (1875). Such works are not only realistic representations of the painful problem that bankruptcy presented for Victorian society; they are novels of bankruptcy in the sense that the idea of bankruptcy permeates the work in subject, plot, structure, language, and meaning as a unifying and controlling image.

BANKRUPTCY AS REPRESENTATIONAL REALISM

Sensing that they possessed in the popular novel a form capable of portraying the social world in more comprehensive and realistic detail than ever before had been attempted, the great Victorian novelists could not fail to comprehend that the new economic conditions of industrial England were a harsh reality that had yet to be assimilated, and that bankruptcy, now a stark fact of life, might provide one of the keys for examining that reality. The episodes of bankruptcy as they appear in the pages of Dickens, Thackeray, and the others involve the same controversies that raged in the contemporary periodicals and parliamentary debates, or surfaced in bathetic paintings, melodramas, and sentimental novels of families being evicted into snow-covered streets.

In the bewildering world of nineteenth-century industrialism, the individual was perceived to be more at the mercy of harsh economic realities than at any time previously, and the major novelists, almost without exception, used the experience of bankruptcy as the perfect image for the economic helplessness of the individual in a harsh industrial world. Most fictional portraits of bankrupts seem to contain an underlying sense of despair at the complexity of the industrial society and the apparent vulnerability of the individual, who seems to need both acuteness and a fair share of "rascality" to survive in a world in which older traditions and personal relationships have given way to the "cash-nexus" of the nineteenth-century economy.

Mr. Tulliver in Eliot's *The Mill on the Floss,* Sol Gills in Dickens's *Dombey and Son,* Mr. Dorrit in *Little Dorrit,* and Colonel Newcome in Thackeray's *The Newcomes* are characters who are simply not equipped to deal with the modern mercantile world, and thus more or less stumble into bankruptcy. Mr. Tulliver, for example, considers himself a man of substance because he possesses land and a mill; the fact of a large mortgage and unpaid debts have not really registered upon his consciousness. His view of the world is a simple one—if he needs water for his mill, for example, then he ought to be entitled to it, " 'as plain as water's water.' " He is aware, however, that the modern mercantile world is a complicated place in which he lacks the necessary skills to survive, and in which a fact of life as simple and as necessary as water cannot be obtained without legal rights. Thus, although he is a strictly honest and honorable man, Mr. Tulliver believes that legal "rascality" is necessary for success in the world. The law, to Mr. Tulliver, is "a sort of cock-fight" in which "the ends of justice could only be achieved by employing a stronger knave to frustrate a weaker."[1] Though not a "schol-ard" himself, Mr. Tulliver wants his son Tom to have an education " 'so as he might be up to the tricks o' these fellows as talk fine and write with a flourish' " (*MF*, 1.2.9). In spite of his willingness to stoop to such "rascality" to obtain water rights, Mr. Tulliver is defeated by a world which proves to be so complex that even hiring a clever lawyer cannot ensure his survival. He is forced to admit in the end that "the raskills" have been too many for him. The novelist considers the question of the guilt of Tulliver's legal opponent: "it is still possible to believe that the attorney was not more guilty towards [Mr. Tulliver] than an ingenious machine which performs his work with much regularity is guilty towards the rash man who, venturing too near it, is caught by some fly-wheel or other and suddenly converted into unexpected mince meat" (*MF*, 3.7.218–19).

The image of Mr. Tulliver caught and crushed in the machinery of an incomprehensible modern world is an echo of Tulliver's own words earlier, in which he expresses his perplexity at the complex and frightening form the world has assumed:

> "not but what, if the world had been left, the way God made it, I could ha' seen my way and held my own wi' the best of 'em—, but things have got so twisted round and wrapped up i' unreasonable words, as aren't a bit like 'em, as I'm clean at fault, often an' often. Everything winds about so—the more straight forward you are, the more you're puzzled." (*MF*, 1.3.18–19)

Thus the old verities have disappeared, and even language itself no longer has any foundation in certainty. When words treacherously refuse to attach themselves to any fixed meaning, and even such an elemental truth as 'water's water' can no longer be relied upon, it is small wonder that Vic-torian literature is filled with characters who have been defeated by the complexities of the modern world.

Uncle Sol Gills of *Dombey and Son* is another naif who is bewildered by modern mercantile methods. (When the final happy ending provides for Mr. Gills's investments to come out "wonderfully well," it seems a rather gratuitous and scarcely credible stroke of authorial manipulation.) With his old-fashioned stock of marine supplies, Uncle Sol is beset by "competition, competition—new invention, new invention—alteration, alteration," and his shop is seized in an execution. Dombey's own failure is in sharp contrast to Sol Gills's. Dombey goes bankrupt because of pride and stubbornness; he has been too much of the world, in contrast to Uncle Sol who has barely understood it.

Another character incapable of finding his footing in the bewildering complexity of economic life is Mr. Dorrit, who languishes in debtors' prison out of a simple inability to understand the muddle he has made out of his finances:

> The affairs of this debtor were perplexed by a partnership of which he knew no more than that he had invested money in it, by legal matters of assignment and settlement, conveyance here and conveyance there, suspicion of unlawful preference of creditors in this direction and mysterious spiriting away of property in that; and as nobody on the face of the earth could be more incapable of explaining any single item in the heap of confusion than the debtor himself, nothing comprehensible could be made of his case . . . to closet him with accountants and sharp practitioners, learned in the wiles of insolvency and bankruptcy, was only to put the case out at compound interest and incomprehensibility.[2]

Clearly Mr. Dorrit is serving a jail sentence for the crime of not being able to cope with the financial maneuvers that the modern world requires.

The most unworldly innocent of all is Thackeray's Colonel Newcome, a simple, honorable old soul, with no personal desire for wealth and power, who is enmeshed in a huge financial speculation, unwittingly becoming the figurehead of a "complicated, enormous, outrageous swindle." Not content to invest every penny of his own in this dubious venture, the good Colonel encourages his friends to plunge their money into the company. He even invests the inheritance of his daughter-in-law in the Bundelcund Bank, a move of questionable legality since he is her trustee and a director of the bank as well. As Thackeray observes, "this worthy old Colonel, who fancied himself to be so clever a man of business, chose to conduct it in utter ignorance and defiance of the law."[3] Colonel Newcome in the end is crushed by the failure of his great bank because he has failed to understand the ground rules of survival in nineteenth-century capitalism. He has trusted rather to the older traditions of noble intentions and an honorable character, and they have failed him.

Even more sophisticated and energetic entrepreneurs often seem powerless in the Victorian novel to control their own economic destiny. Daniel Doyce in *Little Dorrit,* for example, is a practical inventor who might be expected to contribute to the progress of an energetic and inventive industrial society. But Dickens pictures this society as too encrusted with aristocratic patronage to be able to encourage such industry; Doyce is defeated by the gothic bureaucracy of the Circumlocution Office. Other entrepreneurial heroes of the Victorian novel are defeated by the vicissitudes of complicated trade conditions far beyond their control. Robert Moore of Brontë's *Shirley,* for example, is an industrious and knowl-

edgeable manufacturer, but his business fails because of difficulties with
foreign markets due to the fluctuating fortunes of the Napoleonic Wars, a
period of economic stress that also dealt harshly with Amelia Sedley's father
in Thackeray's *Vanity Fair*.

The most industrious and capable entrepreneur of all is Gaskell's Mr.
Thornton in *North and South*, who has built a successful factory by ploughing back all of his profits into enlarging his plant and investing heavily in
new machinery. Even this shrewd man of business is vulnerable to a period
of bad trade, however; beset by one of the "crises" that Marx foresaw would
inevitably plague the capitalist economy, he has to borrow to survive, and is
finally done in by the failure of a house in the American trade "which went
down, along with several others . . . like a pack of cards, the fall of one
compelling other failures."[4] Thus in the interdependent world of Victorian
capitalism (Samuel Smiles to the contrary), individual enterprise and energy often do *not* prove to be enough to ensure success, and the novelists
were quick to comprehend the dramatic emphasis that an episode of
bankruptcy could give to the growing concern over the powerlessness of
the individual.

Although the novelists were not often clear about the finer details of the
legal procedures that surrounded bankruptcy, the full weight of the novel's
most detailed realism is often brought to bear upon the public reaction that
followed a business failure. That such descriptions are realistic is beyond
question. One has only to read accounts of parliamentary debates to ascertain in what terms of scorn the bankrupt is castigated, and novel after novel
depicts with the most faithful verisimilitude this outpouring of public
blame which could make a pariah of the man who failed.

Dickens was quite explicit about the condemnation that would be the fate
of such victims of financial failure as Arthur Clennam: "Those who had not
been deluded being certain to wax exceedingly wroth with them for not
having been wise as they were; and those who had been deluded being
certain to find excuses and reasons for themselves, of which they were
equally certain to see that other sufferers were wholly devoid;—not to
mention the great probability of every individual sufferer persuading himself, to his violent indignation, that but for the example of all other sufferers he would never have put himself in the way of suffering" (*LD*,
2.26.696). Thackeray is equally clear in *Vanity Fair* about why such a man as
Mr. Osborne would find it both necessary and convenient to condemn his
former friend, the bankrupt Mr. Sedley:

> When one man has been under very remarkable obligations to another,
> with whom he subsequently quarrels, a common sense of decency, as it
> were, makes of the former a much severer enemy than a mere stranger
> must be. To account for your own hard-heartedness and ingratitude in
> such a case, you are bound to prove the other party's crime. It is not that
> you are selfish, brutal, and angry at the failure of a speculation—no, no—

it is that your partner has led you into it by the basest treachery and with the most sinister motives. From a mere sense of consistency, a persecutor is bound to show that the fallen man is a villain—otherwise he, the persecutor, is a wretch himself.

And as a general rule, which may make all creditors who are inclined to be severe pretty comfortable in their minds, no men embarrassed are altogether honest, very likely. They conceal something; they exaggerate chances of good luck; hide away the real state of affairs; say that things are flourishing when they are hopeless; keep a smiling face (a dreary smile it is) upon the verge of bankruptcy—are ready to lay hold of any pretext for delay or of any money, so as to stave off the inevitable ruin for a few days longer. "Down with such dishonesty," says the creditor in triumph, and reviles his sinking enemy. "You fool, why do you catch at a straw?" calm good sense says to the man that is drowning. "You villain, why do you shrink from plunging into the irretrievable *Gazette?*" says prosperity to the poor devil battling in that black gulf.[5]

The same self-righteous indignation described by Thackeray is directed at Mr. Dombey for his failure ("The world was very busy now, in sooth, and had a deal to say. It was an innocently credulous and a much ill-used world."),[6] while in *The Mill on the Floss* Mr. Tulliver is condemned by his wife's relations, the Gleggs and Pullets, who constitute a chorus of blame that represents the judgment of the decent citizens of St. Oggs. (Aunt Glegg regards the Tullivers as "'them as have had the same chance as me, only they've been wicked and wasteful'" [*MF*, 3.3.189].)

It is clear that the novelists' sympathies in these scenes are with the bankrupt who has been cast out of respectable society, and that the sharpest satire is being directed toward the hypocrisy and lack of charity of the solvent world. It would be misleading, however, to assume that the great Victorian novelists in no way share the attitude of their contemporaries toward bankruptcy. The novelists, in fact, by and large accepted the prevailing code of commercial honor. Bankruptcy is usually portrayed as a moral failure in the Victorian novel, though perhaps not precisely the kind of moral failure that Samuel Smiles had in mind—that is, failure through lack of energetic endeavor, or lack of prudence. Most of the characters who fail in these novels bring about their own downfall through some moral flaw or blindness. Mr. Dombey allows his assistant Carker to embark on "prodigious ventures" designed solely to flatter his own vanity and ambition, and brings about the downfall of his house by refusing out of stubbornness and pride to contract his enterprises. Colonel Newcome is changed and subtly corrupted by the directorship of the Bundelcund Bank; having assumed this position of power he feels compelled to assume as well the luxurious style of life that estranges him from his son and strains his resources. (He also commits a sin of bad faith in his vindictiveness against Barnes Newcome, which leads, among other complications, to the unnecessary expenditure of a parliamentary election.)

Mr. Tulliver, in *The Mill on the Floss*, is a rash and impetuous man who

views law and business as the survival of the strongest knave, and brings
about his own ruin by his blunders. Lydgate, in Eliot's *Middlemarch,* causes
his own downfall by his moral blindness—the "spots of commonness" that
allow him to overstrain his finances for superficial vanities. In the case of
Dickens's Mr. Merdle in *Little Dorrit* and Trollope's Mr. Melmotte in *The Way
We Live Now,* such fine moral distinctions hardly apply; each man ends in
bankruptcy because he is a swindler, a forger, and a thief.

Thus the treatment of bankrupt characters in the major Victorian novels
does not suggest a radical departure from the standard public rhetoric of
the time. The novelists seem to concur with the evangelical emphasis on
success as a reward for virtue, and its corollary suspicion that failure and
poverty must somehow spring from a moral failure—although admittedly
the moral flaws portrayed vary greatly from novel to novel, and are not
always the standard economic vices (sloth, improvidence, recklessness)
associated with bankruptcy in the public rhetoric. Although the novelists
seem to be attaching a somewhat broader moral parable to bankruptcy than
was the case in other forms of Victorian culture, it is nevertheless apparent
that moral success is often pictured in the Victorian novel as the application
of thrift, industry, and sobriety—the economic virtues farthest removed
from such a profligate condition as bankruptcy. Thus a typical example of
moral success such as David Copperfield becomes "earnest" only when his
aunt loses her money and he must make his way in the world by hard work;
and Nicholas Nickleby demonstrates his strength of character by working
to reestablish the fortune and reputation of his ruined father. Other
earnest young Victorian heros, such as Fred Vincy in *Middlemarch* and Tom
Tulliver in *The Mill on the Floss,* have to learn that success comes about only
through laborious effort and constant industry.

In addition to those earnest characters who succeed by virtue of hard
work and prudence, cautionary examples of characters heavily in debt are
frequently found in Victorian novels. Thackeray is particularly fond of
using scenes in the "spunging-house" for comic effect (as with Rawdon
Crawley in *Vanity Fair,* or Mr. Honeyman in *The Newcomes*), and Thackeray
and Trollope especially satirize that class of businessman, usually Hebraic,
that makes its living from those in debt. However, there is never a doubt in
even the most comic episodes that debt is a moral evil to be avoided or
repented by the judicious. In his well-known disquisition in *Vanity Fair* on
"how to live on nothing a year," Thackeray takes great delight in the comic
rascality of Becky and Rawdon, and yet sees with great clarity the serious
consequences to the victims of the Crawleys' financial irresponsibility.

Rawdon and Becky rent a house from Raggles, who has borrowed from a
fellow butler to purchase it, and will provide their meals and wait on their
table:

This was the way, then, Crawley got his house for nothing, for though
Raggles had to pay taxes and rates, and the interest of the mortgage to

the brother butler; and the insurance of his life, and the charges for his children at school; and the value of the meat and drink which his own family—and for a time that of Colonel Crawley too—consumed; and though the poor wretch was utterly ruined by the transaction, his children being flung on the streets, and himself driven into the Fleet Prison; yet somebody must pay even for gentlemen who live for nothing a year. (*VF*, 37. 360)

Although the irony is at least partially directed at the unfortunate Raggles, who had hoped to earn a profit by catering to this feckless pair, there is nevertheless a strong perception of debt as a moral crime that is all the more heinous because its consequences are felt more painfully by the weak and powerless: ". . . how many great noblemen rob their petty tradesmen, condescend to swindle their poor retainers out of wretched little sums and cheat for a few shillings?" (*VF*, 37. 360).

Fred Vincy, in *Middlemarch*, is taught most painfully that debt is a wrong committed against those whose money is not repaid. Fred had borrowed money for the small pleasures necessary to a college gentleman from the honorable neighbors he sincerely admires; but "he had not occupied himself with the inconvenience and possible injury that his breach might occasion them, for this exercise of the imagination on other people's needs is not common with hopeful young gentlemen."[7] It is only after his failure to make good on his debt that Fred realizes that Mrs. Garth and Mary must inevitably lose the money they had saved through hard work and great sacrifice. The lesson is a painful one for Fred, but it causes him to mend his ways, to learn the value of hard work, and to apply his industry to the repayment of his debts. Fred Vincy's history, in fact, is designed as a deliberate counterpoint to the story of Lydgate's bankruptcy; Fred, with the encouragement of a good woman, adopts the course of energy, industry, and thrift, and successfully establishes himself; while Lydgate, encouraged by a weak woman, entangles himself in debts for needless vanities, and in spite of his willingness to work finds himself sinking into failure.

Thus the attitude of the major Victorian novelists toward bankruptcy and debt is not substantially different from that of their contemporaries. Debt is a moral wrong, and bankruptcy a further aggravation of that wrong because it makes permanent the failure to repay money. Honor is still on the side of those who pay their debts, and, among bankrupts, there is more honor to the man who makes an honest attempt at paying his creditors than to the man who holds back all that he can for himself. Thus it is possible in the novel to make a distinction between such "honorable" bankrupts as Mr. Dombey, Col. Newcome, and Arthur Clennam, and such dishonorable bankrupts as Merdle and Melmotte (a distinction that was less easy to discern factually, as the legislators were to discover). The Victorian novelist, in fact, was likely to use bankruptcy as a kind of moral testing ground, according to the prevailing commercial code of the day, in which the repayment of creditors becomes a badge of honor. So important was this moral obligation that indeed most of the novelists felt compelled to portray their "bankrupt" characters eventually repaying most of their debts. The number of creditors who received satisfaction in these novels in all probability misrepresents the actual state of affairs in Bankruptcy Court, where in fact very few real-life creditors were likely to be repaid in full.

One of the most honorable gestures a man can make is to repay the debts of a bankrupt father, and several characters in the novels drive themselves mercilessly to do just that. Tom Tulliver, for example, in *The Mill on The Floss,* accepts a humble position in his uncle's firm and devotes himself to the repayment of his father's creditors. His motives have at least as much to do with his own honor and reputation as with his father's: "perhaps his father might have helped bringing them all down in the world, and making people talk of them with contempt, but no one should talk long of Tom Tulliver with contempt" (*MF,* 3.2.180). Tom succeeds in recovering his father's reputation by paying back Mr. Tulliver's creditors and even regaining possession of the mill. His modest speech to the creditors ("He was glad that he had been able to help his father in proving his integrity and regaining his honest name" [*MF,* 5.7.310]), is the high point of Tom's life, and in some ways the high point of the novel (it is the apex of the Tullivers' struggles, from which their fortunes once again go downhill).

The author's attitude toward debt is clear; even the somewhat dim-witted Mrs. Tulliver "had been brought up to think that to wrong people of their money, which was another phrase for debt, was a sort of moral pillory" (*MF,* 4.2.244). Debt is a "hateful incubus," a "deep pit," and to rid oneself of it a moral victory; and yet Eliot is profoundly aware of the contradictions in the contemporary attitudes and practices toward debt and bankruptcy:

> These narrow notions about debt held by the old-fashioned Tullivers may perhaps excite a smile on the faces of many readers in these days of wide commercial views and wide philosophy, according to which everything rights itself without any trouble of ours. . . . I am telling the history of very simple people who had never had any illuminating doubts as to personal integrity and honor. (*MF,* 4.2.244)

It is clear that Eliot has no more "illuminating doubts" about honor and integrity in this case than the "old-fashioned" Tulliver family; all of the irony of the passage is directed against the modern spirit of "wide commercial views" that allows business men to rationalize away the dishonor of debt for their own convenience. The irony is particularly effective following as it does the opening chapter of book 4, with its pointed contrast of the ruined and "commonplace" houses of the Rhone with the splendid castles of the Rhine, and its sense of "our own vulgar era" as being sordid and narrow compared to the glories of the past. The irony directed toward the modern commercial spirit also evokes echoes of an earlier description of St. Ogg's during the civil wars: "Many honest citizens lost all their possessions for conscience's sake in those times and went forth beggared from their native town. Doubtless there are many houses standing now on which those honest citizens turned their backs in sorrow; quaint-gabled houses looking on the river, jammed between newer warehouses. . ." (*MF*, 1.12.105). The houses of the religious martyrs are in this description unmistakably juxtaposed with the symbols of commerce and change and the impinging modern world in which people no longer give up possessions for conscience. In these meaner-spirited times the author clearly finds Tom Tulliver's stubborn insistence upon the repayment of his father's debts an admirable gesture.

Other Victorian heroes of novels make similar gestures that establish them in the readers' eyes as men of honor. Charlotte Brontë's Robert Moore, for example, in *Shirley*, is from a family of wealthy merchants of Antwerp made bankrupt by the French Revolution. In spite of the fact that his father's liabilities have been "duly set aside by a composition with creditors," Moore considers these debts "as a legacy; and . . . he aspired one day to discharge them, and to rebuild the fallen house of Gerard and Moore."[8]

The hero of Gaskell's *North and South*, Mr. Thornton, closely resembles Robert Moore (and indeed there are remarkable similarities between the plots of *Shirley* and *North and South*, similarities that may have sprung from the personal relationship between Brontë and Gaskell or simply from an extraordinary conjunction of viewpoints in their work). Like Robert Moore, Gaskell's hero exercises "iron discipline" working to repay the debts of his impoverished father. He is said to have "absolutely lived upon water-porridge for years" until, long after the creditors had given up hopes of seeing their money, Mr. Thornton quietly visits each creditor and repays all of his father's liabilities. As in the case of Eliot's Tom Tulliver, the gesture is meant to confer an aura of nobility upon a hero who lives up to the highest standards of commercial honor, even though the modern world of commerce seems to honor mostly in the breach the standards that it loudly proclaims.

No Victorian character is more admirable in his insistence upon commercial morality, and at the same time more out of step with modern notions of "success" than Eliot's Caleb Garth in *Middlemarch*. Garth is presented as a kind of Carlylean Hero of Work, a man who believes above all in the value of "that myriad-headed, myriad-handed labour by which the social body is fed, clothed, and housed" (*M*, 3.24.185). His goals are not the acquisition of capital, or the accumulation of worldly goods, but rather the satisfaction of a job well-done and an earnest comfort in the nobility of labor for its own sake. His divinities, according to Eliot, "were good practical schemes, accurate work, and the faithful completion of undertakings: his prince of darkness was a slack workman" (*M*, 3.24.185). Garth is perhaps the touchstone by which the fortunes of other characters may be measured; his devotion to labor is contrasted with Fred Vincy, who does not expect to have to earn his keep, and with Lydgate, who delights in intellectual labor, but expects certain luxuries as his natural right. Garth fails in business not because he indulges in luxuries, or because he is unwilling to work, but rather because he is too meticulous in his work to care about his profit—he is a man who knows "values" well but understands nothing about profit and loss. In his bankruptcy Caleb Garth is a model of honorable behavior. He conducted his business "entirely for the benefit of his assignees, and had been living narrowly, exerting himself to the utmost that he might after all pay twenty shillings in the pound" (*M*, 3.23.170).

Such an honest and unselfish course of action was probably not common in real life, but in Victorian novels many of the nobler heroes consider it the "law of honour" when facing bankruptcy to hold back nothing for themselves in order to repay as large a dividend as possible to their creditors. Mr. Thornton, for example, is haunted by the example of his father's less than honorable behavior on the brink of bankruptcy: "His father speculated wildly, failed, and then killed himself, because he could not bear the disgrace. All his former friends shrunk from the disclosures that had to be made of his dishonest gambling—wild, hopeless struggles, made with other people's money, to regain his own moderate portion of wealth" (*NS*, 1.2.87). In contrast to his father's moral weakness, Mr. Thornton is scrupulously honest when facing a similar bankruptcy. Offered the opportunity to redeem himself by speculation, he refuses, because it would risk his creditors' money, a risk "'of ruining many for my own paltry aggrandisement.'" Ironically, the speculation that could have saved his finances is successful, and Thornton is left to take comfort in the virtue that is his only reward. When asked if he must end a "failure" he replies, "'Not a failure. I must give up business, but I pay all men. . . . As I stand now, my creditors' money is safe—every farthing of it; but I don't know where to find my own . . . I dread, nothing . . . I know that no man will suffer by me'"(*NS*, 2.25.423–24).

A similar stand is taken by Dickens's Mr. Dombey when his business fails. The assessment of the situation is by Mr. Morfin, a character whose words have great weight because he is the honorable man of commerce in the novel, the business man with the heart of gold, the only one of Dombey's clerks who has not flattered Dombey, and the only one to stay on after the failure.

> The extent of Mr. Dombey's resources is not accurately within my knowledge; but though they are doubtless very large, his obligations are enormous. He is a gentleman of high honour and integrity. Any man in his position could, and any man in his position would, have saved himself, by making terms which would have very slightly, almost insensibly, increased the losses of those who have had dealings with him, and left him a remnant to live upon. But he is resolved upon payment to the last

farthing of his means. His own words are, that they will clear, or nearly clear, the House, and that no one can lose much . . . vices are sometimes only virtues carried to excess. His pride shows well in this. (*DS*, 58.778)

Arthur Clennam of *Little Dorrit* reacts to bankruptcy with similar rectitude. Rejecting all counsel that advises him to save what he can for himself, Clennam turns his own small savings over to the business, and prints a public declaration taking upon himself all the blame for having squandered the firm's finances in the dubious shares of Mr. Merdle. His response to ruin would have warmed the heart of Samuel Smiles himself: "'I must retain nothing for myself. I must resign to our creditors the power of management I have so much abused, and I must work out as much of my fault—or crime—as is susceptible of being worked out in the rest of my days'" (*LD*, 2.26.693).

Of all the heroes who regain the moral stature they have lost through bankruptcy by the honorable punctiliousness with which they repay their debts, none is quite so noble as Thackeray's Colonel Newcome. Although he has erred in his relationship with his son, the Colonel is not personally responsible in any way for the failures of the Bundlecund Bank—he is, in fact, the lone honest director connected with it, and has forfeited his own fortune in trying to make good to shareholders the losses of the bank. Even public opinion, usually so merciless, acquits the Colonel:

> It was shown that he had been egregiously duped in the transaction; that his credibility had cost him and his family a large fortune; that he had given up every penny that belonged to him; that there could not be any sort of stain upon his honest reputation. The judge before whom he appeared spoke with feeling and regard of the unhappy gentleman; the lawyer who examined him respected the grief and fall of that simple old man. (*N*, 71.722)

The integrity of Colonel Newcome is contrasted to the scheming of the other directors, who, having managed to withdraw in time with huge fortunes intact, are now living in luxury.

The Colonel, on the other hand, is never more honorable than in the ruin of his fortune. When the bailiffs take possession of his home, Newcome orders the servants to remove only a few necessaries, carefully making inventory of his valuables, so that as much as possible will remain for his creditors. All of his bills to servants and tradespeople are repaid at great personal sacrifice. The Colonel's own private military pension and life insurance are sold to cover debts he has incurred in a parliamentary election—despite the pragmatic advice of his friends. In particular the canny, good-natured money-lender Sherrick is at a loss to understand such unheard-of nobility. Sherrick has prudently counseled the Colonel to let his election bills be included in his imminent bankruptcy, "'but he wouldn't, sir—he went on like an old Bengal tiger, roaring about his honour, he paid the bills every shilling . . . and it's my belief that at this minute, he ain't got fifty pounds a year of his own to spend' " (*N*, 72.733). Sherrick is disconsolate at the Colonel's lack of self-interest in having deliberately left himself penniless to avoid inconveniencing his creditors. Although he is one of the novel's less savory characters (making his living on the outer edges of respectability and preying upon the financial miseries of others), Sherrick speaks of the Colonel's conduct with tears in his eyes and apparent sincerity. In his judgment:

> "There's none of them so good as old Newcome. . . . That was a good one—that was an honest man if ever I saw one—with no more guile, and no more idea of business than a baby. Why didn't he take my advice, poor old cove? —he might be comfortable now. Why did he sell away that annuity . . . I got it done for him when no body else perhaps could have got it done for him—for the security ain't worth twopence if Newcome isn't an honest man; but I know he is, and would rather starve and eat nails off his fingers than not to keep his word, the old trump." (*N*, 72.733)

Nor is Sherrick the only one to find the Colonel's financial integrity perplexing. Clive Newcome's wife Rosie and her redoubtable Mama, Mrs. MacKenzie, defy the Colonel's orders to leave all valuables behind for the creditors; unable to comprehend Newcome's insistence upon strict financial honor, these "female robbers" pack their trunks with silver forks, spoons, ladles, and other trinkets to spirit them off the premises and away from the auctioneer's block. Although Clive fully supports his father's actions in spending his own money to repay creditors, Rosie and Mrs. Mackenzie are outraged that the Colonel has left them penniless. For Clive and the Colonel, the rules of honor are relatively simple ("How could he do otherwise than meet his engagements?") but apparently the feminine mind is less able to appreciate such fine scruples: " 'For the women are very angry,' said the poor Colonel; 'You see they do not understand the laws of honour, at least as we understand them' " (*N*, 72.736).

In the interests of realism and verisimilitude, it is perhaps only natural that the Victorian novelist should depict women like Rosie and her Mama, isolated as they were from the economic whirlwinds of the industrial economy, as less finely attuned than men to the necessity for honor in financial affairs. Dickens seems to have had some similar concept in mind when he portrayed Little Dorrit, an otherwise sainted character, as espousing an attitude toward commercial honor that falls short of the accepted standard. Even so muddle-headed a man of business as her father sees immediately, upon being restored to his fortune, that his first obligation is to recompense all who have aided him, and to repay all his old debts. Little Dorrit, however, does not quite comprehend the logic of commercial honor: " 'It seems to me hard,' said Little Dorrit, 'that he should have lost so many years and suffered so much, and at last pay all the debts as well. It seems to me hard that he should pay in life and money both;' " (*LD*, 1.35.409). This timid objection is rejected by Clennam as the slight "taint" of prison on an otherwise uncorrupted mind ("the last speck Clennam ever saw of the prison atmosphere upon her" [*LD,* 1.35.472]), a "little spot" of weakness which makes her purity all the more beautiful and touching.[9]

As we have previously seen in contemporary periodicals and parliamentary debate, however, the Victorian attitude toward bankruptcy and debt was hardly monolithic. And if so virtuous a character as Little Dorrit could be portrayed as having some doubt as to the sacredness of the commercial code of honor, then it is hardly surprising that there would be authors who would question it as well. Interestingly (but perhaps naturally enough), it is the *women* novelists who seem occasionally to challenge the priority of commercial honor.[10] Although Eliot, Brontë, and Gaskell accord admiration for those of their characters (Tom Tulliver, Robert Moore, Mr. Thornton) who work with single mind and "iron discipline" to repay the debts of their bankrupt fathers, it is in each case evident that the character has given up a higher good in his narrow pursuit of commercial honor. And in each case the hero is by the end of the novel made aware of some higher virtue that he has ignored—usually the social good of the community, and usually through the tutoring of the heroine.

From the beginning of their father's ruin, it is apparent that Maggie and Tom Tulliver in *Mill on the Floss* are motivated by very different emotions. Maggie is all compassion for her father, and indignation toward the aunts and uncles who tyrannize over them; Tom, on the other hand, feels humiliated by the family downfall, and rather agrees with the aunts' and uncles' harsh condemnation of his father, agreeing with their severity "all the more because he had confidence in himself that he should never deserve that just severity" (*MF,* 3.5.199). In the process of driving himself to repay the debts of his father, Tom becomes even more self-righteous and his work becomes a single-minded endeavor that shuts out all other emotions, while his sister's thoughts continue to yearn for some more noble path in life. The narrowmindedness of Tom's pursuit of commercial honor and "good name" deprive him of all sensitivity and compassion, and inevitably separate him from Maggie: "Maggie had an awe of him against which she struggled as something unfair to her consciousness of wider thoughts and deeper motives" (*MF,* 5.2.271). The final catastrophe of the story, in which Tom and Maggie die in the flood reenacting the legend of St. Ogg and the Virgin, has been criticized for being sensational, as indeed it is, but it is also an effective reversal of their customary positions. As Maggie, with unexpected reserves of courage and devotion, risks her life to rescue her brother, he is finally struck with "awe and humiliation," learning in the final moments before their deaths, that there have been deeper strength and higher motives in Maggie's idealism than in his own narrow rules of commercial rectitude and social morality.

Gaskell's Mr. Thornton and Brontë's Robert Moore are also characters who have constricted their lives to repay their fathers' debts, and who must be taught by the heroine that there are higher duties than simply behaving with honor in financial dealings. Mr. Thornton has a sweeping view of industry—he sees it as a "war which compels . . . all material power to yield to science" (*NS*, 1.10.81), but Margaret Hale believes that this vision is still too narrow. She says critically, "'When he spoke of the mechanical powers, he evidently looked upon them only as new ways of extending trade and making money'" (*NS*, 1.11.87). Margaret herself would prefer to see the new economic order harnessed for the social good. For Thornton, however, commerce has a more worldly power:

> Architect of his own fortunes, he attributed this to no especial merit or qualities of his own, but to the power, which he believed that commerce gave to every brave, honest, and persevering man, to raise himself to a level from which he might see and read the great game of worldly success, and honestly, by some farsightedness, command more power and influence than in any other mode of life. Far away, in the East and in the West, where his person would never be known, his name was to be regarded, and his wishes to be fulfilled, and his word pass like gold. That was the idea of merchant life with which Mr. Thornton had started. "Her merchants be like princes," said his mother, reading the text aloud, as if it were a trumpet-call to invite her boy to the struggle. (*NS*, 2.25.419)

Mrs. Gaskell is among Victorian novelists perhaps the one to understand most generously the commercial character in its virtues and energy as well as in its vices. Nevertheless, she contrasts the Christian view of Margaret to the more worldly one of Mr. Thornton, and observes that in his struggles for such "distant" things as power and influence, he has overlooked things closer at hand—what he might be "among his own people." Only after coming under the influence of Margaret does he begin to appreciate the opportunity his position gives him of using his wealth to ameliorate the lives of his workmen, and to attempt a few social experiments among them.

Like Mr. Thornton, Brontë's hero Robert Moore initially is blind to the importance of human relationships, seeing, in Carlyle's words, "cash payment as the sole nexus" of his relation to his men. Like Thornton, Moore has grown up under the burden of a father's bankruptcy and debt, and it has dried up his more tender emotions, and hardened him into the narrow path of commercial honor and ambition. He admits to having "three gods," "'my trade, my mill, and my machinery'" (*S*, 2.57). Concerned solely with recouping his family's fortunes, "he had a tendency to isolate his individual person from any community amidst which his lot might temporarily happen to be thrown . . . and he felt it to be his best wisdom to push the interests of Robert Gerard Moore, to the exclusion of philanthropic consideration for general interests; with which he regarded the said Gerard Moore as in a great measure disconnected" (*S*, 2.60).

A stranger to the Yorkshire neighborhood of his mill, and a foreigner by birth, Moore is slow to understand the peculiar nature of his workers, and cares little about the unemployment his new machines will cause among weavers: "he never asked himself where those to whom he no longer paid weekly wages found daily bread" (*S*, 2.61). As his cousin Caroline points out to him, he exhibits no compassion for his men, " 'as if your living cloth dressers were all machines like your frames and shears' "(*S*, 5.100). This single-minded pursuit of commercial success has stunted Moore's emotional life as well. He cares nothing for personal popularity, the word *friend* irritates him, he has no time for the "softer" emotions. In spite of a very real inclination toward Caroline, he considers his financial obligations too pressing to allow him the luxury of romance. He cautions Caroline to exclude from her heart " 'one who does not profess to have any higher aim in life than that of patching up his broken fortune, and wiping clean from his bourgeois scutcheon the foul stain of bankruptcy' " (*S*, 7.144).

For Charlotte Brontë, the full extent of Moore's inability to rise above his own selfish interests is measured by the fact that he opposes the Napoleonic War (and thus Brontë's hero, Wellington) because the war is bad for his trade. Moore's attitude leads to an authorial disquisition on the selfishness and short-sightedness of the British merchant: "These mercantile classes certainly think too exclusively of making money; they are too oblivious of every national consideration, but that of extending England's (i.e., their own) commerce" (*S*, 10.183). Sunk like others of his class in his own narrow interests, Moore is thus unable to extend his imagination or compassion toward his fellow man, and unable even to acknowledge the depth of his own emotional involvement with Caroline.

He is fortunate, however, in having as a spiritual and moral guide, *two* heroines who awaken his finer instincts. Caroline and her friend Shirley have been described as Charlotte Brontë's representations of her sisters Anne and Emily;[11] it seems at least as plausible, however, to assume that they are both reflections of the psyche of the author in its passive and active phases. It is clear, at any rate, that in many ways the heroines constitute two halves of the same consciousness, and that in their relationship to Robert Moore, they act from the same perspective. It is Caroline who preaches a wider human vision to Moore, and who awakens deep emotions in him. But it is the more active Shirley who administers the chastening blow, by scornfully rejecting the marriage that he proposes to her purely for mercenary reasons. The moral conversion that Moore experiences under the tutoring of these two heroines is a thorough one in which he finally transcends the narrow limits of the commercial code of honor.[12] The crestfallen hero admits to his neighbor, " 'Something there is to look to, Yorke, beyond a man's personal interest . . . *beyond even the discharge of dishonouring debts* [emphasis added]. To respect himself, a man must believe he renders justice to his fellow-men. Unless I am more considerate to ignorance, more forebearing to suffering, than I have hitherto been, I shall scorn myself as grossly unjust'" (*S*, 30.506).

Even his feeling about the dishonor of his approaching bankruptcy has been transformed under the softening moral guidance of Shirley and Caroline: "'All slavish terrors of embarrassment have left me: let the worst come, I can work . . . for an honourable living; in such doom I yet see some hardship, but no degradation. Formerly, pecuniary ruin was equivalent in my eyes to personal dishonour. It is not so now. I know the difference'" (*S*, 35.555). Thus the prevailing code of commercial honor has its dissenters; at least among the female novelists of the Victorian period, there were those who could accept the necessity for repayment of debts as a moral obligation, and yet envision a higher and nobler duty that had nothing to do with obligations belonging purely to the marketplace.

In its several attitudes toward bankruptcy and debt, then, the novel is at least as contradictory as other forms of Victorian art and rhetoric. What emerges clearly, however, is the necessity that realism forced upon the novel to consider the painful subject of bankruptcy, and to try, with whatever success, to make some sense of its wide devastation of Victorian economic life. With the novel's emphasis upon verisimilar representation of such unsettling elements of modern life as the urban scene and the financial maneuverings of entrepreneurial capitalism, it was inevitable that bankruptcy would become a central concern of the novel—not only for its effect upon the domestic hearth (as in other arts), but for its equally interesting effect upon the individual personality, and its very far-reaching consequences for the social community. As episodes of bankruptcy become more frequent, moreover, the *idea* of bankruptcy seems to permeate the novel in ways that go far beyond its use as a realistic detail, and begins rather to influence the novel in its language, meaning, symbolism, and structure.[13] While the remaining chapters of this study will be devoted to studying the emergence of bankruptcy as an important metaphor in the Victorian novel, it will be necessary first to examine briefly the way in which the idea of bankruptcy influences the theme and structure of the novel.

BANKRUPTCY AS THEME AND STRUCTURE

Although there are endless variations, there seems to be an archetypal pattern in the Victorian novel of economic prosperity, loss, debt, and then final catastrophe. In its stark drama, as we have said in the introduction, the catastrophe seems to evoke echoes of the old medieval parables of Fortune's wheel, or of even older legends of the downfall of heroes. As the Victorian novelist follows the rise and inevitable fall of the protagonist from prosperity to poverty and despair, bankruptcy functions as the traditional reversal of fortune, the turning point upon which the fortunes of the hero and the structure of the novel is organized. Moreover, as bankruptcy becomes a central structural device, it is inevitable that the idea of downfall becomes central to the theme and meaning of the novel. The fall of the hero invariably evokes suggestions of the vulnerability of the individual in an age of harsh economic realities, and beyond this, of the many uncertainties of human existence in the Victorian era. Theme and structure are thus inseparably intertwined in these novels of bankruptcy.

Of the novels discussed in this study, *Middlemarch* and *Vanity Fair* use bankruptcy only peripherally, insofar as the structure of the novel is concerned, although certainly the acquisition and loss of money is a unifying motif in both, and reverberates in each case with ironies directly connected to the essential themes of these works. In the remaining novels, *The Mill on the Floss, Dombey and Son, The Newcomes, Shirley, North and South, Little Dorrit,* and *The Way We Live Now,* bankruptcy is crucial to both the structure and the theme of the work.

Eliot's *The Mill on The Floss* would seem at first glance to use bankruptcy in the most clichéd fashion, as the initial catastrophe that launches the misfortunes of a persecuted heroine. (Eliot, in fact, used the standard devices of melodrama with surprising frequency; in *Daniel Deronda,* for instance, the ordeals of Gwendolyn Harleth are initiated by the loss of her family's fortune.) On closer observation, however, the use of bankruptcy in *The Mill on the Floss* turns out to be more pivotal. The first two books of the novel contain the childhood of Maggie Tulliver, a world of innocence, security, and stability. The last three books are by comparison a world of struggle and bitter experience. Between these two worlds is the crucial episode of Mr. Tulliver's bankruptcy, which occupies books 3 and 4 ("The Downfall" and "The Valley of Humilation"). The bankruptcy thus exists at the center of the novel, a bitter passage of pain, loss, and defeat, that marks the journey from childhood to adulthood, from innocence to experience, and from certainty to doubt. Mr. Tulliver's failure marks not only the turning point in the fortunes of the Tulliver family, but the turning point of the novel as well, a structural device that separates the two halves of Maggie's experience into an early idyll of innocence and then the painful battles of life after the fall.

In *Shirley* and *North and South* the business misfortunes of the hero actually constitute the main action of the plot. The heroes, Robert Moore and Mr. Thornton, are developed as personalities in good measure by the way in which they conduct their business. Their early strivings for success, their conduct toward their men and other members of the social community at the height of their prosperity, their threatened downfall due to circumstances beyond their control, and their final success in reestablishing their companies are the mainsprings of the plot, and other key elements such as character development and the emotional relationship with the heroine are closely linked with the fluctuations in the heroes' solvency. In each case, the bankruptcy that has been threatening through many chapters finally emerges as the turning point, the crucible in which the hero painfully reevaluates his feelings for the heroine, and a whole range of economic and social values as well, and emerges stronger in character, more responsive in his human relationships, and more concerned for his moral obligations to the community.

The dramas of Mr. Dombey and Colonel Newcome are even closer to the old mythic pattern structured around the downfall of a hero. In each case the final bankruptcy of the central character of the novel creates a structure similar to those medieval tales of a fall from fortune, which were meant to impress the listener with the transitory nature of the glories of this world. Mr. Dombey is introduced to us at the height of his pride and folly like some foolish old king of legendary fame, wasting his power on opulence, blind to his own arrogance and lack of humanity. By the end of the novel (in a chapter fittingly entitled "Retribution"), the wheel of fortune has turned and cast Dombey from its height, leaving him, a pitiful and broken old bankrupt, to contemplate his past sins. The story of *The Newcomes,* on the other hand, is more of a protracted rise and fall. When we make our acquaintance with the Colonel he is a simple army man, rather straitened in circumstances, due less to a lack of funds than to an inability to handle his money wisely. We follow his spectacular rise as director of the great Bundel-cund Bank, and witness the subtle changes of character that power evokes in the once-simple Colonel. At the climax of the novel the dramatic smash-up of the bank signals the fall of the Colonel from the heights of fortune to its depths, and we are left to contemplate the vanity of worldly power. *The Newcomes,* like *Dombey and Son,* is a kind of morality tale, in which bankruptcy is the reversal of fortune that properly chastens the hero.

Little Dorrit and *The Way We Live Now* revolve around even more spectacular failures, calamitous bankruptcies that bring about the fall of many of the novels' characters; indeed, by the end of these novels an entire social structure has come crashing down. Mr. Merdle is not the central character of *Little Dorrit,* but he is interesting as a counterpoint to Mr. Dorrit. Their fortunes, in fact, appear to be intersecting lines, one falling as the other rises. The first half of the novel (Book the First: "Poverty") introduces us to Mr. Dorrit at the nadir of his fortunes, a permanent prisoner in the Marshalsea. We meet at the same time Mr. Merdle, the fabulous entrepreneur and Pillar of Society, who is at the height of Fortune's wheel. The climax of Book the First is the rise of Mr. Dorrit when he suddenly acquires a fortune; the climax of Book the Second, "Riches," is the spectacular bankruptcy of Mr. Merdle, which also occasions the fall of many other of the characters, including the hero Clennam and the Dorrit family. Merdle's bankruptcy is not merely a personal downfall; it seems to suggest a kind of general ruin as in the old legends when the fall of a king brought devastation to his people.

The disaster created by Melmotte's bankruptcy in *The Way We Live Now* is even more widespread. Here the rise and fall of Mr. Melmotte *is* the central structure of the novel, and the destiny of almost every other character is in some way attendant upon the fortunes of the speculator. Subplots seem to echo the structure of the main plot; the initial flourishing and subsequent bankruptcy of the Beargarden social club, for example, is a reflection of the more spectacular rise and fall of Melmotte's enterprises. The bankruptcy of Mr. Melmotte is a stunning reversal toward which everything in the novel has been building; bankruptcy has become at once the controlling image, theme, structural device, and metaphor in *The Way We Live Now.*

BANKRUPTCY AS METAPHOR

It is apparent, then, that bankruptcy in these novels is far more than an incidental detail of plot, that it expands instead into a central metaphor in more than one novel. In an age painfully coming to grips with economic realities of an unprecedented nature, it is not surprising that bankruptcy would be seen by the artist as a symbolic event to which all sorts of meanings might well be attached. Indeed, novelists were not the only writers to see the potential metaphorical value in the experience of bankruptcy. Tennyson used the bankruptcy of a father (by the villainy of a neighbor) in the opening stanzas of *Maud* (1855) as a cataclysmic upheaval that suggested by extension a "World of plunder and prey."[14] Even earlier, however, Thomas Carlyle evidently sensed that the great symbolic virtue of bankruptcy was that it overturned all *surface* reality, either to expose the dreadful void beneath the facade, or to restore a truer reality. In *The French Revolution* (1837) Carlyle made explicit the connection between the corrupt state of the French monarchy and its inability to pay its bills, linking the financial bankruptcy of the state to the coming revolution:

> Great is Bankruptcy: the great bottomless gulf into which all Falsehood, public and private, do sink, disappearing; whither, from the first origin of them, they were all doomed. For Nature is true and not a lie. No lie you can speak or act, but it will come after longer or shorter circulation, like a Bill drawn on Nature's Reality, and be presented there for payment—with the answer, *No effects.* Pity only that it often had so long a circulation: that the original forger were so seldom he who bore the final smart of it![15]

"Bankruptcy," "circulation," "Bill Drawn," "payment," "No effects," "forger"—the language is the argot of the marketplace, but the suggestions are apocalyptic. Bankruptcy is pictured as some monumental force of nature, stripping away falsehood and sham. Carlyle warns that the corruption and arrogance of the royal court will be overturned by the neglected misery of the "Twenty Millions": "Such is the law of just Nature—bringing, though at long intervals, and were it only by Bankruptcy, matters round again to the mark."[16] Whatever is false will eventually be exposed by the tendency of truth to prevail, and bankruptcy is a kind of agent of truth, setting aside pretensions and facades:

> Honour to Bankruptcy; ever-righteous on the great scale, though in detail it is so cruel. Under all falsehoods it works, unweariedly mining. No falsehood, did it rise heaven-high and cover the world, but Bankruptcy, one day, will sweep it down, and make us free of it.[17]

Carlyle's use here of the image of Bankruptcy has little to do with the public rhetoric that pictured bankruptcy as a public shame and moral disgrace. His use of bankruptcy as a metaphor seems to oppose directly the niceties of the code of commercial honor, or rather, manages to disregard the public horror of bankruptcy as irrelevant.

The major novelists of the period (all to some extent under the aura of Carlyle's influence) seem to use financial failure in a very similar fashion. On the most realistic level the commercial attitude is given credence in varying degrees by the upright actions of the hero facing bankruptcy (or the craven behavior of others). But when the novelists employ the experience of bankruptcy metaphorically (as opposed to realistically) it emerges as a kind of providential life force that exposes the reality which lies below the surface of Victorian society.

The use of the economic metaphor is of course not new to the language of literature. The novel, in particular, obsessed as it has always been with the place of money in human life, has traditionally employed economic language to ironic and symbolic effect. The rhetoric of the Victorian novel is, if anything, even more prone to using financial terminology to imply broader meanings, and bankruptcy frequently occurs in these rhetorical metaphors. Thackeray, for example, uses "bankruptcy" to refer to relationships between human beings that are built upon falsehood and pretense, and are suddenly proven to be hollow. Thus in *The Newcomes* the marriage of Lady Clara and Barnes Newcome is described in terms of bankruptcy. Lady Clara has been "sold" by her family to a husband who lacks all human feeling and who regularly mistreats her. When she runs off with another man, Thackeray assesses their marriage: "When the whole of the accounts of that wretched bankruptcy are brought up for final Audit, which of the unhappy partners shall be shown to be the most guilty?" (*N*, 58.617).

He uses the same economic metaphor in *Vanity Fair* for the relationship between Becky and Rawdon. After Rawdon has discovered Becky's treachery, and abandoned her, the author asserts: "All her lies and her schemes, all her selfishness and her wiles, all her wit and genius had come to this bankruptcy" (*VF*, 53.517).

Dickens uses the term in an even broader sense to imply any kind of institution or attitude that turns out to be hollow. He waxes heavily ironic over the reaction of the world to Mr. Dombey's bankruptcy:

> There was no other sort of bankruptcy whatever. There were no conspic-
> uous people . . . trading far and wide on rotten banks of religion,
> patriotism, virtue and honor. There was no amount worth mentioning of
> mere paper money in circulation, on which anybody lived pretty hand-
> somely, promising to pay great sums of goodness with no effects. There
> were no short-comings anywhere, in anything but money. The world was
> very angry indeed; and the people especially, who, in a worse world,
> might have been supposed to be bankrupt traders themselves in shows
> and pretenses, were observed to be mighty indignant. (*DS*, 58.773–74)

Thus the Victorian novelist, in such verbal metaphors, would use financial language in general, and the idea of bankruptcy in particular, to
symbolic effect. But of far greater interest, for the purposes of this study, is
the tendency among the great novelists of the early and middle Victorian
years to expand their usage of bankruptcy into a kind of *structural* metaphor, in which plot construction, theme and meaning, and symbolic overtones all revolve around the act of financial failure. In the novels under
consideration in these pages, the Victorian novelist seems to use the image
of bankruptcy as Carlyle envisioned it—a kind of elemental life force that
was capable of sweeping away the carefully gilded surface of life to expose
the reality—or the void—beneath. The remaining chapters of this study
will deal with some specific variations of this metaphor: bankruptcy as a
threat to the idea of self; bankruptcy as moral regeneration or spiritual
rebirth; and bankruptcy as social apocalypse.

5

Bankruptcy as Metaphor: The Threatened Self
(*The Mill on the Floss* and Others)

In the world of the Victorian novelist, the most painful problem of the age often seems to be the need for some accommodation between the private subjective life of the individual and the urgent demands of the public, objective world. As modern industrial society emerged, the pressures upon the individual became correspondingly harsher, and the universal terror of financial failure becomes all too comprehensible in the light of the effect that economic failure could have upon the private self. On the very simplest level, the personal bankruptcy of an individual reveals the void beneath a supposedly prosperous economy. The economic identity of the Victorian turns out to be strangely vulnerable, and its destruction is likely to have the most devastating consequences.

Bankruptcy in the Victorian novel is a crushing experience from which the victim rarely, if ever, regains his sense of self. After their failures such bankrupts as Mr. Sedley, Mr. Tulliver, Colonel Newcome, and Mr. Dombey all creep pathetically through the ensuing chapters of their novels, lost in a kind of befuddled twilight, literally a shadow of their former selves. Such destruction of human personality, though it appears on the surface to be caused by a simple loss of money, suggests that the Victorian fear of bankruptcy was, in reality, the key to a far deeper terror, a crisis in economic, emotional, social, sexual, and religious values that shook the Victorians to the core and threatened to reveal beneath the obvious prosperity and optimism of the nineteenth century a chasm that imperiled the very reality of self.

CRISIS OF ECONOMIC IDENTITY

Among the Victorian writers, George Eliot was perhaps foremost in her ability to convey the interaction of private lives and objective social conditions, and *The Mill on the Floss* most graphically illustrates the threat to private identity that could be so shockingly represented by a loss of economic identity. The novel begins:

> A wide plain, where the broadening Floss hurries on, between its green banks to the sea, and the loving tide, rushing to meet it, checks its passage with an impetuous embrace. On this mighty tide the black ships—laden with the fresh-scented fir-planks, with rounded sacks of oil-bearing seed, or with the dark glitter of coal—are borne along to the town of St. Ogg's . . . (*MF*, 1.1.7)

The first sentence seems to locate us in a rural environment, the world of Maggie and Tom's childhood idyll, the world of Dorlcote Mill which is dominated by the rhythms of the river and the seasons. By the second sentence, however, the river has carried us into the town of St. Ogg's, and has taken on a distinctly mercantile character, transformed into a channel of trading vessels, carrying lumber, seed, and coal to the emerging center of industry. Indeed, in spite of its apparently bucolic setting, *The Mill on the Floss* is a novel about economic activity, about the labor necessary to do the work of the world. (Our introduction to the Tullivers in chapter 2 begins with Mr. Tulliver's words about giving Tom a good education " 'as'll be a bread to him.' ")

Eliot is not, of course, writing specifically about the changes that the Industrial Revolution brought to Victorian England; the novel is distinctly placed in the 1830s. Nevertheless, she is conscious of the changes that will be wrought by economic development, and there is already a suggestion of new values replacing older traditions, or, as N. N. Feltes puts it, "the tension . . . between old and new economic forms."[1] Mr. Tulliver is of the old economic tradition. His occupation as a miller and maltster suggests an activity that had hardly changed in its technology and tools in a thousand years; indeed, the mill has been in his family for many generations, and Mr. Tulliver wishes to die where his father was born. For the miller, a sense of place and family tradition is at least as important as the profits of Dorlcote Mill. He is attached to the mill because "The Tullivers had lived in this spot for generations," and he believes almost mystically in a personal connection between the mill and himself. (" 'The old mill 'ud miss me . . . There's a story as when the mill changes hands the river's angry. I've heard my father say it many a time' " [*MF*, 3.9.233].)

Eliot contrasts Mr. Tulliver's attachment to place with the "instructed vagrancy" of her own day; Tulliver and the world of Dorlcote Mill repre-

sent an older, more personal tradition. Opposed to the traditional values of
the Tullivers and the mill, as the opening sentences of the novel make clear,
is the emerging mercantile center of St. Ogg's, where Mr. Deane and his
firm represent the more impersonal values of the modern economy, and
where Tom Tulliver must go to expiate the economic failings of his father.
Mr. Deane's firm, Guest and Co., is clearly going to be able to accommodate
itself to the world of nineteenth-century capitalism—it is a firm that "did
not carry on its business on sentimental grounds." The change of values is
difficult for a more traditional mentality to comprehend. Mrs. Tulliver
suggests to Mr. Deane that in order to save Dorlcote Mill as a home for the
Tulliver family, the firm of Guest and Co. might like to purchase the mill
and retain Mr. Tulliver to run it, because

> ". . . Mr. Tulliver's father and grandfather had been carrying on Dorl-
> cote Mill long before the oil-mill of that firm had been so much as
> thought of." Mr. Deane, in reply, doubted whether that was precisely the
> relations between the two mills which would determine their value as
> investments. (*MF*, 3.7.215)

Thus an ominous new economic value, the "cash-nexus" of the industrial
world, is already beginning to replace an older world of family traditions
and personal relationships.

Mr. Tulliver is apparently crushed by his inability to understand the
more competitive practices of this new economic world, and his failure is all
the more terrible because his economic identity is so very crucial to his
sense of personal worth:

> he was held to be a much more substantial man than he really was. And as
> we are all apt to believe what the world believes about us, it was his habit
> to think of failure and ruin with the same sort of remote pity with which
> a spare long-necked man hears that his plethoric short-necked neighbor
> is stricken with apoplexy. He had been always used to hear pleasant jokes
> about his advantages as a man who worked his own mill and owned a
> pretty bit of land, and these jokes naturally kept up his sense that he was
> a man of considerable substance. (*MF*, 1.8.69)

His first concern when faced with financial loss is to "avoid the appearance
of breaking down in the world . . . and remain Mr.Tulliver of Dorlcote
Mill" (*MF*, 3.1.172). Mr. Tulliver, to a great extent, *is* "Mr. Tulliver of
Dorlcote Mill," a "substantial man"; and without the mill, it seems, Mr.
Tulliver has no substance at all. His loss of identity is symbolized by the
stroke that wipes his memory clean and robs him of his senses. The hot-
tempered, dominating miller is described in illness as "apathetic," "passive,"
"prostrate," and "infantine"; he is compared to a baby and his daughter
Maggie becomes his nurse. The author speaks of his "bruised, enfeebled
powers" and his "heart-cutting childish dependence," and Mr. Tulliver

compares himself to "'a tree as is broke,'" and adds later that "'what's broke can never be whole again.'" His sense of dislocation and dispossession have completely sapped from him all possibility of action: "'I'm nought but a bankrupt,'" he complains, "'it's no use standing up for anything now'" (*MF*, 3.8.231).

Even after his recovery from the stroke, Mr. Tulliver no longer bears much relationship to the individual referred to as "Mr. Tulliver of Dorlcote Mill." His loss of power is apparent as soon as he loses his lawsuit. In chapter 2 the rash and strong-willed miller has been shown determining to educate his son, and scornfully rejecting his wife's plea to consult with the rest of the family. After his reversal of fortune, however, he lies ill upstairs, while a conclave of aunts and uncles decides upon the destiny of the family in a singularly high-handed manner. With his pride thoroughly crushed by the bankruptcy, Tulliver even agrees to work for his old enemy Wakem. His personality, moreover, has undergone a total transformation. Once a proud, hasty, hot-tempered but kind-hearted father, Tulliver sinks into a sullen depression. All social intercourse with his fellow man has been strangled by his humiliating loss of economic identity; he slinks away from contact with his neighbors and "in all behavior towards him, whether kind or cold, he detected an allusion to the change in his circumstances" (*MF*, 4.2.243).

All of his energy is now channeled into the seemingly hopeless task of repaying his creditors, and under this compulsion his formerly open-handed hospitality dries up until he grudges every morsel his family eats. Above all the old habit of predominance has been crushed: "he had lost some of his old peremptoriness and determination to be master" (*MF*, 5.2.272). The repayment of his debts brings about an almost miraculous restoration of his identity; at the dinner for the creditors

> he looked more like the proud, confident, warm-hearted, and warm-tempered Tulliver of old times, than might have seemed possible to anyone who had met him a week before, riding along, as had been his wont for the last four years since the sense of failure and debt had been upon him—with his head hanging down, casting brief, unwilling looks on those who forced themselves on his notice. (*MF*, 5.7.320)

Tulliver's manner on leaving the dinner is a reassertion of his old identity as a man of substance: "He did not choose any back street today, but rode slowly, with uplifted head and free glances, along the principal street. . ." (*MF*, 5.7.311).

The recovery of identity proves to be illusory, however. Mr. Tulliver is felled by one final spasm of violence and shock, and dies muttering brokenly of his defeats. "'This world's . . . too many . . . honest man . . . puzzling'" *MF*, 5.7.315). His death, in a sense, has already been prepared and prefigured by the original economic loss and defeat. His long illness, described in terms of "insensibility" and "rigidity," has already been "a living death," and his subsequent life "a long descent under thickening shadows" (*MF*, 3.4.198). Thus the loss of money, with its dissolution of all sense of personal identity, has been a foretaste of death. "Mr. Tulliver of Dorlcote Mill" has in fact ceased to exist at the moment that his bankruptcy dispossesses him from the economic status on which his fragile sense of personal identity rests.

CRISIS OF SOCIAL IDENTITY

The experience of bankruptcy does not destroy simply the economic identity; there is a much wider consequence in all of the individual's social relationships. If bankruptcy is a prefiguration of death in its annihilation of the economic identity, it is equally a great leveling force upon the social identity of the individual, which, dependent as it is upon financial status, is easily dissolved in the disgrace of bankruptcy. Novel after novel depicts the bankrupt and his family (the Sedleys, the Tullivers, the Dorrits, the New-comes) sinking in social class as a result of financial ruin. (Frequently, of course, the social postures of Victorian society are seen as having been based on pretension and hypocrisy in the first place. Dickens is particularly good at using bankruptcy as a kind of Carlylean force that exposes the false identity and false position of such characters as the Veneerings and Lammles in *Our Mutual Friend* and the Merdles and the Dorrits in *Little Dorrit*, while Trollope does something very similar with the great imposter Melmotte in *The Way We Live Now*.)

Eliot is equally aware of the wider social repercussions of bankruptcy. "Allocaturs, filing of bills in Chancery, decrees of sale," she writes, "are legal chain-shot or bomb-shells that can never hit a solitary mark, but must fall with wide spread shattering" (*MF*, 3.7.215). Thus the failure of one individual, in legal and economic terms, must have far-reaching implications for the bankrupt and his family in all of their social relationships, and will inevitably have an impact upon the social community as a whole. The bankruptcy of Mr. Tulliver is a "tragedy" to his hand Luke because it upsets "that sense of natural fitness in rank" that is essential to his understanding of the social community. It is a painful surprise to Bob Jakin who has treasured memories of the young Tom Tulliver's condescending fellowship as something out of the ordinary in his hard-knock existence. And it is a mortifying blow to the Pullets, Gleggs, and Deanes, who consider it a dreadful blot upon their family name.

Mr. Tulliver is painfully aware of the social consequences of his failure. He is, as we have seen, a man whose identity is strongly affected by his social position. Mr. Tulliver's sense of his own reality has always been derived in part from the view of the world that he was a man of substantial means, and his first thought upon receiving news of his loss of fortune is how to avoid "the appearance of breaking down in the world." His most painful moments occur in his forced social intercourse with old acquaintances and creditors, a contact that is necessarily fraught with reminders of his degraded social position.

Indeed the social significance of financial failure is painfully obvious to the Tullivers; it affects their very sense of social identity in relation to one another and to the community:

> Tom had never dreamed that his father would "fail:" *that* was a form of misfortune which he had always heard spoken of as a deep disgrace, and disgrace was an idea that he could not associate with any of his relations, least of all with his father. A proud sense of family respectability was part of the very air Tom had been born and brought up in. (*MF*, 2.7.168)

Tom's sense of who he is, and who his father is, and what is their natural place in the world is uncomfortably shaken by the appearance of a bailiff in the Tulliver home:

> To "have the bailiff in the house" and "to be sold up" were phrases which he had been used to, even as a little boy: they were part of the disgrace and misery of "failing," of losing one's money, and being ruined—sinking into the condition of poor working people. (*MF*, 3.2.178)

The discovery that his father will "fail," that is, pay less than twenty shillings in the pound to his creditors, is a "continual smart" to Tom, for it implies a stain upon his father's reputation as an honest man, a downfall that is moral as well as economic and social, and the exclusion of the Tulliver family from the part of the mercantile community which considers itself upright and respectable. Even Mrs. Tulliver, not generally perceptive, is keenly aware that "while people owed money they were unable to pay, they couldn't rightly call anything their own" (*MF*, 4.2.244), and she is painfully aware of the disgrace of having household linens marked with her name sold at public auction to go "into strange people's houses."

Thus the Tullivers are painfully conscious of their social disgrace, and were they not so, it would evidently be the duty of the social community to instill such a consciousness. Mrs. Tulliver's Dodson relatives descend upon the unfortunate family like a flock of harpies, comprising a chorus of blame and scorn that represents the opinion of the respectable world of St. Ogg's. Aunt Glegg, in particular, arrives on the scene filled with "the high moral purpose of instilling perfect humility into Bessy and her children"(*MF*, 3.3.183), and her speeches are among the finest examples of Eliot's facility with social comedy:

> "You must bring your mind to your circumstances, Bessy, and not be thinking o' silver and chany; but whether you shall get so much as a flock

bed to lie on, and a blanket to cover you, and a stool to sit on. You must remember, if you get 'em, it'll be because your friends have bought 'em for you, for you're dependent upon *them* for everything; for your husband lies there helpless and hasn't got a penny i' the world to call his own. And it's for your own good I say this, for it's right you should feel what your state is, and what disgrace your husband's brought on your own family, as you've got to look to for everything—and be humble in your mind." (*MF*, 3.3.185)

The smug, self-righteous, hectoring tone is just right: Aunt Glegg, who is by far the most "having" character of the novel, is absolutely sincere in her scornful rejection of her sister's fretful pleas for her silver and china. She represents here the collective wisdom of the respectable community. The Tullivers *deserve* to live in poverty and humility; the price of failure in mercantile honor and mercantile success is exclusion from the community of the solvent. Nor is the blow to family pride to be taken lightly; the highly prized Dodson gentility is clearly threatened by "that too evident descent into pauperism which makes it annoying to respectable people to meet the degraded member of the family by the wayside" (*MF*, 3.8.225).

The disgrace of bankruptcy destroys the social position of Mr. Tulliver and his family, leaving them in a kind of limbo from which relatives shrink, and friends fall away.

There is a chill air surrounding those who are down in the world, and people are glad to get away from them as from a cold room: human beings, mere men and women, without furniture, without anything to offer you, who have ceased to count as anybody, present an embarrassing negation of reasons for wishing to see them, or of subjects on which to converse with them. At that distant day there was a dreary isolation in the civilised Christian society of these realms for families that had dropped below their original level. (*MF*, 4.2.245)

Poor Mrs. Tulliver's instincts about her need for "silver and chany" are correct after all; in her own dim way she perceives accurately that such valuables are not only an indication of economic status, but the very fabric of which social position is woven. Without them the Tullivers indeed "cease to count as anybody." To be "mere men and women, without furniture" is to have lost the many small ornaments out of which we construct our social identities in "civilised Christian society."

By the end of the novel Tom's heroic efforts to repay his father's creditors have restored the family to the social community once again. In the eyes of the Dodson family, the "change in the fortunes of the Tullivers . . . were likely finally to carry away the shadow of their demerits . . . and cause their hitherto obscured virtues to shine forth in full-rounded splendour" (*MF*, 6.12.395). The restoration of social identity is not quite complete, however. The Tullivers remain people who have had "troubles" and been "down in the world." Both Maggie and Tom have been scarred and set apart by the experiences of the past, and continue to impose a kind of social isolation upon themselves, Tom by devoting himself to business and ignoring the social pleasures of life, and Maggie by her decision to remain an outsider in the community of St. Ogg and to exile herself to distant employment.

CRISIS OF SEXUAL IDENTITY

That the restoration of economic status cannot completely restore the Tullivers to the social community is evidence that an emotional toll has been exacted from them that is far more complicated than the simple loss of money and social position. Destruction of economic identity seems to have resulted in an emotional upheaval in family life, which suggests a crisis in sexual roles and sexual identity potentially more threatening than actual poverty. Of course, the Tulliver "family romance" is readily apparent long before the financial crisis; Mr. Tulliver admires Maggie's cleverness and defends her against the criticisms of her mother and aunts, while Mrs. Tulliver favors Tom and has only peevish remonstrances for her daughter. Moreover, we discover early that one of Mr. Tulliver's motives for educating his son for a profession other than his own is a fear that " 'he'd be expectin' to take to the mill an' the land, an' a hinting at me as it was time for me to lay by an' think o' my latter end . . . I shall give Tom an eddication . . . as he may make a nest for himself, an' not want to push me out o' mine' " (*MF*, 1.3.15).

The effect of the bankruptcy, nevertheless, is to instantly magnify the existing family tensions and bring the dynamics of this sexual conflict to the surface. Thus Mr. Tulliver's first reaction to the knowledge of his losses is a "craving which he would not account for to himself to have Maggie near him" (*MF*, 3.1.174), and he writes for her to come home from school. In his delirium and illness he gives no sign of recognizing his wife but calls repeatedly for "the little wench." Mrs. Tulliver, on the other hand, is the one who sends for Tom, and "seems to be thinking more of her boy even than of her husband" (*MF*, 3.1.177). Her tears, as she weeps over her linens and china, are all for Tom, for whom these treasures were to be saved— Maggie is relegated to second best in everything.

The emotional responses of Tom and Maggie in this crisis also display a heightening of the sexual tensions already existing within the family relationship. Tom is moved by his mother's grief and a sense of her wrongs to reproach his father. Maggie, on the other hand, is motivated by compassion and tenderness for her father, and feels no inclination to blame. In addition, the bankruptcy of Mr. Tulliver places a strain on the emotional relationships of the family in other and more prosaic ways. Without the "softening accompaniment of an easy prosperous home" the "peculiarities" of Mr. and Mrs. Tulliver become suddenly grating to their son and daugh-

ter, who now see their parents' defects with clearer eyes. Even the abundant
tenderness of Maggie is sorely tried by the daily irritations of her father's
sullen depression.

That Eliot should have depicted a lack of money wreaking such havoc in
sexual relationships is hardly surprising, for the Victorians seem to have
had a clearly felt (if seldom articulated) notion about the connection between money, sex, and power in personal relationships. Steven Marcus has
explained "the informing idea of sexuality in the era before Freud" as being
based upon economics: "the body is regarded as a productive system with
only a limited amount of material at its disposal. And the model on which
the notion of semen is formed is clearly that of money."[2] Thus a common
Victorian euphemism for orgasm was "to spend" and a man who indulged
in excessive sexual activities could be said to face "ruin . . . he goes bankrupt
and is sold up . . . like the head of a company who has invested wildly in
shares." (Marcus correctly perceives behind this imagery "a universal personal and cultural experience of poverty—and fear of it."[3])

With the connection between loss of money and loss of sexual potence so
clearly established in the language of the culture, it is small wonder that a
loss of fortune could have disturbing effects upon emotional and sexual
relationships. As Marcus points out, "One of the principal components in
male sexuality is the desire for power, the desire to dominate. In modern
society money is one of the two or three most important instruments of
personal power, and the association of sex and money through the medium
of power is an inevitable one."[4]

We have already observed the way in which the painting, melodrama,
and sentimental fiction of the Victorian period chronicled the economic
dependence of women upon men; the art of the time is particularly vivid
concerning the plight of the woman whose man has failed to protect her,
thus making her vulnerable sexually as well as financially. (One of the
problems of the love story in *The Mill on the Floss* is that it so clearly derives
from this hoary cliché of the impoverished young girl whose financial
problems make her vulnerable to the blandishments of the wealthy local
squire.) The Victorian novelist was equally aware of the connection between economic power and sexual power, but, ironically, it was the women
novelists who seem to have understood with the greatest clarity that if the
acquisition of money means sexual dominance, then conversely the loss of
money could be equated with impotence.

Thus Eliot observes the effect of bankruptcy upon the hot-tempered and
passionate Mr. Tulliver, and describes him after his financial ruin in terms
of passivity, helplessness, and impotence. His loss of power is evident in all
of his family relationships. The wife toward whom he once displayed such
condescending superiority now emerges as a woman clearly wronged.
Much is made of the fact that Mrs. Tulliver's precious linens and china,
which must be sold at auction, were bought with her own money, and that

the money Tulliver has foolishly lost was primarily Mrs. Tulliver's fortune. He has thus been chastened in his relationship to his wife by the loss of her money, and is forced to defer to her even upon such crucial questions as accepting Wakem's offer of employment. Toward his son as well, Tulliver is no longer able to prevail with his old authority. Once Tom has taken over the responsibility of repaying Tulliver's debts, the miller is "in some awe" of his son, and finds himself deferring to Tom's wishes. Eliot carries the dynamics of financial loss and sexual impotence even further in *Middlemarch,* where the power struggle between Lydgate and Rosamund is climaxed by Lydgate's financial ruin and his figurative emasculation by his wife.

Thus bankruptcy seems to expose a potential crisis in the very nature of sexual identity, and to raise some disturbing questions about what it means to be male or female in the nineteenth century. An interesting (and surprisingly similar) exploration of these questions is contained in Charlotte Brontë's *Shirley* and Elizabeth Gaskell's *North and South,* both novels that consider the problem of male dominance, and end in a dramatic reversal of the economic roles brought about by the potential bankruptcy of the hero. Much attention has been devoted lately to the "feminism" of Charlotte Brontë and to the struggle for dominance between her heroes and heroines. M. A. Blom has identified Brontë's "basic theme" as "woman's agonized search for social and sexual identity in a male-dominated society,"[5] and has described Brontë's "ambivalence" toward the culturally induced stereotypes of feminine passivity, while F. A. C. Wilson sees Brontë's heroes and heroines as working toward an essentially "androgynous" solution, "an ideal of love and union by which both partners freely alternate between "masculine" or controlling and "feminine" or responsive roles."[6]

The ending of *Jane Eyre* has of course provided abundant material for such reflections. Typically, Blom regards the ending as a "total victory" for the feminine principle; Jane "confronts and dominates Rochester whom Charlotte Brontë has symbolically emasculated for her heroine."[7] Wilson, on the other hand, believes that rather than emasculating Mr. Rochester, Jane has "liberated" him, remaking her lover "into the androgynous being which he potentially is."[8] Both authors, however, agree in seeing *Shirley* as a retreat from the idea of feminine independence, and agree that "Captain" Shirley Keeldar's marriage to Louis at the end of the novel is an acknowledgment by Brontë of women's need to be "mastered."

Both critics also reject the Caroline-Robert story as the less interesting romance and less central to the novel, and it is here, I believe, that they have missed the crucial point of *Shirley.* For the chastisement of Robert Moore by both Shirley and Caroline is surely the major focus of the plot; Louis Moore does not even make his appearance until two-thirds of the novel has passed, and his character is poorly imagined in comparison with that of his brother. Blom considers *Shirley* a flawed work which "though it ostensibly deals with the threat of civil war posed by the Yorkshire machine breaking in 1812, actually focuses on an examination of the internecine war between male rulers and their repressed and sometimes rebellious subjects."[9] To see the novel in terms of such dichotomies, however, is to ignore a connection that Brontë clearly establishes: the theme of economic conflict between men and masters, and the struggle for female independence from male dominance are clearly joined in the figure of Robert Moore. As Arnold Shapiro has observed, "One cannot separate the public and private themes of *Shirley,* just as one cannot separate the public and private lives of its central characters . . . Robert Moore, who reflects society's values, is the very embodiment of the social criticism of *Shirley.*"[10] Moore is the arrogant and domineering master of the rebellious factory hands, but he is arrogant and masterful in his relationships with women as well. Robert Heilman has observed how thoroughly Robert Moore is described in terms of maleness: "He is the great lover of the story."[11] Robert is admired by Caroline: " 'Has he not fine eyes and well-cut features, and a clear, princely forehead?' " (*S*, 12.255), and by Shirley: " 'He is handsome and manly and commanding. . . . Prince is on his brow, and ruler in his bearing' " (*S*, 31.518). His commanding, masculine presence is insisted upon over and over:

> Mr. Moore appeared at the door. His figure seemed very tall as he entered, and stood in contrast with the three ladies, none of whom could boast a stature much beyond the average. . . . (*S*, 13.239) . . . he made no petty effort to attract, dazzle, or impress. He contrived, not withstanding . . . to command a little, because the deeper voice, however mildly modulated, the somewhat harder mind, now and then, though involuntarily and unintentionally, bore down by some peremptory phrase or tone the mellow accents and susceptible, if high, nature of Shirley. (*S*, 13.254)

Moore's masculine attributes exert a "secret power" over both Shirley and Caroline. Caroline's more passive feminine nature, however, is not simply a sign of the author's sentimentality; Brontë makes sufficiently clear that Caroline's economic dependence leaves her almost no alternatives. And the author allows her heroine certain bold ruminations upon the bitter lot of single women barred from honest employment by social pressures which are certainly far-seeing for the period in which the novel was written.

The character of Shirley seems, on the other hand, to be a kind of wish-fulfillment figure; what would a woman be like if economic independence freed her from social constraints? (" 'Shirley Keeldar, Esquire, ought to be my style and title. They gave me a man's name; I hold a man's position: it is enough to inspire me with a touch of manhood. . . . they ought to make me a magistrate and a captain of yeomanry . . .' " [*S*, 2.213].) The fact that Shirley is Robert's *landlord* is crucial to the novel's resolution; the economic role reversal is one of the most striking features of the plot. Robert is felled by a bullet from the mutinous "hands" whose human needs he has ignored, and his pride is humbled by Shirley's rejection of marriage, but one of the most crucial factors in his transformation seems to be his economic defeats and the necessity of accepting money from Shirley to save his mill. Brontë is explicit about the thoroughness of Robert's punishment. The "princely," "manly" hero is chastened by illness and defeat. He is now described as "a tall, thin, wasted figure," a "meagre man," his state of mind "dark, barren, impotent." In his own words, " 'See what a poor, pale, grim phantom I am—more pitiable than formidable' "(*S*, 35. 651). Such chastisement, however, proves to be beneficial. By the end of the novel Robert has reconsidered his relationships with the community at large and has acquired a more compassionate set of values. He is now able to express the softer side of his nature toward Caroline, and his mill will apparently become a philanthropic enterprise (" 'the houseless, the starving, the unemployed shall come to Hollow's mill from far and near' " [*S*, 37.598]).

In his new resolution to conduct his business on more humane principles he acknowledges the moral ascendancy of Caroline (" 'I *will* do good," he tells her, "you shall tell me how' " [*S*, 37.596]), but significantly it is Shirley's money which will finance this happy ending. That the novel ends with conventional Victorian marriages should not mislead the reader. Brontë could scarcely have given her heroines' romances any other ending, but the dynamics of the sexual power struggle emerge quite clearly in Robert's downfall. Whether the hero's fate constitutes an "emasculation" or a liberation of his more "androgynous" nature is for the purposes of this study beside the point. What is clear is that Brontë has succeeded in posing questions concerning the very nature of masculinity and femininity. Robert's position as mill owner makes it quite clear that the question of economic justice and the question of sexual equality are related; his threatened bankruptcy and consequent necessity of accepting money from Shirley clearly threaten the economic basis of male dominance. In one small but telling scene in the novel, Caroline foolishly offers financial help to a laborer who is offended by the implications of such an offer. " 'Look at t' difference between us: ye're a little, young, slender lass, and I'm a great strong man . . . It's not *my* part then, I think, to be under obligations (as they say) to ye . . .' " (*S*, 18.329). Brontë is clearly aware of the psychological consequences at work in such a reversal of economic roles.[12] The reversal of roles in this situation is plainly fraught with threatening implications for the nineteenth-century male identity, and thus Brontë clearly uses the episode of bankruptcy as a kind of cataclysmic force capable of exposing a crisis of sexual identity at least as shattering as the threat of poverty or social disgrace.

It is fascinating, but not altogether surprising, to note the similarities in the treatment of this theme in Brontë's *Shirley* and Gaskell's *North and South*.

Charlotte Brontë had sent Mrs. Gaskell a copy of *Shirley* as early as 1849. The two first met in 1850, and Gaskell was enormously impressed with Brontë's character and circumstances. At least one author has suggested that the writing of *North and South* was a sort of preparation for the biography of Charlotte, and that the character of Margaret Hale is informed with "Charlotte Brontë's secret haunting presence."[13] John Pikoulis suggests that "behind *North and South* lie Charlotte's novels, including *Shirley*, in which the theme of women searching for an expansion of the possibilities for living that are open to them is combined with the theme of dispute between masters and men."[14] Like Brontë, Gaskell joins the questions of economic justice and sexual equality in the figure of the domineering factory owner, whose threatened descent into bankruptcy transforms his views on social and economic justice at the same time that it reverses the dynamics of his relationship with the heroine.

In the character of Margaret Hale, Gaskell further establishes the connections between economic and sexual tensions; as a woman suffering the limitations forced upon her by a male-dominated society, it is only natural that Margaret should identify with the equally powerless industrial workers. Her relationship with Mr. Thornton is a prolonged struggle for dominance (or at least equality) in which their dialectical argument over political economy is every bit as important as their sexual attraction. Pikoulis has correctly established the motivating forces behind the crucial scene in which Margaret shields Thornton from the fury of a mob of striking workers as the wish-fulfillment of the powerless, "a reverie in which the lonely, slighted, and obscure project themselves into heroic activity."[15] But surely an even more striking example of feminine wish fulfillment (and one that perhaps seriously flaws the novel) is the ending in which Thornton's landlord dies, leaving all his property to Margaret Hale, thus enabling the heroine to lend Thornton the money with which to save his mill.

With this stroke Gaskell has gone Brontë one better. Robert Moore ended in *Shirley* with one heroine as his conscience and another as his landlord; in *North and South* Margaret Hale becomes both conscience and landlord, spiritual guide and financial creditor—a moral arbiter who also holds the purse strings. The relationship of the hero and the heroine has been critically transformed by a striking reversal of their economic roles, and although the incident may strike the reader at best as rather improbable, it allows Gaskell more scope in which to work out a balanced sexual relationship than the realities of the nineteenth century would generally have permitted. The novel suggests a dawning perception that the role of money may well be crucial as the basis of social and sexual roles. It suggests as well that beneath the stubbornly traditional attitudes of Victorian society there is emerging a crisis in sexual identity, a crisis which an abrupt loss of money such as bankruptcy can glaringly expose.

RELIGIOUS CRISIS

Thus far we have considered the ways in which bankruptcy is used by the Victorian novelist to suggest a contemporary crisis in the selfhood of the individual—the increasing vulnerability of the human identity in its economic, social and sexual manifestations. But by far the most terrifying crisis of Victorian life was the spiritual malaise that was beginning to afflict the average Victorian. Evidence for this last is somewhat more difficult to discern within the context of these novels. The Victorian novelist was far more likely to depict the characters in their own homes, or even in the marketplace, than in their churches; and religion for the Victorians, although a potent force, was probably more a matter of underlying assumptions and unarticulated attitudes than a question of any particular religious dogma.

In *The City of Dickens* Alexander Welsh perceptively discusses the secular iconography of the Victorian period, in which the city, dominated by images of materialism and greed, becomes St. Augustine's earthly city.[16] The condition of urban man is seen as increasingly alienated and powerless, and his environment increasingly associated with decadence and death. (Both Dickens and Thackeray refer to London as "Babylon," and in *Dombey and Son* Harriet Carker perceives the city as a "monster" of death that swallows up all who enter.) Opposed to this earthly City of Man, the closest that the Victorian culture can come to a vision of the Heavenly City is in its celebration of hearth and home. As a symbol of shelter and warmth that predates Christianity itself, the cozy hearth is the antithesis of the urban environment. It represents the religious values that are in retreat elsewhere in Victorian life, and is generally presided over by a Good Angel in the person of the female of the house. Welsh is persuasive on the "make-believe angelology" of the Victorian home;[17] in all forms of Victorian art it is the "quasi-religious position of women" that sanctifies the home and establishes it as the repository of the City of God.[18] Coventry Patmore's *The Angel in the House* is one of many Victorian works that glorify the earthly love of women as a prefiguration of divine love,[19] and the home established under such beneficent protection becomes a veritable image of paradise. According to Welsh, "One of the signatures of Victorian literature, in truth, is the frequent reference to 'household gods.'"[20] George Eliot, in fact, devotes an entire chapter of *The Mill on the Floss* to the grief of Mrs. Tulliver as she weeps over her "teraphim, or household gods" (gods which in this case are specifically located in her silver tea pot and best china, her "spoons and skewers and ladles").

It is Dickens, however, who is most clearly associated with this tendency to glorify the sacred hearth as a refuge from the monstrous city of man, and the religious significance of the cozy hearth perhaps explains his fondness for a figurative techinque described by J. Hillis Miller as "the use of houses to symbolize states of souls,"[21] or, as Henri Talon phrases it, "houses as synecdochic expressions of human beings."[22] *Dombey and Son* is particularly rich with scenes of cozy firesides exuding warmth and security, which are contrasted to a series of false and uncomfortable homes. In this novel in which "houses are natural metaphors for their inhabitants,"[23] the home of Mr. Dombey is particularly important. The cold, blank aspect of the Dombey home is stressed, especially after the death of Paul, when the unused house is covered with the mold and dust of neglect. The absence of love and comfort are particularly noticeable in the scenes at the dinner table (always a crucial index in Dickens's iconology). The frozen atmosphere of Paul's christening is embellished with a "dead dinner lying in state," while at the ironically named "housewarming" of Dombey and Edith, the bride and groom preside over dinner separated by a "long plateau of precious metal."[24] Dickens allows himself an ironic (if rather obvious) comment on the elegance of the Dombey home after the marriage: "what an altar to the Household Gods is raised up here!" (*DS*, 35.478).

A similar scene of elegant discomfort is portrayed in the home that Edith's mother borrows from her relative for the wedding party. Plates, china, and butlers have been hired to fill up the "dead sea of mahogany" that surrounds the wedding party. The scene of disorder and discomfort after the wedding is specifically given symbolic overtones reflecting the emotional state of the bride and groom:

> The hatchments in the dining room look down on crumbs, dirty plates, spillings of wine, half-thawed ice, stale discoloured heel-taps, scraps of lobster, drumsticks of fowls, and pensive jellies, gradually resolving themselves into a lukewarm gummy soup. The marriage is, by this time, almost as denuded of its show and garnish as the breakfast. (*DS*, 31.435)

Mrs. Skewton's inability to provide her guests with comfort and hospitality is a telling defect. As Talon observes, "in this novel the failure to make a home . . . [is] always the sign of a want of heart and of sins against the spirit."[25]

Another such sinner is Mrs. Skewton's lower-class doppelganger, Mrs. Brown, who lives with her daughter amid filth and poverty. Still another such sinner lives in gracious comfort, and yet the home of Carker the Manager is hardly a sacred hearth: "there is something in the general air that is not well" (*DS*, 33.454). His furnishings are "voluptuous" but empty— Mr. Carker has been more successful than his employer in establishing physical comfort, but like his wealthier employer, Carker lacks the emotional resources to establish a home of spiritual comfort. His home is specifically contrasted in chapter 33 to that of his less fortunate brother: "It is a poor, small house, barely and sparsely furnished, but very clean; and there is even an attempt to decorate it, shown in the homely flowers trained about the porch and in the narrow garden" (*DS*, 33.455). This poor but cozy home betrays a "woman's touch" in those trailing flowers; it is of course significant that Harriet Carker has chosen to follow her downfallen brother into exile. It is the presence of her "cordial face" that sanctifies his poor hearth, as the presence of a good woman usually imparts a religious sanctity to the family fireside. Similarly, the cozy home of the "apple-cheeked" Toodles family revolves around the nourishing figure of the mother Polly, who is wet-nurse, earth mother, and the center of the family's domestic bliss. The most important fireside is the cozy hearth of the Wooden Midshipman, in which Florence eventually takes refuge from the coldness and discomfort of her father's home. The scene of Captain Cuttle preparing a snug chamber for Florence, and cooking with a "diminutive frying-pan, in which some sausages were hissing and bubbling in a most musical manner" (*DS*, 49.650), exudes the warmth and security that are the antithesis of Dombey's earthly City, and prefigures the domestic haven in which Florence will eventually harbor her father and the company of the Midshipman in an idyllic paradise suggestive of the City of God.

If the domestic hearth is the Victorian equivalent of earthly paradise, then it is obvious that bankruptcy represents a shattering cataclysm which disrupts the home and annihilates the heavenly vision. The destruction of the comforting household which has been a sanctuary and haven from the city of man is tantamount to an expulsion from paradise; small wonder that it was painful for Victorians to contemplate such a violation of the hearth. Thus for Maggie and Tom Tulliver in *The Mill on the Floss*, the first wrenching revelation of their father's failure comes when Tom returns home to find "there was a coarse, dingy man . . . sitting in his father's chair, smoking, with a jug and glass beside him" (*MF*, 3.2.178). The sense of dispossession and violation is perfectly clear. The "coarse" stranger in the father's chair is a harbinger of the Tullivers' exclusion from their own hearth; the disgrace of "having the bailiff in the house" is deepened by the invasion of the sacred fireside and the dislocation of the domestic haven. Nor can such traumatic events be dismissed as merely the fanciful drama of fiction, for the Victorian reader would have been only too aware of their painful reality.

That such scenes struck at the very heart of Victorian emotional and spiritual life may be verified by the findings of the Parliamentary Commission of 1854, which investigated the unsatisfactory nature of bankruptcy proceedings. Discussing the function of the court messenger (who had come to replace the bailiff), a solicitor testified:

> This is also another reason why bankruptcy is so distressing and painful to a large class of persons. The domestic sanctity of the home is violated, not by a well-conditioned public officer, but by a man of the very poorest class, a man not always temperate, nor always clean. Just imagine the horror and disgust arising from such a man as that being introduced into

a well-ordered establishment, in the midst of trouble! I have known, again and again, (I am now stating this from my own personal experience) a man struggle more against bankruptcy in consequence of the pain that he knows his wife and family will endure by the introduction of this messenger's man than from any publicity which he will have to undergo.[26]

The bailiff's man in Eliot's *The Mill on the Floss* is not a villain. He has a "rough, embarrassed civility" which shows that he is uncomfortable in his role. But often in Dickens, Thackeray, and Trollope, the unsavory aspect of the brokers who seize a home and prepare it for auction suggests the sleaziness of this type of action and emphasizes the sense of a corrupt materialistic economic system grinding down the vulnerable individual. Furthermore, the frequent emphasis upon the Hebraic character of such brokers suggests that the popular Victorian novelists were not above taking advantage of the ethnocentrism and anti-Semitism of their audience to heighten the dramatic effect of these pillages of sacred Christian hearths.

Thus Thackeray speaks of "dingy guests of oriental countenance" who invade the Sedley home in *Vanity Fair*, gentlemen who offend even the insensitive Becky: "'Look at them with their hooked beaks,'" she says. "'They're like vultures after a battle'" (*VF*, 18.166). In *The Newcomes* Thackeray pictures "swarms of Hebrew gentlemen with their hats on" taking over Colonel Newcome's home, and the image is echoed in the illustration of Richard Doyle, which shows several gentlemen with hooked noses examining the ill-fated cocoa-nut tree, which is marked "Lot 70" (*N*, 72.733). Similarly in *Dombey and Son* Dickens pictures "a gentleman of a Mosaic Arabian cast of countenance" as one of the "shabby vampires" who pick over the Dombey home. (And in Frith's painting *The Road to Ruin*, too, the broker and his men who are taking possession of the family home are portrayed with physical features meant to suggest Jewish origins.)

This vision of the sacred hearth violated by strangers of an alien order increases the sense of dispossession and desecration—the loss of the spiritual haven. Fairly often in fact, the Victorian novel details the scene of seizure and auction in what becomes almost a set piece, described in images of "plunder" and "desecration."[27] In the Sedley home in *Vanity Fair* "old women and amateurs have invaded the upper apartments, pinching the bed-curtains, poking into the feathers, shampooing the mattresses, and clapping the wardrobe drawers to and fro" (*VF*, 17.159), while at the Newcome's auction "swarms of Hebrew gentlemen . . . are walking about the drawing rooms, peeping into the bedrooms, weighing and poising the poor silver cocoa-nut tree, eying the plate and crystal, thumbing the damask of the curtains, and inspecting ottomans, mirrors, and a hundred articles of splendid trumpery" (*N*, 70.721).

The painful nature of such violation and invasion of privacy is clear. If one's home is the face that one presents to the world, then an auction of one's beloved possessions becomes a devastating exposure. The ripping away of the facade to allow the humiliating public gaze into the innermost secrets of the family combines with the noise and confusion, and the dirty shoes and unclean hands of strangers, to negate the very image of the sacred hearth. The warmth and security that are the natural function of the domestic scene have been destroyed, and in their place is only a comfortless house filled with disorder and ruin. Dickens (who is a master of describing clutter) provides a bravura description of the Dombey auction:

> The men in the carpet caps go on tumbling the furniture about; and the gentlemen with the pens and ink make out inventories of it, and sit upon pieces of furniture never made to be sat upon, and eat bread and cheese from the public-house on other pieces of furniture never made to be eaten on, and seem to have a delight in appropriating precious articles to strange uses. . . .
> Then, all day long, there is a retinue of mouldy gigs and chaise-carts in the street; and herds of shabby vampires, Jew and Christian, over-run the house, sounding the plate-glass mirrors with their knuckles, striking discordant octaves on the Grand Piano, drawing wet forefingers over the pictures, breathing on the blades of the best dinner-knives, . . . There is not a secret place in the whole house. Fluffy and snuffy strangers stare into the kitchen-range as curiously as into the attic clothes-press. Stout men with napless hats on, look out of the bedroom windows and cut jokes with friends in the street. . . . The swarm and buzz, and going up and down, endure for days. . . .
> Then there is a palisade of tables made in the best drawing-room; and on the capital, french-polished, extending telescopic range of Spanish mahogany dining tables with their legs, the pulpit of the Auctioneer is erected; and the herds of shabby vampires, Jew and Christian, the strangers fluffy and snuffy, and the stout men with napless hats, congregate about it and sit upon everything within reach, mantel-pieces included, and begin to bid. Hot, humming and dusty, are the rooms all day; and—high above the heat, hum, and dust—the head and shoulders, voice and hammer, of the Auctioneer, are ever at work. (*DS*, 59.790–91)

It is ironic that in this novel about commerce, the auction is the only commercial activity besides the building of the railroad that is fully described. Unlike Dickens's description of the railroad, however, there is no ambiguity in his attitude toward the scene of the auction. With its greed and confusion, its dislocation of precious objects from their natural functions, its violations of all that the domestic scene stands for, the auction is a bizarre ritual, a kind of inverted religious ceremony in which a congregation of lost souls gathers beneath the "pulpit" of the Auctioneer to celebrate damnation rather than salvation. Dombey has been excluded from the only earthly Paradise that the Victorian world can offer—his own fireside—and the craven vultures who pick over its ruin are clearly in no greater state of grace than the dispossessed owner.

Interestingly, there is a companion piece to Dickens's description of the auction, in an earlier description of the shop of Mr. Brogley, broker and appraiser. Mr. Brogley's second-hand shop is the destined resting place of the possessions of all those who fall victim to the complexities of the Victorian economy. Uncle Sol has a near brush with Mr. Brogley, and some of Dombey's possessions will doubtless find their way to this shop "where every description of second-hand furniture was exhibited in the most uncomfortable aspect, and under circumstances and in combinations the most completely foreign to its purpose" (*DS*, 9.113). There are the familiar anthropomorphic images of disorder and disarray, the ironic junkheap of a failed materialism: "Dozens of chairs hooked on to washing stands, which with difficulty poised themselves on the shoulders of sideboards, which in their turn stood upon the wrong side of dining tables: (*DS*, 9.115). There is the same jumble of objects that have been separated from their natural functions, "motionless clocks," "a set of window curtains with no window belonging to them," and, most significantly, "a homeless hearthrug severed from its natural companion the fireside," while "various looking-glasses accidentally placed at compound interest of reflection and refraction, presented to the eye an eternal perspective of bankruptcy and ruin" (*DS*, 9.116).

The sacrilege involved in the sale of such "household gods" is readily apparent. Clearly bankruptcy represents a violation of the self in that it takes from the individual those beloved possessions upon which is based his or her sense of personal identity and vision (or illusion) of the hearth as spiritual sanctuary. In the above-mentioned description of bankruptcy and auction, the narrative usually dwells lingeringly upon familiar objects imbued with great emotional significance that are roughly removed by strangers: Amelia Sedley's "little" piano, Paul Dombey's "little" bedstead, Col. Newcome's silver cocoa-nut tree, Mrs. Tulliver's china and linens, Maggie Tulliver's books.

The loss of possessions is critical: the auction, in fact, becomes the perfect economic metaphor for lives that have been measured by the price of possessions, and will henceforth be valueless in the eyes of the world. There is often an ironic intention in such portraits of economic dispossession; such treasured objects as the portrait of Jos Sedley on an elephant which is auctioned in *Vanity Fair* and Colonel Newcome's hideous silver cocoa-nut tree are hardly designed to enlist our sympathies, while the elegant households of the Dombeys and Newcomes that are destroyed by bankruptcy are only feeble imitations of domestic warmth. But there is surely no irony intended in the loss of Paul Dombey's death bed, Colonel Newcome's old campaign chests, Amelia's piano, or Maggie's *Pilgrim's Progress*. The loss of such treasured objects makes it clear that bankruptcy in the Victorian novel is an emotional and spiritual dispossession as well as an economic one.

The scene of auction and the loss of beloved objects are, as one might expect, more restrained in George Eliot than in Dickens. The reader is not present at the sale at all, but experiences it, along with the Tulliver family, from the remote sickbed of Mr. Tulliver. The dirt, noise, and confusion of the sale are represented merely as distant metallic raps and "the trumping of footsteps on the gravel." Instead of the bustle of the sale, we confront Mrs. Tulliver's anguished supsense as she sits by the side of her senseless husband, and we view the consequences of the auction upon the household through the determined effort of the housemaid to disguise the true nature of the calamity by removing the dirty footprints of strangers:

> She was not scrubbing indiscriminately, for there would be further dirt of the same atrocious kind made by people who still had to fetch away their purchases; but she was bent on bringing the parlour, where that "pipe-smoking pig" the bailiff has sat, to such an appearance of scant comfort as could be given to it by cleanliness, and the few articles of furniture brought in for the family. Her mistress and the young folks should have their tea in it that night. . . .(*MF*, 3.6.209)

The "scant comfort" that the auction has left in its wake is a sufficient clue to the cataclysmic disruption of the sale.

Similarly, Eliot does not dwell upon the rough handling of beloved treasures, or their violent removal. What is emphasized instead is the absence of these objects, the void which they leave behind. The parlor is "altered" with a "new strange bareness." In the place where the book case had been, "there was now nothing but the oblong unfaded space on the wall," and Maggie mourns her *Pilgrim's Progress:* "'I thought we should never part from that while we lived'" (*MF*, 3.6.212). The absence of her possessions is a source of eternally recurring grief to Mrs. Tulliver, who complains, "'I go and look at the bare shelves every day, and think where all my things used to stand'" (*MF*, 3.7.221). For Mr. Tulliver the shock is delayed by illness, but when he finally descends to his parlor the cruel sunshine shows him only "the empty places, and the marks where well-known objects once had been" (*MF*, 3.8.225), and he looks with despair "at all the bare places, which for him were filled with the shadows of departed objects—the daily companions of his life" (*MF*, 3.8.229–30).

The bankruptcy and auction not only create a void in the Tulliver home, they are wrenching dislocations that startlingly reveal the terrible mutability of human life. The loss of possessions marks a sudden and bitter discontinuity with the past. As Maggie mourns over the loss of her books, "'The ends of our lives will have nothing in it like the beginning'" (*MF*, 3.6.212). The early experiences of Maggie and Tom are a kind of childhood idyll, in spite of the tensions between them, because neither of them is yet aware of the transient nature of the human condition:

> It was one of their happy mornings. They trotted along and sat down together, with no thought that life would ever change much for them:

they would only get bigger and not go to school, and it would always be
like the holidays; they would always live together and be fond of each
other. And the mill with its booming . . . the Ripple, where the banks
seemed like home . . . above all, the great Floss . . . these things would
always be just the same to them. (*MF,* 1.5.37)

But time and bankruptcy work their changes, and Maggie and Tom must
confront the bitter knowledge of human mutability. The loss of the past
and the discontinuity of the present that bankruptcy brings are like a
foretaste of death; Maggie acknowledges such burdens when she proclaims
about her old friendship with Phillip Wakem which is no longer possible, "I
may not keep anything I used to love when I was little. The old books went;
and Tom is different—and my father. It is like death" (*MF,* 5.1.263).

Thus bankruptcy has opened up a spiritual void within Maggie. It has
stripped from her the spiritual comfort and sanctity of the domestic
hearth, it has exposed the possibility of dislocation, mutability, and death. It
has dispossessed her economically and spiritually, and plunged her into a
religious crisis that will change the nature of her experience for the rest of
her life. Bewildered and despairing, Maggie can find no comfort in the
simple, unthinking "semi-pagan" theology of St. Ogg's. ("The religion of the
Dodsons consisted in revering whatever was customary and respectable"
[*MF,* 4.1.239].) Seeking the guidance that is lacking in the orthodox religion
of her time, Maggie turns to a narrow and fanatical asceticism which she
has dreamily gleaned from the works of Thomas à Kempis. "Making a faith
for herself without the aid of established authorities" (*MF,* 4.3.256), she
concludes that the "secret of life" is to be found in elaborate plans of self-
humiliation and martyrdom.

This religious crisis is crucial to the events which follow. Maggie's sacrifice
of the joys of the present world comforts her, but leaves her ill-prepared to
deal with worldly temptations. Even when Maggie "falls" by her half-
consent to elope with Stephen Guest, however, she is tormented by her
former ideals, "the divine presentiment of something higher than mere
personal enjoyment, which had made the sacredness of life" (*MF,* 6.13.402).
The vision of the Virgin of the Flood, which awakens her conscience,
recalls to her her earlier "longings after perfect goodness," and prepares
the way for the final act of self-sacrifice during the flood in which Maggie
suddenly finds herself "alone in the darkness with God." It must be acknowledged that the divine intervention of the flood results in an ending to
the novel that is problematical at best, but the authenticity of Maggie's
religious quest is not to be denied.[28] Her confusion and seeking for truth
mirror what seems to have been a fairly representative experience for such
Victorians as Carlyle and Eliot herself, a rejection of established religious
verities, a period of agonizing doubt, a painful search for spiritual comfort,
and the attempt, not altogether successful, at reestablishing belief "without
the aid of established authorities."

Thus in *The Mill on the Floss* the dislocations of economic bankruptcy have exposed a crisis of religious identity that seems to have been a significant part of the Victorian experience. Like other great Victorian novelists who wrote about bankruptcy, Eliot uses the financial catastrophe to reveal a void that seems to lurk beneath the confident surface of Victorian life. In such novels bankruptcy becomes a metaphorical upheaval that exposes a crisis of economic, social, sexual, and religious values that threatens to annihilate the very existence of the individual self.

6

Bankruptcy as Metaphor: Moral and Spiritual Rebirth
(Dombey and Son, The Newcomes)

Clearly some of the major Victorian novelists saw in the experience of bankruptcy an ominous portent of the destruction of the human self by the forces of materialism unleashed by the Industrial Revolution. Such a despairing view was, however, quite counter to the prevailing Victorian belief in industrial progress. In the rapid changes and expanding technology of the nineteenth century, proponents of industrialism believed, there were new possibilities and opportunities arising, as well as old values and traditions decaying. Even the novelists were not immune to such hopes, although their optimism was at once more guarded and more subtle than that of the "official" view. In several novels of the late 1840s and early 1850s, then, bankruptcy functions ironically as a harbinger of better things to come, a chastening experience that contains within itself an opportunity for the restitution of old wrongs, and a chance for moral regeneration as well. In *Dombey and Son* and *The Newcomes,* and to a lesser extent in *Shirley* and *North and South,* bankruptcy becomes a kind of fortunate fall in which all the old falsehoods, false values, and mistaken goals are swept away and a new and purer beginning is possible.[1]

Much of this hopefulness may be laid at the door of Thomas Carlyle, whose influence upon such novelists as Brontë, Gaskell, and Dickens was profound. Carlyle saw clearly the materialism and corruption of the Victorian world, but in *Chartism* (1839) and *Past and Present* (1843) he had not yet begun to despair of setting things right. On the contrary, the increasing productivity of the Victorian economy seemed to Carlyle to offer new hope for an equitable and just solution to the problem of the "Condition of England." The English people, he wrote in *Chartism,* had two tasks in World History: "the grand Industrial task of conquering some half or more of the

Terraqueous Planet for the use of man; then secondly, the grand Constitutional task of sharing, in some pacific endurable manner, the fruit of said conquest, and showing all people how it might be done."[2] Manufacturing was potentially a noble endeavor, for "is not the spinning of clothes for the naked intrinsically a most blessed thing?"[3]

Thus "Disorganic Manchester" had an enormous capability for good, once harnessed and properly channeled. Again in *Past and Present* Carlyle exhorts manufacturers to the "heroic life." The cotton manufacturer is potentially a Hero of Work:

> he was a Captain of Industry, born master of the Ultimate genuine Aristocracy of this Universe, could he have known it! These thousand men that span and toiled round him, they were a regiment whom he had enlisted, man by man, to make war on a very genuine enemy: Bareness of back. . . .[4]

For this noble endeavor, labor must be organized by true leaders, wise and valiant men capable of rising above the lure of the "cash-nexus" to attain higher goals: "A man has other obligations laid on him, in God's Universe, than the payment of cash. . . ."[5]

The social themes of Carlyle had enormous currency in the early Victorian years; writers such as Brontë and Gaskell were thoroughly familiar with his gospel of the nobility of Work and the Aristocracy of Talent. Like Carlyle, Brontë and Gaskell believed that the commercial world contained within itself the possibilities of salvation, and they attempted in their "industrial" novels, *Shirley* and *North and South,* to work out a plausible model for the way in which such a salvation might be enacted. Each author created an industrialist hero who is chastened by the experience of bankruptcy (and by the superior moral integrity of the heroine) into a kind of economic and social rebirth, in which he comes to realize that his economic resources and commercial energy may be channeled into beneficial change for the good of the greater community. Like the Captains of Industry, whom Carlyle envisioned as ennobling labor by finding order and purpose in it, Brontë's Moore and Gaskell's Thornton each begins to see in his relationship to his workers the possibility of going beyond the mere "cash-nexus," and each accepts in the end his larger responsibilities within the social order. Like Carlyle, Brontë and Gaskell see manufacturing as a potentially noble endeavor, an enterprise that might some day cover the naked backs of the world. (It is probably not a coincidence that both Moore and Thornton are manufacturers of cloth.)

Of the two novels, Brontë's *Shirley* is not quite as insistent as Gaskell's *North and South* about the saving grace possible under a new economic order. Brontë clearly condemns the self-interest of the mercantile world, which places financial gain above national honor and private emotion. Just as clearly, the author pleads for a change of heart among the manufacturing class that would create more compassionate human relationships. Thus her hero Moore is forced to recognize the humanity of his workers, and his new awareness of his fellowship with them leads to a new determination to conduct his business with regard for "the houseless, the starving, the unemployed." In the conclusion of *Shirley,* as Arnold Shapiro has noted, "history and private life come together" in the figure of the reformed manufacturer,[6] and Moore's conversion seems to offer the possibility of salvation through moral rebirth within the structure of the existing society. It must be noted, however, that Brontë's conclusion is not a very forceful one. Robert Moore's mill will prosper, but the beautiful countryside will suffer for it. Moreover, hard times will return on occasion; a moral regeneration will not solve all of the problems of economic fluctuations, and even for a morally awakened Captain of Industry, life will continue to be a struggle. The muted quality of the conclusion suggests that while Brontë was clearly inspired by the social gospel of Carlyle, she remains aware of the painful obstacles to be overcome before the new Chivalry of Work can prevail.

Elizabeth Gaskell, on the other hand, seems to have held a more robust belief in the possibilities inherent in capitalism. Like Carlyle, she admires the vitality of the new industrialism. Her hero Thornton "represents something specifically contemporary, an explosion of energy, an extension of consciousness, which reinforces her belief that man may master his fate."[7] Like Brontë's Moore, Mr. Thornton is chastened by his experience of financial loss and by the redemptive love of the heroine into a new understanding of his human connection to his workers. (The rhetoric is specifically Carlylean here: Thornton speaks of "cultivating some intercourse with the hands beyond the mere cash-nexus!" [*NS*, 2.26.431].) Gaskell clearly believes that the energy and vitality of her hero (and of the new social forces that he represents) are capable of overcoming the painful crises of the industrial world; the problem, at least for the present-day reader, is whether or not she is capable of making such a solution credible.

On the whole, critics have tended not to be impressed with the conclusion of *North and South.* According to John Pikoulis, the author's control wavers when she insists upon the triumph of humanitarianism; Thornton's relationship with the working-man Higgins, his establishment of communal kitchens, his denial of the "cash-nexus" are "no more than verbal victories."[8] Pikoulis believes that Thornton's character loses force with his conversion, and that the imaginative strength of the book lies in its very insistence upon a grim portrait of industrial relationships which is then belied by the facile ending. John Lucas takes a strikingly similar view, charging that the power of the novel is in its depiction of the way in which class interests inevitably separate even well-meaning men, and that "again and again the pattern of reconciliation intrudes into and mocks the real imaginative strengths."[9] In her defense of industrialism (or, as Lucas terms it, "sticking up for her own class") the author is guilty, according to Lucas, of "constant simplification of issues whose real complexities are scarcely glimpsed before they are skirted."[10]

Such criticisms cannot be dismissed out of hand, for they are likely to echo the modern reader's experience of resistance to the happy conclusion of *North and South.* It is important to keep firmly in mind, however, the fact that our pessimism about private philanthropy as the solution to the problems of capitalism is likely to be based upon knowledge that was not available to Gaskell. Stephen Gill has ably defended the ending of the novel by pointing out the necessity for viewing Gaskell within the context of her own time. According to Gill, the author not only possessed a strong Christian faith in the efficacy of good works, but would have had available to her many inspiring examples of Victorian benevolence.

Gill resurrects one such example of capitalist philanthropy that was likely to have influenced the writing of *North and South:* an article in *The Quarterly Review* of 1852 enthusiastically praising a *Special Report by the Directors to the Proprietors of Price's Patent Candle Company.* In this report, James Wilson, a director of Price's Patent Candle Company at Belmont, Vauxhall, describes the establishment of four schools upon the factory premises, with an enrollment of five hundred to eight hundred working children, apparently paid for out of Wilson's own pocket. The director justifies such activities on the grounds that a company's responsibilities to its workers goes beyond mere economic compensation. Gill observes:

> Carlyle's presence is felt in every line of the *Report,* for Wilson is presenting the case for the necessity of human relationships within the commercial system which had been most forcefully stated by Carlyle during the Chartist years and had since become a commonplace amongst economic and social commentators.[11]

Mr. Wilson was actively pursuing his benevolent reforms at Price's Patent Candle Company between 1847 and 1852. Mrs. Gaskell apparently made his acquaintance during this period; she is known to have visited the Belmont factory with Harriet Beecher Stowe and Lady Hatherton in May 1853 to view this example of individual capitalist benevolence, and she began the writing of *North and South* at the end of 1853.[12] It seems highly probable, then, that Elizabeth Gaskell wrote with the example of what could be accomplished by individual commitment clearly before her in the efforts of Wilson and others. Carlyle's vision of the Captain of Industry who would lead mankind to master his fate may well have seemed attainable to Gaskell, could the individual industrialist but experience a change of heart and be brought to understand the noble possibilities of his role.[13] In her eyes, therefore, the conversion of Mr. Thornton to a humanitarian point of view is neither unrealistic nor futile—and it would be less than generous to fault her because one hundred years of further industrial development have proven her (and Mr. Wilson) to have been overly optimistic about the efficacy of private benevolence.

Thus for Charlotte Brontë and Elizabeth Gaskell, salvation is still possible within the context of a mercantile world. Bankruptcy functions as a kind of redemptive suffering from which the industrialist hero emerges morally reborn. Such a hero must remain in the world of commerce and industry to shoulder his social responsibilities and to atone for his past wrongs. Other Victorian heroes, such as Dickens's Mr. Dombey and Thackeray's Colonel Newcome, experience bankruptcy as a spiritual death through which they must pass in order to achieve salvation; for such heroes, the commercial world can never again be their proper home—it must be renounced as antithetical to spiritual rebirth and regeneration.

Such a conclusion is of course hardly new to literature. The traditional view of money in literature is that money is an evil to be rejected by those who seek salvation. Money is seen in traditional Christian terms as a temptation, a moral testing ground; those who are corrupted by it, as in Chaucer's *Pardoner's Tale,* are forever damned.[14] Clearly Dickens is linked to this tradition in many of his novels; as Ross Dabney observes, the ending of all of the later novels points up the same Christian lesson: "Let us be poor and happy."[15] Alexander Welsh refers to "the under-lying religious basis of Dickens' attack on moneyed society."[16] For Welsh it is clear that "the antipathy to money in Dickens is essentially Christian."[17] There is general critical agreement that *Dombey and Son* is patterned upon this traditional Christian theme: J. Hillis Miller, for one, is convinced of the presence of an authentic religious motif in the novel.[18] In actuality there may well be more ambivalence in Dickens's attitude toward money than the obviously Christian themes of the novel would at first suggest; when we consider the happy ending of *Dombey and Son* it will be necessary to examine Dickens's lingering fondness for the Dick Whittington myth of success and self-help which perhaps undermines the overtly Christian solution of the novel. But there can scarcely be any doubt that Dickens consciously intended his tale of bankruptcy to bear a Christian reading. (His intentions are echoed dramatically in Browne's frontispiece for the novel, which prominently features a host of heavenly figures.)

Within this structure of religious belief, then, bankruptcy occurs as a providential judgment, a redemptive experience of loss and suffering that leads in turn to spiritual salvation. Unlike the heroes of Brontë and Gaskell who continue to toil in the marketplace, trying to impose a Christian solution upon the economic problems of the nineteenth century, Mr. Dombey (and Colonel Newcome) in the end turn completely from mercantile activity to the sacred world of hearth and family. In terms of underlying Victorian religious motifs, they choose the City of God over the City of Man.

The Christian ending of *Dombey and Son* is all the more striking because of the power with which Dickens has portrayed Dombey as a man enmeshed in mercantile values. As critics have often pointed out, Mr. Dombey's sin is not really pride as much as it is his belief in a callous sense of values that measures all human relationships in economic terms.[19] The very first chapter brilliantly conveys the force of the merchant's obsession; Dombey sees the world in terms of profit and loss: "The earth was made for Dombey and Son to trade in. . ." (*DS*, 1.2). All human relationships are judged according to their monetary value. A son is highly desirable because he will perpetuate the firm of Dombey and Son; a girl, on the other hand, has no economic value at all. "In the capital of the House's name and dignity, such a child was merely a piece of base coin that couldn't be invested. . ." (*DS*, 1.3).

Marriage too is seen as a commercial relationship, in which Mrs. Dombey receives a certain social position, in return for presiding over the merchant's household and providing him with an heir to his empire. Thus he is able to face the prospect of his wife's death with a certain equanimity in which regret for her as an object of value is paramount. When it becomes necessary to replace his deceased wife in her function of wet nurse, Dombey proceeds in a characteristically business-like manner: "I desire to make it a question of wages, altogether . . . a mere matter of bargain and sale, hiring and letting. . ." (*DS*, 2.18). Having settled the question of salary with Polly Toodles, Dombey renames the nurse and warns her against forming an attachment to the baby in a stubborn effort to negate her human identity and to limit her relationship with the child to a purely mercenary one. His failure in this regard is apparent after Paul's death; he is humiliated by finding Polly's husband with a piece of new crepe in his cap in memory of Paul: "every one set up some claim or other to a share in his dead boy, and was a bidder against him!" (*DS*, 20.275). The emotion is genuine, but the language ("claim," "share," "bidder") is purely mercantile. Even in mourning his son, Dombey is incapable of seeing him as anything but an object of value that he desires to have in his sole possession.

In Dickens, as with most Victorian writers, marriage is the most sacred human relationship, and when it is tainted by materialistic values, as it is in *Dombey and Son*, it indicates a sin of the gravest order. As Dabney puts it, in the Dickens canon mercenary marriage is the "most important example of the wickedness involved in mixing economic advantages into relations which ought to be based on affection and human need." [20] Dombey's relationship with his first wife was clearly based upon economic motives; his second marriage is an even more blatant display of commercial enterprise. Edith Dombey declares of her prospective husband, "he has bought me . . . He has considered of his bargain; he has shown it to his friend; . . . he thinks it will suit him, and may be had sufficiently cheap. . ." (*DS*, 27.381). The economic bargain between Dombey and Edith is so unmistakable that it hardly needs the added emphasis of Cousin Feenix's blunder at the wedding feast, when he tells the story of another mercenary marriage: "She is regularly bought, and you may take your oath, he is as regularly sold" (*DS*, 36.493).

Dombey's corrupted values are highlighted by the purity and innocence of his son, whose view of money is a Christian one ("the old, old fashion"). Paul's innocent question, "Papa! what's money?" creates great difficulty for the merchant:

> He would have liked to give him some explanation involving the terms circulating-medium, currency, depreciation of currency, paper, bullion, rates of exchange, value of precious metals in the market, and so forth . . . (*DS*, 8.93)

But financial terms mean little to Paul, who has other ideas about money: "I mean . . . to put my money all together in one Bank, never try to get any more, go away into the country with my darling Florence, have a beautiful garden, fields, and woods, and live there with her all my life" (*DS*, 14.190). All of Dombey's fevered efforts to educate his son as the pride and hope of the firm have been futile. Paul has no interest in accumulating more earthly goods. As Welsh has pointed out, Paul's word "Bank" is a "code word" for Heaven "typical of Victorian indirection in matters of religious faith." [21] Paul obviously belongs not to the City of Man but to the City of God.

To the City of God Dombey himself must be brought, but first he must pass through a kind of spiritual death that will purge him of his worldliness. From the beginning, there has been a subtle connection between death and money, an association that Dickens would enlarge upon in later novels. Mr. Dombey's office is close to the Bank of England "with its vaults of gold and silver 'down among the dead men' underground" (*DS*, 4.36). The novel emphasizes the frequency with which men drown in the course of such commerce as that carried on by Dombey and Son, and within Dombey's office the books and papers and clerks appear to be "assembled at the bottom of the sea" (*DS*, 13.170).

The comparison of bankruptcy itself with death is quite explicit. After the failure of the firm, the clerks speak in whispers, "as if the corpse of the deceased House were lying unburied in the next room" (*DS*, 58.744). Mr. Dombey shuts himself up within his gloomy mansion, where he is rumored to be dying, and wanders through the empty rooms "like a ghost." Saved by Florence's return from the suicide he has been contemplating, Dombey is stricken so ill that he lies close to death. His illness is a spiritual passage necessary for his redemption and rebirth. In wrestling with death, Dombey grasps at last the import of Paul's question "What is money?" and emerges from the crisis reduced from a cold, proud, powerful merchant to a "faint, feeble semblance of a man" purified at last of his false values. The bankruptcy of Dombey and Son is described in a chapter entitled "Retribution" and the economic failure is indeed a punishment, a kind of providential judgment against him. The broken figure upon whom the novel closes has been chastened but purified. Stripped of his pride, he begs forgiveness from Florence, who appears as an Angel of Mercy, offering him a new vision of his dead child (her own son Paul) as a token that he has indeed been redeemed by love and suffering.

Dombey's spiritual rebirth is of course the great aim toward which the novel has been working; it is important to note, however, that Dombey is not the only sinner saved by grace. Alice Brown is converted from her evil ways by the perfect goodness of Harriet Carker. At Alice's deathbed Harriet presides as a benevolent Angel of Death, reading to Alice from "the eternal book for all the weary, and the heavy-laden; for all the wretched, fallen, and neglected of this earth" (*DS*, 58.785), and Alice dies "murmuring the sacred name that had been read to her" (*DS*, 58.746). (Florence, of course, is also adept at ministering to the dying, and is referred to by Edith, to whom she has offered the blessings of Heaven, as "my better angel.") Dickens cannot bear to allow even the villain Carker to die in complete spiritual darkness. As Carker flees his pursuers, urged on by fear and guilt, Dickens suggests that he is touched in the moment before his death by "some weak sense of virtue upon Earth, and its reward in Heaven" (*DS*, 55.743). There is even a suggestion of "tenderness and remorse" in the thought of his sister and brother, but Carker, unlike Alice and Dombey, has no ministering angel to grant salvation. Redemption is rewarded as a special grace apparently through the medium of the love and goodness of an angelic woman.

Thus *Dombey and Son* seems to conclude with the triumph of Christian values, the victory of love over money. Walter and Florence walk through the City on the way to their marriage:

> Riches are uncovering in shops; jewels, gold, and silver, flash in the goldsmith's sunny windows; and great houses cast a stately shade upon them as they pass. But . . . they go on lovingly together, lost in everything around; thinking of no other riches, and no prouder home, than they have now in one another. (*DS*, 58.767)

Around Walter and Florence grow up a company dedicated to these Christian virtues. Susan Nipper wants to return to work as Florence's maid without wages; she proudly announces that she cannot "sell" her love and duty. Polly Toodles, who stays at the Dombey house when all other servants depart, also comes to Florence when needed; she is another who does not sell her services. The snug circle of the Wooden Midshipman includes Uncle Sol and Captain Cuttle, Polly, Susan Toots, and even Miss Tox, but its most prized convert is Mr. Dombey himself. At the end of the novel he sits cozily toasting Walter and Florence along with Captain Cuttle and Uncle Sol, amidst "a blithe and merry ringing, as of a little peal of marriage bells" (*DS*, 62.829). Dombey appears to be suitably chastened: "Ambitious projects trouble him no more. His only pride is in his daughter and her husband" (*DS*, 62.829), and the novel closes with a glimpse of the "white-haired gentleman" and his grandchildren by the sea. Deleted portions of the first proof read:

> The voices in the waves speak low to him of Florence, day and night . . . of Florence and his altered heart; of Florence and their ceaseless murmuring to her of the Love, eternal and illimitable, extending still, beyond the sea, beyond the sky, to the invisible country far away. (*DS*, 62.833)

Thus Dickens clearly intended his closing chapter to end on a note of Christian affirmation and eternal love. Those who have accepted the immutable values of Florence and Paul are among the saved, and, as Henri Talon points out, it is only these characters who seem capable of reproducing themselves. (Walter and Florence have children, so do Susan and Toots, and so, in abundance, do the Toodles.) The future belongs, it seems, "to these supporters of the ancient Christian values."[22]

The case for salvation by bankruptcy seems clear enough. The loss of money has chastened and redeemed Mr. Dombey; he emerges from his baptism of suffering a true believer. Nevertheless, for the modern reader, disquieting questions are likely to remain. How persuasive is the author in presenting this fable of salvation? Do we really accept Dickens's vision of the repentant bankrupt ending his days in piety and love, or does the author betray some ambivalence toward his Christian solution? In order to consider this question fully, we must first refer briefly to an issue often raised by critics of Dickens, the charges that Dickens and other Victorian authors could not portray their characters in time. For the credibility of the ending of *Dombey and Son,* and the success of those final episodes of bankruptcy and salvation, are related directly to Dickens's success (or lack of success) in portraying convincingly the changes that time and mutability wreak upon his hero.

G. K. Chesterton was perhaps the first to criticize Dickens for his apparent inability to portray his characters developmentally. According to Chesterton, "It was not the aim of Dickens to show the effect of time and circumstance upon a character. . . . It was his aim to show character hung in a kind of happy void, in a world apart from time. . . ."[23] Contemporary critics have often concurred in this view, charging that Dickens's (and Thackeray's) novels are spatial pictures with no movement, static canvases with no dramatic development. But surely a novel about bankruptcy must by its very nature deal with the effect of time and circumstance upon character, and *Dombey and Son,* of all of Dickens's novels, would seem to be concerned with change and mutability. John Lucas has stated that "*Dombey and Son* is about change, about society in transition. Everything shifts and becomes impermanent as the implicitly stable society of the past is pursued to extinction by the new."[24] Steven Marcus points out that "more than any of Dickens' previous novels, *Dombey and Son* directs its attention to the important changes that take place in human life—to birth, marriage, and death, to separations and reconciliations, to shipwrecks and bankrupt-cies."[25]

Moreover, Dickens appears to have been quite consciously portraying the effects of time upon his characters. The very first page of the novel presents Mr. Dombey and his newborn son already confronting time and change:

> On the brow of Dombey, Time and his brother Care had set some marks, as on a tree that was to come down in good time—remorseless twins they are for striding through their human forests, notching as they go—while the countenance of Son was crossed and recrossed with a thousand little creases, which the same deceitful Time would take delight in smoothing out and wearing away with the flat part of his scythe, as a preparation of the surface for his deeper operations. (*DS*, 1.1)

Thus from the very first moment, we are presented with the chief charac-ters in the context of the "deeper operations" that time will work upon them. Dickens, in fact, is relentless in his reminders of the passage of time; bankruptcy is only the last of many changes that mark the course of time in the novel. We are confronted continually with watches and clocks, with the remorseless speed of the railroad, the ever-quickening flow of the river, and the ceaseless rhythm of the ocean waves.

Both Stephen Marcus and Henri Talon have pointed out how crucial is time as a moral gauge to the individual characters; the good characters and bad characters experience time quite differently in this novel. For those who are afflicted with worldly values, time is something to be used for material purposes. Thus Mrs. Skewton tries to freeze time by imitating the dress and manners of youth, and Mr. Dombey tries to hasten time by force-feeding an education to his son to speed him along in the process of taking possession of his mercantile empire. Both of these attempts are of course doomed to failure. Time proceeds upon its fatal course, oblivious to petty human strategems, and both Mrs. Skewton and Mr. Dombey fall victim to its inexorable advance. Time, in fact, wreaks a terrible revenge on such characters. Mrs. Skewton descending into senility and death, Mr. Carker the Manager pursued by guilt, Mr. Dombey chastened by bankruptcy and contemplating suicide—time and memory have caught up with them all. The present merges into the past, and they must face at last the bitter knowledge that the only escape from the remorseless efforts of time is in death.

The good characters, on the other hand, "do not wish to disintegrate time, nor do they want it to run differently for themselves."[26] Those who are saved experience time as a natural flow to which they willingly submit, and yet they are granted a kind of immunity from the effects of time in the love and memory that are strong enough to exist outside time. Thus Walter and Florence depart upon the sea, to the accompaniment of the ceaseless voices in the waves that speak to Florence of the love of Walter and the memory of Paul, whispering "of love, eternal and illimitable, not bounded by the confines of this world, or by the end of time, but ranging still, beyond the sea, beyond the sky, to the invisible country far away" (*DS,* 57.773). The passage is almost identical to the one with which Dickens originally planned to end the novel (see p. 118 above). Clearly Dickens was consciously setting out in his tale of a merchant's fall to portray the effects of time; just as clearly he wanted to create a sense of the immutable values that could exist beyond the reach of mortal time.

Such considerations bring us back inevitably to the original problem: does Dickens succeed in portraying his hero in time, does the portrayal of the bankruptcy and its consequences convince us that Mr. Dombey has found a way to make peace with time and yet has gained some intangible goal which is timeless? Chesterton, for one, did not believe that Dickens had succeeded; he charges that "when ever he tried to describe change in a character, he made a mess of it, as in the repentance of Dombey . . . ."[27] Henri Talon agrees that Mr. Dombey's emotional development is not convincing: "His change is no 'becoming.' It is willed by the novelist because he firmly believes that the child can and must redeem the parent—but there is no process of growth."[28] It must be admitted, indeed, that the happy ending of *Dombey and Son* often strains our credulity. We are told in the space of one last hasty chapter that Mr. Dombey cherishes his daughter, that he is now an intimate of the Wooden Midshipman, that he has given up worldly ambitions, and that he dotes upon his grandchildren. Uncle Sol is discovered to have investments that turn out "wonderfully well" and Walter is apparently going to succeed as a capitalist where Dombey has failed. A little community of the loving, compassionate characters will live in prosperity and blessedness, in harmony with the waves that speak to them a message of eternal love.

One must, of course, make allowance for the change in literary styles; Dickens's florid sentimentality is a problem for the modern reader, although hardly an insurmountable one. Much more serious than any objection to his prose style, however, is the sense that the ending belies the vision established earlier in the novel, betraying perhaps the underlying conflict of the author in confronting the problems of ambition and success in Victorian society. Having overcome his earlier financial misfortunes and earned unparalleled financial success with his novels, Dickens may well have experienced a painful ambivalence toward the whole issue of wealth. The author appears to have partially shared the Victorian worship of success at the same time that he satirized it fiercely.

Throughout most of the novel the full power of Dickens's genius has been focused in an uncompromising indictment of Dombey's materialism.

The ending, on the other hand, seems to betray an uneasy hankering after simpler answers and more comfortable solutions. More than any supposed inability to develop characters through the passage of time, the novel seems to be flawed by the author's desire to impose a happy ending that he has not earned. Dickens has succeeded so masterfully in portraying the hard, proud, materialistic character of the merchant that the obligatory repentance brought about by bankruptcy strikes us as somewhat forced. That Dombey should be reconciled with his daughter seems both necessary and right; that he should be transformed into the cozy drinking companion of Uncle Sol and Captain Cuttle, and a lovable, affable old grandfather into the bargain, places a burden on the ability of even the most generous reader to suspend disbelief.

The blessed domesticity upon which the novel closes does not somehow satisfy us; for one thing, Dickens is honest enough to know that it cannot apply universally. Curiously, the most effective rebuttal of the happy ending is not the melodramatic plot revolving around Edith Dombey and Carker, but in the comic subplot. In his desire to wrap up all of his characters' destinies, Dickens allows Captain Cuttle's friend Bunsby to be shanghaied into marriage by the formidable landlady, Mrs. MacStinger, and the Captain notes with trepidation the "deadly interest" that the Mac-Stinger daughter Juliana exhibits in the marriage ceremony. The Captain envisions in this "promising child, already the image of her parent . . . a succession of man-traps stretching out infinitely; a series of ages of oppression and co-ercion, through which the seafaring line was doomed" (*DS*, 60.815). Dickens cannot resist here giving us the other side of the coin. Woman is the ministering angel whose love redeems mankind, but she is also a shrew and a man-trap, a domineering termagant who makes man's life a living hell. The comic intensity and spleen of this brief scene belies somewhat the triumph of Florence's angelic goodness. Dickens may impose a beatific ending upon the story of Dombey's bankruptcy, but it is undercut by the knowledge, which Dickens is incapable of repressing completely, that life will not always conform to Christian sweetness so conveniently.

Thus it is not only the reader who has trouble accepting the solution of domestic felicity that Dombey's bankruptcy brings about. Dickens himself seems to have had difficulty in maintaining such a solution with any consistency. The problem of the happy ending is of course not unique to Dickens; it is a distinctive and problematic feature of almost every Victorian novel. The Victorian audience believed in domestic bliss and wanted its novels to end with this affirmation; the pressure on the novelist to conform could be quite explicit. It is fascinating to reflect that Dickens originally intended to give his novel quite another conclusion. In the original conception Walter Gay was destined to fall victim to the corruption of the Dombey world. Dickens wrote to Foster early in the progress of the novel, declaring his intention of disappointing the expectations aroused by the appearance of

Walter, and allowing him to fall into "idleness, dissipation, dishonesty, and ruin."[29] (This intention accounts for the strange personal interest that the repentant embezzler Carker the Junior takes in Walter, an interest not accounted for by the novel as it eventually worked out.) In spite of his original intention, Dickens apparently felt obligated in the actual writing to conform to the standard Victorian ending. Walter remains the honest hero of self-help and is rewarded with financial success and his employer's daughter.

It is ironic that Thackeray, in *The Newcomes,* also changed the ending he originally contemplated. It seems obvious that the events of the novel (Clive's marriage and the Colonel's bankruptcy) must separate Clive and Ethel forever. Thackeray, however, allowed the appeals of his public to override his better judgment. Obligingly, he killed off Clive's wife Rosie and managed, without explicit statements, to suggest the future happiness of Clive and Ethel. ("What could a fellow do?" he wrote later. "So many people wanted 'em married."[30]) Even this concession did not completely satisfy the Victorian public; James Hain Friswell wrote a supplementary chapter for *Sharpe's Magazine* showing the married future of Clive and Ethel in more elaborate and sentimental detail than Thackeray had been able to bring himself to provide.[31] (The change, which Thackeray acknowledged to be an "artistic blunder," is strongly reminiscent of Bulwer-Lytton's recommendation that Dickens followed in reuniting Pip and Estella in *Great Expectations.* But whereas a case might be made for Dickens's second ending as appropriate to the thematic structure of *Great Expectations,*[32] the convenient reunion of Clive and Ethel cannot fail to jar the modern reader suspicious of conventional contrivance to achieve a "happy-ever-after.")

Thus in both *Dombey and Son* and *The Newcomes* the downfall by bankruptcy ironically helps to bring about a resolution of Christian love and domestic harmony prized so highly by the readers of the time. To say that Dickens and Thackeray imposed domestic happiness upon the endings of their novels purely to satisfy the illusions of the reading public, however, would be to underestimate the force that this vision of the sacred hearth had upon the authors themselves. As Angus Wilson has stated:

> The happy ending is an unfortunate distortion in Dickens' work as it is in that of the other great Victorians, but, despite the change made to *Great Expectations,* it goes deeper than a mere capitulation to the whims of readers. With Dickens, as with Thackeray, though for different reasons, the contemporary idea of domestic happiness as the resolution of, or perhaps more fairly one should say, the counterpoise to social evil, was a strongly held personal conviction. Even more vital to Dickens was the idea of pure love as the means of redemption of flawed, weak, or sinful men.[33]

That Dickens believed—or wanted to believe—that Dombey's bankruptcy would lead to salvation is clear; the problem obviously lies in his inability to convey to the reader the likelihood of such an event. Julian Moynahan has presented the case against the ending of *Dombey and Son* most effectively, complaining that the novel slips from complexity into "weltering simplicity" with the establishment of the little company of the Wooden Midshipman, a community that is clearly inadequate as an alternative to the City of Dombey. According to Moynahan:

> The "little society of the back parlour" which Dickens sets up as an alternative form of organization to the hard actuality of mid-nineteenth century England and its Industrial Revolution consists of two retired female servants, a near-imbecile, a virtuous and very funny retired ship pilot, a vendor of obsolete nautical instruments, and a boring young man named Walter. Florence is less *of* the company, than its object of worship.[34]

The values of this little community are "simple good-nature and simplemindedness" and to enter it Dombey must experience a second childhood. Moynahan finds the spectacle "depressing" and even unwholesome.[35] His views are echoed heartily by Michael Steig, who complains of Dickens's "diagrammatic moral structuring" in creating characters so clearly either good or evil, and charges Dickens further with the "polarization of humanity into the heartless and the mindless."[36] And John Lucas argues that in establishing the good folks of the Wooden Midshipman as a repository of the values of the past, and pretending that they will somehow continue to survive (and even flourish) in the present, Dickens has been guilty of "a plain faking of the issues."[37]

It would seem indisputable that Dickens's happy ending is not adequate to the forceful vision of the rest of the novel; it seems equally clear that the weakness of the ending is not due to the author's inability to portray time and change. Not only Dickens, but Brontë, Gaskell, and Thackeray, as well, were all keenly aware of the importance of the changes going on about them. *Dombey and Son*, *Shirley*, *North and South*, and *The Newcomes*, are works that are informed by an overwhelming sense of the enormous dislocations and upheavals of the time, and an equally strong sense of the force with which the passing of time sets its mark upon individuals and social groups. The problem seems to lie not in a failure to recognize the existence of change, but in the desire to believe, at least at this early stage of the Victorian experience, that the change could be *beneficial*. Desperately, in these early years, the Victorian novelists, like their contemporaries, seem to have wanted to believe that the Industrial Revolution would improve the lot of mankind, and that its inherent problems and dangers could be overcome solely by the faith and love of individuals.

That this vision proves to be inadequate and sentimental may be due at least in part to a failure within Victorian religion itself. Moynahan has argued that there is in fact no genuine religious vision in *Dombey and Son* at all:

The book seems to me to exhibit Protestant piety divorced from its doctrinal foundations, Christian sentiments divorced from the rigors of a creed and from Christian practice. Religion has become a set of loose analogies and tropes employed to conceal faulty arguments by analogy: people who act like saints will be rewarded like saints in the end. The meek shall inherit the Industrial Revolution.[38]

The religious platitudes of the period are indeed alarmingly feeble when pitted against the energy and magnitude that Dickens has depicted in the building of the railroad, or the hostility and conflicts that Brontë and Gaskell pictured between laboring hands and masters. In all these novels, it seems, the very clarity with which the author sees the upheavals of the changing economy seriously undercuts the effectiveness of the sentimental religious solution imposed by the author's conclusion.

For all the courage of such authors in exploring the changes in industrial England, then, there seems always to be an eleventh-hour change of heart, a last-minute retreat from the clear-sighted realities of the novel into the soothing hopefulness of Christian sentiment. There is, at bottom, a fundamental failure to come to grips with the problem raised so fearlessly in the body of the novel, questions about the equitable distribution of property, about the proper relationship between labor and management, and ultimately, questions about the place of wealth in human lives.

It is this failure to deal squarely with the question of money that most seriously flaws the endings of the novels in question. Characters go bankrupt and become virtuous thereby; money corrupts and therefore bankruptcy must purify and save. And yet no one ends up poor in *Shirley,* or *North and South,* or *Dombey and Son,* least of all Mr.Dombey. Fate, in the person of the author, intervenes to insure that the merchant, who has now been purged of all materialistic desires, will never suffer for the want of a good income. We learn in the last chapter that Uncle Sol Gill's investments have turned out "wonderfully well" after all, and that his money "is turning itself over and over pretty briskly," while Walter is reported to be appointed "to a post of great trust and confidence . . . mounting up the ladder with the greatest expedition" (*DS,* 62.832). In triumph Mr. Toots reports that "under the very eye of Mr. Dombey, there is a foundation going on, upon which . . . an edifice . . . is gradually rising, perhaps to equal, perhaps excel, that of which he was once the head. . ." (*DS,* 62.832).

Dombey has been saved by losing his money, but he is not left to savor this fate, poor but happy. Instead the author intervenes to reveal that the saved bankrupt can be rich and happy after all, and that, in spite of the forceful evidence presented to the contrary, it seems that a merchant can be both rich and virtuous—if only he is lovable like Walter, instead of proud like Dombey. At bottom Dickens is still a firm believer in the myth of Dick Whittington and all the self-help virtues that his story implies. Indeed, as Robin Gilmour has pointed out, Dickens was an exact contemporary of

Samuel Smiles, and his own life could well have served as one of the inspiring biographies that abound in Smiles's books. And certainly in the early novels, the careers of such characters as David Copperfield exemplify the qualities of hard work and perseverance that lead to success. According to Gilmour, Dickens's affirmation of these values in the early stage of his career

> enables him to articulate his criticism of the repressive, life-denying forces in contemporary life (the Dombey/Murdstone forces) while at the same time proclaiming his allegiance to the new forces of the changing world embodied in the railroad in *Dombey*. The ethic of self-help, that is to say, is congenial to a Dickens who is still open-minded about contemporary society, still genuinely affirmative of some manifestations of Victorian progress.[39]

In later novels Dickens would reject the industrial society for being incompatible with human values and ideals of individual self-worth. But in *Dombey and Son* he is still insisting upon the more hopeful aspects of this new world, and that determined optimism leads in the end to the gross simplification of economic issues. In his attempt to be fair to the emerging society, to see hope for social progress in industrial advances, Dickens is yet unable to imagine an economic community in which his good characters can survive, and so he allows them to escape the world entirely into a little Christian community of their own, a community that survives solely by the sleight-of-hand of the author.

One indication of Dickens's failure to provide a reasonable alternative for those of his characters who are "saved" is the frequency with which he must resort to the fairy-tale motif.[40] Florence is the little lost heiress, the princess shut up in her lonely home and kidnapped by a wicked witch in the person of Good Mrs. Brown. Captain Cuttle is the "good monster" who protects the princess, and Walter is at once the shining knight who rescues the princess and another Dick Whittington who rises from the lowly condition of apprentice to marry his master's daughter. It is only through the medium of this fairy-tale imagery that Dickens can comfortably envision the radiant transformation of Mr. Dombey from evil merchant to saintly (and very solvent) bankrupt, or the triumph of such virtuous but inept characters as Uncle Sol, Captain Cuttle, Walter Gay, and Mr. Toots.

Thus *Dombey and Son* (and in a sense *Shirley* and *North and South*) seems to be incapable, in the end, of solving the problem of money. Money corrupts, but it is also unquestionably useful, and so there is a recurring search, within these novels, for a conclusion that will clearly repudiate greed and materialism and at the same time somehow sanction the possession of a comfortable fortune. As John Pikoulis notes of Mrs. Gaskell's novel, *"North and South"* is full of dirty money becoming clean."[41] Mrs. Gaskell is suitably censorious about Mr. Thornton's preoccupation with earning money, but

she allows him to return from bankruptcy to prosperity when it is clear that
he has been converted to the Christian principles of the heroine. In the
same way Brontë plainly considers Mr. Moore's greaest sin to be his single-
minded pursuit of money, but he is allowed to prosper once his heart has
been purified and it is clear that the money will be used in part for Christian
philanthropy. And Dickens who began his novel with a brilliant satire of the
way in which the Firm of Dombey and Son has distorted all human relationships with mercenary values, ends triumphantly with a "new edifice"
arising that will rival the old establishment in financial success, but that will,
by some mysterious and not very convincing providence, manage to become a more humane enterprise than its predecessor.

The necessity for rationalizing the hero's return to prosperity after his
spiritual redemption by bankruptcy strikes in varying degrees a false note
in each of these novels. It is with interest, then, that we turn to examine
another novel of bankruptcy from the same period, Thackeray's *The Newcomes,* for Thackeray is fully conscious of this problem of "dirty money." In
fact, it has been suggested that all of Thackeray's novels are in one way or
another about just this theme of making dirty money clean.[42] There is a
subtle difference in Thackeray's statement of the problem, however. In *The
Book of Snobs* he describes the custom in aristocratic clubs of washing silver
coins before they are presented as change to members; to Thackeray, the
cleansing of money has as much to do with social class as with morality.[43] In
The Newcomes, as in his other novels, money is "clean" only when its pos-
sessor has traveled a great enough distance from the actual soil of trade and
commerce to assume the aristocratic mien of the gentleman. (The Newcomes are in a sort of transitional stage, in which their origin in the success
of a country weaver is still recent enough to be remembered as a blot, and
yet remote enough to be eradicated by aristocratic marriages.) Thackeray is
thus at once more open and more cynical about the process by which dirty
money becomes clean, and he is far less confident about imposing such a
solution on the novel. Colonel Newcome is cleansed and saved by the loss of
his money; unlike Dickens, Thackeray does not fudge the ending by allowing his hero a gratuitous return to prosperity. Colonel Newcome dies
poor—dies, in fact, a humble charity pensioner—and if the problem of
money is not squarely faced, it is at least not faked by a dubious happy
ending.

Does Thackeray succeed, then, where Dickens has failed, in portraying
the repentance and salvation of a bankrupt merchant prince? Contemporary audiences, at least, seemed to think so; Colonel Newcome was one of
the best-loved characters Thackeray ever created, and, in the eyes of his
readers, served to vindicate the author from charges of cynicism.[44] Some
later critics have concurred in this view. Alexander Welsh, for example, is
impressed by Thackeray's achievement with such a character; he writes that

Thackeray "believes more strongly in the possibility of repentance" than other Victorian authors.[45]

Thackeray's religious vision, however, does not seem on the surface to differ greatly from Dickens's. Society in *The Newcomes* is corrupt because it is tainted with economic relationships, and bankruptcy, because it removes the source of corruption, leads to salvation. *The Newcomes* is the story of a banking family, as *Dombey and Son* is the story of a merchant's family, and the origin of the family's wealth is of some significance:

> Thomas Newcome, who had been a weaver in his native village, brought the very best character for honesty, thrift, and ingenuity with him to London, where he was taken into the house of Hobson Brothers, cloth-factors; afterwards Hobson and Newcome. This fact may suffice to indicate Thomas Newcome's story. Like Whittington, and many other London apprentices, he began poor and ended by marrying his master's daughter, and becoming sheriff and alderman of the City of London. (*N*, 2.14)

The reference to Dick Whittington is instructive. We are located in the world of Hogarth's industrious apprentice, and of Samuel Smiles's self-made men. (Note, for example, the presence of those sturdy self-help virtues, "honesty, thrift, and ingenuity.") Virtue leads to financial success which in turn leads to power and position, and the value of the individual is therefore judged by the size of his bank account. When Colonel Newcome returns home from India at the beginning of the novel, still a relatively poor man, he is shocked by his brothers' failure to welcome him hospitably: "Thomas Newcome had overdrawn his little account. There was no such balance of affection in that bank of his brothers, as the simple creature had expected to find there" (*N*, 6.64). The economic terminology is appropriate; in the Newcome family money is the only real basis for human relationships. (Years later when the Colonel returns to England a second time, now a man of considerable wealth, he is greeted with a great deal more civility: "Tom Newcome of the Bundelcund Bank is a personage to be conciliated; whereas Tom Newcome of the Bengal Cavalry was not worth Mr. Barnes' attention" [*N*, 51.535].)

As Juliet MacMasters has pointed out, money is even more important in *The Newcomes* than in other of Thackeray's works. It influences the language, imagery, character development, and plot. Relationships depend upon the size of a bank account, and financial transactions such as the closing of an account, the overdrawing of a cheque, or the rise and fall of stock shares, are major events in the story. Love, morality, art, and faith are all converted into the language of the market place.[46]

In *The Newcomes,* as in *Dombey and Son,* marriage is the most prominent of the sacred relationships corrupted by the desire for money. The chief sinner of *The Newcomes* in this respect is Barnes Newcome, an odious young man who has "ruined" one woman by refusing to marry her, and proceeds to purchase the aristocratic Lady Clara in a marriage of convenience that ends with tragic consequences to all. But the most visual emblem of the theme of economic marriage is the green ticket that Ethel Newcome removes from a painting exhibit and wears on her dress at the family dinner table to indicate that she is available for purchase. Indignantly she rails against the "mammon-worship" that condemns her to be married to the highest bidder: "We are as much sold as Turkish women . . . there is no freedom for us. I wear my green ticket, and wait till my master comes. But every day as I think of our slavery, I revolt against it more" (*N*, 32.338). But in spite of what Lady Kew terms "the fine speeches of a schoolgirl," Ethel is a part of her world. As her aunt knowingly tells her, "you belong to your belongings, my dear, and are not better than the rest of the world" (*N*, 32.338).

The philosophy of Lady Kew is the most cynical in the novel. It is one of the ironies of *The Newcomes*, therefore, that her words turn out to be as true of the simple, naive old Colonel as of the worldly Ethel. For Colonel Newcome is changed by the success of his bank and the acquisition of a fortune. Like Ethel, he too eventually "belongs to his belongings." With the success of the Bundelcund Bank, the Colonel (who is never more than a naive figurehead for this enterprise) is trapped by the marketplace into accepting its values. As a director of the bank, he feels obligated to further its prestige by maintaining a luxurious home, giving sumptuous feasts, and standing for parliament. Colonel Newcome, of course has no other object in these projects but to ensure the happiness of his son Clive; ironically the Colonel's financial success and his lavish way of life only alienate the artistic Clive. Estranged from his son and disappointed in his plans for their splendid new life, the Colonel lapses into the sin of vindictiveness, turning against Barnes Newcome and the rest of the Newcome family, and spending a large fortune to defeat Barnes in a parliamentary election notable for its nastiness. The Colonel's fall from grace is clear; bent upon destroying Barnes's reputation, he rejects the counsel of that "sweet Christian pleader," Laura Pendennis, and feeds instead upon his own desire for revenge.

The Colonel's downfall is clearly the result of the evil influence of his wealth. Thackeray creates the perfect visual image for the Colonel's ill-fated treasure in a hideous silver cocoa-nut tree. This marvelous object is presented to Clive's wife by the Colonel's business acquaintances:

> There was a superb silver cocoa-nut tree, whereof the leaves were dexterously arranged for holding candles and pickles; under the cocoa-nut was an Indian prince on a camel giving his hand to a cavalry officer on horseback; a howitzer, a plough, a loom, a bale of cotton on which were the East India's Company's arms; a Brahmin, Britannia, Commerce with a cornucopia were grouped around the principal figures. (*N*, 63.657)

The illustration by Richard Doyle does not nearly do justice to this beguiling concoction, but one can only sympathize with the predicament of the illustrator; such an object almost defies visualization. Like the immortal portrait in *Vanity Fair* of the corpulent Jos Sedley upon an elephant, the cocoa-nut tree is a monument to Victorian colonial plunder, and also to Victorian bad art. (Barbara Hardy has suggested that the elaborate design of the silver tree is a deliberate parody of the intricate symbolism of the Albert Memorial.[47]) As the men of commerce and trade toast the health of British artists "*à propos* of this splendid specimen of their skill," Clive Newcome sits "silent and gloomy" while his friend J. J. Ridley eyes the testimonial "with a queer expression on his shrewd face" (*N*, 63.658). The response of the novel's two artist figures is significant, for both of them understand that false art equates with false values.

The tree appears throughout the novel as an emblem of the state of the Colonel's fortunes and of the condition of his soul as well. As the shares of the Bundelcund Bank begin to fall, the glory of the cocoa-nut tree becomes bitterly ironic as many of the subscribers whose names are engraved upon the tree fail to show up at the Colonel's grand dinners. When the Colonel announces his ruin, the tree is one of the objects with which Rosie and her mother try to abscond; in spite of its empty symbolism and bad taste, it is an object of solid worth to these greedy and shallow women. The testimonial tree makes its last appearance on the auction block after the Colonel's bankruptcy. It has become at last the emblem both of his ruin and of his salvation as well, for in the bankruptcy of his fortune and in the stubborn integrity with which he insists upon parting with every object of value for the benefit of his creditors, the Colonel at last regains the honor and rectitude that were temporarily numbed by the possession of too much money.

Clearly it seems unlikely that Colonel Newcome can be spiritually redeemed and wealthy at the same time; money is an indication (a negative indication) of his spiritual grace as well as of so many other things. Mac-Masters states that "No novelist makes a man's income seem more significant than Thackeray—the amount of it, how he gets it, how he spends it, and what his own circle in society thinks of how he gets it and spends it."[48] (And, one might add, how he loses it.) Thackeray is anatomizing the acquisitiveness of his society in *The Newcomes* as in no other of his works. Jean Sudrann has compared Thackeray to Carlyle, Tennyson, and Dickens in his protest against "a world unified by 'the cash nexus' "; she believes that "*The Newcomes* takes its place with *In Memoriam* and *Bleak House* as a part of the Victorian attempt to express the sickness of the age."[49] In his disgust with the rampant materialism of his times, Thackeray manages to invert what he perceives as the false values of society.

In the world of the respectable Newcome family, as MacMasters has

observed, "money is virtue and bankruptcy is damnation,"[50] but the fate of
Colonel Newcome ironically reverses this view. For the Colonel, money
leads to corruption, and no commercial venture is more corrupt or more
spectacular than the Colonel's ill-fated Bundelcund Bank. This outrageous
swindle draws scoundrels and charlatans to it, and infects even sensible
people with the disease of speculative fever. Its lucrative shares, its testimonial dinners, and the emblematic cocoa-nut tree are proved to be merely
empty forms, however, the shams that must be swept away when reality is
restored by bankruptcy. The hero endures his financial loss as a kind of
redemptive suffering that he must undergo in order to free himself of
earthly ambitions. Like Mr. Dombey, Colonel Newcome emerges from his
trials purified and whole, fit less for the city of man than the City of God.

As in other Victorian novels of bankruptcy, financial loss becomes in *The
Newcomes* a kind of symbolic death. The Colonel is weakened physically by
his bankruptcy. Pendennis records his shock at the sight of the Colonel
after his ruin. "As he advanced a step or two toward me I could see that he
trembled in his walk. His hair had grown almost quite white. He looked
now to be more than his age—he whose carriage last year had been so erect,
whose figure had been so straight and manly" (*N*, 72.734). The wealthy
director of the Bundelcund Bank, the lavish host, the triumphant member
of Parliament is reduced to living in mean and squalid circumstances. Like
other bankrupt heroes, the Colonel finds that bankruptcy threatens his
identity in its social, moral, and sexual aspects as well as in the more obvious
economic ones. Far more humbling than the financial downfall is the
knowledge that he has been the means of ruining innocent people, that his
conduct, blameless in financial matters as he has been, has caused the moral
stigma of bankruptcy to stain his good name. The Colonel is tormented by
"some things which were said to him in the Bankruptcy Court by one or two
widows of old friends who were induced through his representations to
take shares in that infernal bank" (*N*, 73.741).

The shame and moral disgrace of bankruptcy are also heightened by the
kind of sexual reversal that we have noted in other novels. The Colonel,
once a "straight and manly figure" and a good catch financially as well, is
now a broken and feeble pensioner, existing on Rosie's small settlement and
her mother's pension. Economic dependence upon these women puts the
Colonel and Clive completely at the mercy of the vulgar, sarcastic Mrs.
Mackenzie, and this redoubtable mother-in-law, who had once tried all her
feminine wiles to entice the Colonel into marriage, now proceeds to bully
him unmercifully, "using the intolerable, undeniable advantage which her
actual wrongs gave her to tyrannize over these two wretched men" (*N*,
72.740).

Broken by his reversals and defeats, the Colonel flees Mrs. Mackenzie's
home and takes refuge as a pensioner at the Grey Friars school. The use of
the Grey Friars is a masterly stroke on Thackeray's part, for it epitomizes

the continuing flow of time in which the Colonel moves. (Chesterton wrote that unlike the characters of Dickens, "Newcome, throughout the book, is in an atmosphere of time,"[51] and Jean Sudrann believes that all of Thackeray's works are a "vision of the human condition as man's life in time."[52]) From the first mention of the Grey Friars we are confronted with the flux of change and circumstance, for Grey Friars was the memorable scene of the school days of Pendennis who, now grown and presumably matured, narrates the present novel. The early visit of the Colonel to his son and the description of the school prepare us for the conclusion that only time can bring about:

> Under the great archway of the hospital he could look at the old Gothic building; and a black-gowned pensioner or two crawling over the quiet square, or passing from one dark arch to another. The boarding-houses of the school were situated in the square, hard by the more ancient buildings of the hospital. A great noise of shouting, crying, clapping forms and cupboards, treble voices, bass voices, poured out of the school-boys' windows: their life, bustle, and gaiety contrasted strangely with the quiet of those old men, creeping along in their black gowns under the ancient arches yonder, whose struggle of life was over, whose hope and noise and bustle had sunk into that grey calm. There was Thomas Newcome arrived at the middle of life, standing between the shouting boys and the tottering seniors. . . . (*N*, 8.68)

The passage is indeed rich with suggestions of the passage of time, for Thomas Newcome "arrived at the middle of life" has spent his boyhood at Grey Friars and will die an old man there. The boardinghouses of the school are "hard by" the "ancient buildings" of the hospital, as the black-gowned old pensioners creep along the square "hard by" the "hope and noise and bustle" of the school boys. The commotion of the boys is at once mocked and subtly undermined by the "grey calm" of the old men that prefigures age and death for the young students as surely as for Colonel Newcome.

It is marvelously fitting, then, at the end of the novel, that Pen returns for Founders Day ceremonies to this place of age and youth, and discovers the Colonel among "the swarm of black-coated pensioners" just as the congregation utters the words of the twenty-seventh Psalm:

> 23. The steps of a good man are ordered by the Lord, and he delighteth in his way.
> 24. Though he fall, he shall not be utterly cast down, for the Lord upholdeth with his hand.
> 25. I have been young, and now am old, yet have I not seen the righteous forsaken, nor his seed begging their bread. (*N*, 75.760)

To this lowly station the Colonel has resigned himself with Christian patience, "to humble his soul, and to wait thankfully for the end" (*N*, 75.761).

His Spartan room is reminiscent of a monk's cell, and, indeed, the pensioners are referred to as "Poor Brothers." The Christian humility and penitence of the Colonel are exemplary: he willingly wears the black gown of the pensioners and says his prayers "with a thankful heart." The Colonel's final illness wipes clean his memory; it is a sign of his approaching death, as well as the final cleansing of his soul: "Now, as in those early days, his heart was pure; no anger remained in it; no guile tainted it; only peace and good will dwelt in it" (*N*, 80.802).

The Colonel's downfall through bankruptcy, like that of Mr. Dombey, has been a kind of providential judgment against worldliness, pride and vindictiveness. Having atoned for his sins through redemptive suffering, the Colonel dies sanctified by his trials:

> At the usual evening hour the chapel bell began to toll, and Thomas Newcome's hands outside the bed feebly beat time. And just as the last bell struck, a peculiar sweet smile shone over his face, and he lifted up his head a little, and quickly said "Adsum!" and fell back. It was the word we used at school, when names were called; and lo, he, whose heart was as that of a little child, had answered to his name, and stood in the presence of the Master. (*N*, 80.804)

Once again, the Colonel is presented within the flux of time and change. His death scene is filled with images of youth and choirboy scenes, emphasizing the aspects of human life that are both subject to time and change and at the same time eternally changeless.

Unlike the repentance of Mr. Dombey, then, the Colonel's salvation somehow strikes us as part of the natural fitness of things. How does Thackeray manage to convince us where Dickens has failed? The answer, I believe, lies at least in part with the narration of Arthur Pendennis. The narrator of *Dombey and Son* is omniscient and arbitrary; he is more than a little inclined to preach to us. But Pendennis is a fallible narrator in that he does not always have perfect knowledge, and the saga of the Colonel's salvation is told through the filter of Pen's somewhat impetuous judgment. Pen has been moved by the ritual of Founders Day until he discovers Colonel Newcome among the Poor Brothers:

> The steps of this good man had been ordered hither by Heaven's decree: to this almshouse! Here it was ordained that a life, all love, and kindness, and honour should end! I heard no more of prayers, and psalms, and sermon, after that! How dared I to be in a place of mark, and he, yonder among the poor? (*N*, 75.761)

Pen's horror as a narrator here seems to negate the comfort and consolation that the Colonel claims to have found in this haven. But of course Pen is a very worldly narrator (and in the novel that bears his name, a very worldly character) while Colonel Newcome, from his first appearance in the novel (at the Cave of Harmony, chastising an astonished habituée for singing a risqué song) has been very unworldly indeed.

In later scenes the Colonel explains to Pen his reasons for entering the Hospital and manages to convince him, with the further aid of the Thirty-seventh Psalm, of his contentment. Pen submits finally to the Colonel's wisdom: "And who that saw him then, and knew him and loved him as I did—who would not have humbled his own heart, and breathed his inward prayer, confessing and adoring the Divine Will, which ordains these trials, these triumphs, these humiliations, these blessed griefs, this crowning love?" (*N*, 75.763). Pen's apparently reluctant conversion goes a long way toward allaying the natural skepticism of the reader. It points as well toward another reason for the success of the Colonel's redemption; it has a dramatic function in the novel that Mr. Dombey's salvation lacks.

Mr. Dombey's fate is contrived so as to return him once more to a position of triumph; the other characters have only to congratulate him on his good fortune. But the Colonel's fate has a dramatic function at the end of *The Newcomes* as a kind of moral litmus test. It separates the worldly characters from those who are saved. The responses of the characters to the Colonel's new life are clearly indicative of the states of their souls: Colonel Newcome, Clive, Florac, Florac's mother, Laura Pendennis, and eventually Arthur Pendennis see no dishonor in the Colonel's accepting alms. The Newcome relatives, on the other hand, feel that the family has been disgraced, and the formidable Mrs. Mackenzie berates the Colonel for living as a pauper and speaks of his "*mean* and *unworthy* and *degraded* conduct" in entering a "workhouse" (*N*, 79.786). Most important of all, when Ethel Newcome discovers the fate of her uncle and visits his cell to take up his homely Pensioner's cloak and kiss its hem, her response indicates that, like her uncle, she has repented of her worldly ambitions, and dedicated herself to the City of God. Thus the dramatic use to which Thackeray puts the Colonel's repentance unifies the conclusion of *The Newcomes* in a way that Dickens was not able to achieve in *Dombey and Son*. (Another significant factor of Thackeray's success with the Colonel, however, must not be overlooked. Unlike Dickens, Thackeray was able to restrain himself from forcing a solution of "clean money" upon his repentant hero. Ethel's trumped-up legacy comes too late to penetrate the Colonel's understanding, and he dies believing himself to be poor but blessed.)

Nevertheless, the ending of *The Newcomes* somehow remains a problem,[53] just as the conclusion of *Dombey and Son* somehow fails to satisfy the reader. It is particularly interesting, for example, that Thackeray chose to set his presumably realistic portrait of social life within the same context of fairy-tale imagery that Dickens used for *Dombey and Son*. One critic has defended this fabular framework as being absolutely essential to the novel. Thackeray's works, according to Jean Sudrann, are merely episodes "in the perpetually retold story of human life."[54] In the design of the title page,[55] the opening chapter with its potpourri of animal fables, the references to classical legends and fairy tales, Thackeray presents his vision of the individual life within the context of the past and present history of the human race.[56]

However, it cannot be denied that the novel's happy ending presents a problem, one that the author himself seems to have recognized. Pressed by his readers to permit the marriage of Ethel and Clive, Thackeray coyly allows his characters to "fade away into Fable-land" before Pendennis's narration can settle their fates. With a rather poor grace, the author submits to his audience's wishes: "My belief then is, that in Fable-land somewhere Ethel and Clive are living comfortably together" (*N*, 80.805). But beyond this he will not be pushed, and he washes his hands rather contemptuously of further responsibility for the sentimental details:

> You may settle your Fable-land in your own fashion. Anything you like happens in Fable-land. . . . the poet of Fable-land rewards and punishes absolutely. He splendidly deals out bags of sovereigns, which won't buy anything; belabours wicked backs with awful blows, which do not hurt; . . . makes the hero and heroine happy at last, and happy ever after. Ah, happy, harmless Fable-land, where these things are! (*N*, 80.805–6)

The conclusion strikes us as insincere as it is peculiarly illogical. Pushed into an ending he clearly knows is not justified by his tale, Thackeray disclaims all responsibility. ("You may settle your Fable-land in your own fashion. Anything you like happens in Fable-land.") The insistence upon artifice and the denial of responsibility is lame, however, either as protest or as irony. As Juliet MacMasters has pointed out, the happy Fable-land ending of *The Newcomes* fails precisely because it promises a poetic justice that the main body of the work denies.[57] In the world of *The Newcomes* bags of sovereigns buy a great deal, and blows hurt terribly; by denying the truth of his fable, Thackeray fails to sustain the terrible vision that operates so powerfully throughout most of the novel.

Nor is the marriage of Clive and Ethel the only problem not squarely faced. By allowing the Colonel to die after his bankruptcy, Thackeray does his best to avoid the problem of "dirty" money altogether. The Colonel loses his money and therefore saves his soul; Thackeray courageously allows the Colonel to remain poor once he has found salvation. But to leave Colonel Newcome in poverty is relatively simple—he is, after all, on his deathbed. For those who continue to live in the perplexing world of *The Newcomes*, the problem is more complicated. Ethel is still quite well-off, and presumably the same considerations of class that kept her from marrying Clive earlier do not disappear as long as he is penniless. Thackeray cannot refrain from making Clive comfortable again with a convenient old legacy, or from further ensuring financial stability all around with some additional legerdemain concerning wills. Once his characters have receded into the make-believe of Fable-land:

> Mrs. Mackenzie cannot have the face to keep that money which Clive paid over to her, beyond her lifetime; and will certainly leave it and her savings to little Tommy. I should not be surprised if Madame de Mont-contour left a smart legacy to the Pendennis children; and Lord Kew stood godfather in case—in case Mr. and Mrs. Clive wanted such an article. (*N*, 80.805)

Money in Thackeray's vision is dangerous and corrupting, but it is also quite necessary. The bankruptcy of the Colonel operates metaphorically as a spiritual rebirth and regeneration, but for Clive and Ethel, for Laura and Pen, and for their children, Thackeray is unable to envision any solution but the old one—the hope that private benevolence and Christian faith will not prove incompatible with the possession of a comfortable fortune.

In each of the novels discussed in this chapter, then, there is a sense of a problem not quite solved, an issue not squarely faced. Bankruptcy saves the hero from losing his soul to materialism, and yet the novel manages somehow to imply that certain characters will by some special grace remain both virtuous and comfortably well-off after all. Brontë, Gaskell, Thackeray, and the early Dickens were of course writing at a time when it was still possible to believe that industrialism would allow man to master his fate, and it is difficult to fault them for not having believed otherwise. As Stephen Gill has pointed out in the case of Mrs. Gaskell, the novelist in the early Victorian years could not have seen the shape that industrialism would finally take, and would perhaps have believed with some confidence that the good intentions and Christian benevolence of the private individual were going to succeed in avoiding the dangers inherent in capitalism. The early Victorians, in fact, may have been the last generation to have fostered such hopes.

7

The Development of Corporate Capitalism

By the late eighteen-fifties, only a few years after the publication of *North and South,* it was beginning to be apparent to the writers of Victorian fiction that optimistic assessments of the potential benefits of industrialism, and faith in the benevolence of the individual industrialist, might prove at best to have been premature. The shape of corporate capitalism was emerging more clearly in the decades of the fifties and sixties, as waves of wild speculation in stock shares were followed by catastrophic financial panics and revelations of corruption on the most shocking scale. Novels written in the late 1850s and afterwards were likely, therefore, to be even more satiric about the corrosive influence of wealth and ambition than their predecessors, and correspondingly more pessimistic about the social and moral effects that corporate capitalism would have upon English society. Elizabeth Gaskell had chosen to believe, on the evidence of specific examples of Victorian benevolence and her own Unitarian ideals, that a change of heart among the manufacturing classes would be sufficient to transform industrial capitalism into an equitable and harmonious social system. The ending of *North and South* represents, as John Pikoulis has observed, "a refusal to regard human history apocalyptically."[1] Within a very few years, however, it would become increasingly difficult for novelists to regard either industrialism or the industrialist in such a sanguine light; a later literary sensibility would in fact deal with new economic developments in a manner indeed suggestive of apocalypse. Before exploring in the next chapter the metaphorical uses of bankruptcy in such later novels as *Little Dorrit* and *The Way We Live Now,* therefore, it would be helpful to examine in some detail the economic developments of the fifties that were instrumental in generating a less hopeful perception of industrial progress and the benevolence of its individual captains.

136

The Laws of Limited Liability

In order to comprehend the public concern over the nature of the corporate capitalism that emerged in the late fifties and thereafter, it will be necessary to trace briefly the extension in these years of the laws of limited liability. Unlike the other industrial countries of Europe, England, from 1720 on, had operated upon the assumption of unlimited liability: that is, that every man or woman with the smallest investment in an enterprise, no matter how large or small his share in the actual managment of such a business, would be responsible for its debt to the full extent of his own private property. Thus Mr.Tulliver in his small agrarian business, Mr. Thornton and Mr. Moore at the head of their cotton mills, and Mr. Dombey as the head of a large City firm, would each be obliged to make his own private property liable for debts incurred as business expenses. It is because of unlimited liability that Colonel Newcome must strip himself of private pensions to repay the debts of the Bundelcund Bank. Arthur Clennam and Daniel Doyce feel a very personal responsibility for the debts of their partnership, while corporate entrepreneurs such as Merdle and Melmotte, on the other hand, feel no obligation at all.

In spite of such hardships on the ordinary capitalist, unlimited liability was presumed to be the normal manner of doing business until the middle of the nineteenth century. Corporations could be formed only by royal charter or private Act of Parliament, and they were granted generally only to huge enterprises, such as railroads, that required more capital than could be raised by a few private investors. As the Victorian economy expanded, however, there was perceived to be a need for investment capital that could not be raised under the restrictions of unlimited liability, and the success of the railway shares made the further acceptance of the corporation inevitable.[2] It is important to note that much of the agitation for limited liability came from the middle and working classes, who felt that unlimited liability worked to the disadvantage of small capitalists and entrepreneurs. If small investors could limit their responsibility to the amount of their own investment, then the capital of such men could be utilized in industrial expansion, and the wealth generated by such enterprises would be more equitably distributed.[3] Moreover, men who possessed skill and ingenuity but few financial resources would be more likely to find financial backing if they could offer small investors the chance to employ their savings without risk.

The advent of limited liability, however, did not elicit universal enthusiasm. A great deal of opposition was voiced, in Parliament and journals, almost entirely upon moral grounds. British commercial greatness was said to be founded upon the principle that every man would be personally responsible for the debts of his enterprise. To change such a law would, it was charged, give rein to moral slackness in the conduct of business, and impair the reputation and credit of England forever. As one member of Parliament put it, the bill for limited liability would

> enable persons to embark in trade with a limited chance of loss, but with an unlimited chance of gain. That was a direct encouragement to a system of vicious and improvident speculation. . . . The first and most natural principle of commercial legislation was that every man was bound to pay the debts he had contracted, so long as he was able to do so.[4]

Another member denounced the bill as a "snare and a delusion" that would "entrap persons into improvident and dishonest speculation," while a third claimed that such a bill would be disastrous for a stable economy:

> men having small capital would invest it in undertakings of the nature of which they would be totally ignorant and would have to intrust the sole management of their property to the body of directors, who, instead of being the servants, would be the masters of the company.[5]

Many of the opponents of limited liability were of course successful businessmen themselves, "proud of their triumphs in life and of their ability to bear the honorable burden of unlimited liability."[6] There was an implicit assumption of moral superiority in their insistence that their opponents wanted merely to make money without working for it or taking responsibility for it. Nevertheless, there was also a widespread fear on the part of many responsible men of business that limited liability would encourage speculation and fraud, and weaken individual enterprise.

In spite of such opposition, limited liability was clearly an idea whose time had come. The Companies Act of 1844 gave legal status to joint-stock companies and required them to register, and the Limited Liability Act of 1855 and the Joint Stock Companies Act of 1856 provided that shareholders of registered "limited" companies would be liable only for the unpaid portion of their shares. Such laws were extended to banks and other enterprises in 1858 and 1862. The importance of the change thus facilitated in the nature of economic activity can hardly be exaggerated. With the advent of corporate capitalism, economic life turned once and for all from a simple endeavor for a livelihood to a quest for the highest possible return for investment.[7] Leland Jenks has pointed out the way in which "the concept of a business concern as an entity apart from the individuals engaged in carrying it on" has tended to depersonalize business:

> The final step to stock-and-bond capitalism was taken when the liability of shareholders for the conduct of their company was made purely pecuniary and limited to the amount of their investment. The number of proprietors of a concern might now expand indefinitely. The number of concerns in which one proprietor might safely engage received indefinite

extension. Capital was organized into Company, engaging in economic activity with not so much as a sign of the Capitalist to be seen.[8]

The one-man concerns and the partnerships, which had been chiefly responsible for economic progress in England until the 1850s, had been organizations of some stability. Their proprietors had prided themselves upon their proven character, and their credit was rated primarily upon personal attributes such as the punctiliousness with which their debts were repaid. Bankruptcy to such businessmen was a momentous calamity, a declaration to the world that they had failed in their moral responsibility to the mercantile community. With the growth of the corporation, however, individual reputation was no longer at stake, and individual responsibility was no longer valued. Bankruptcy could be merely a convenient way of evading debts, and economic investment became correspondingly more risky.

Moreover, the limited liability company, with its hierarchy of salaried managers, produced a class of shareholders with almost no responsibility for, or knowledge of, the day-to-day affairs of the company. The shareholder was unlikely to have any contact at all with the workmen employed by the company in which he invested, and personal relations between master and worker, such as Carlyle, Brontë, and Gaskell had envisioned, were no longer a reasonable or likely alternative.

In addition, the advent of a corporate economy hastened the evolution already in progress in the nature of wealth itself. According to the new economic principles, wealth was no longer founded upon such tangible realities as old country seats or good corn crops. Wealth was based instead upon the more abstract and theoretical foundations of paper money, shares, cheques, etc. Aptly Thomas Carlyle had dubbed Victorian England "The Age of Scrip"; the widespread acceptance of chimerical forms of paper wealth seemed to alarmed observers like Carlyle to suggest the unreality of England's prosperity, a prosperity that seemed to be dangerously founded in illusion and corruption.

THE DANGERS OF CORPORATE CAPITALISM

The effect of the laws of limited liability upon British capitalism was immediate and dramatic. The number of corporations registered annually in Great Britain leaped from 227 in 1856 (with a nominal capital of 14 million pounds) to 1,014 in 1865 (with a capital of 203 million pounds).[9] The annual formation of companies seems to have remained at this level throughout the seventies, and doubled again in the eighties.[10] But the numbers alone do not tell the story; the very nature of the corporations being registered was an innovation in British economic life. Many were formed as finance companies on the model of the *Credit Mobilier* founded in

Paris in 1852 for the purpose of mobilizing the capital of small investors for
large-scale enterprises. Companies grew up "whose owners were themselves impersonal entities, owned by other limited liability companies, in
infinite series. A whole society of creatures of stocks and bonds was inter-
posed between capitalists and production."[11] Many of these concerns were
"promoters' companies," involved in foreign investments of the most speculative sort. They supplied short-term commercial loans to endeavors in
which the risk was great and the price of money exorbitant.[12]

The danger of such enterprises are of course obvious; the rate of failure
was bound to be high. Limited liability proved to be a blessing in that it
made possible large-scale undertakings requiring enormous investments
that could not have been raised by private investors. It also provided a
convenient means of investment for holders of small amounts of capital
that would otherwise perhaps not have entered the economy at all. On the
other hand, limited liability, at least in its early years, undoubtedly encouraged a good deal of careless speculation,[13] as well as some downright
dishonesty and fraud. The high rate of failure could be disastrous in a
credit economy that depended upon public confidence; the fifties and
sixties were plagued by calamitous panics which brought ruin to large
numbers of people. The money panic was not, of course, new to the
economy. "Bubbles" and subsequent failures had been buffeting the economy since the origins of capitalism. But the panics of the Victorian period,
beginning with the Railway Panic of 1847–48 were particularly virulent.

The railway market had become glutted in the late 1840s with impossible
schemes and fly-by-night speculations. Hundreds of companies were promoted without ever being registered at all, the profits quickly disappearing
into the pockets of promoters. It has been estimated that it would have
required more capital than the country possessed to build all of the railways
projected.[14] When the bubble burst in 1845, the devastation was widespread. Thousands were ruined by their losses in railway shares, and by
1847 the panic had become more generalized, claiming in its wake many
old, established firms.

Unfortunately such widespread panics were to become endemic in the
middle of the nineteenth century with the coming of corporate capitalism.
In the panic of 1857, the year after the law of limited liability was passsed,
many speculative ventures went under. Of thirty-one firms that testified
before a Parliamentary select committee, only two had had capital of more
than one hundred thousand pounds, and yet all together had managed to
fail with total unsecured liabilities of thirteen million pounds![15] By the
sixties, the British market was once again glutted with the bills of speculative enterprises. The failure of the super-finance company of Overend
and Gurney in 1866 set off another panic; according to Leland Jenks, "the
whole brood of finance and contracting companies were swept into the

court of chancery," and top financiers "went the way of the Bundelcund Bank and Dombey and Son."[16]

The instability and recurring failures of such enterprises were reason enough for the opponents of limited liability to claim that their worst fears had been realized. But even more dismaying than the insecurity of these corporations was the dishonesty and fraud to which they appeared to give rise.[17] Throughout the fifties and sixties England was to be perpetually shaken by revelations of the most venal corruption in the marketplace but the first, and in many ways the most dramatic scandal of the Victorian period concerned George Hudson, the Railway King of the forties.[18]

This pioneer of corporate enterprise had begun life as a linen-draper in York but rapidly rose to power and wealth as a promoter of railroads. Within a relatively short time he was amalgamating old railway companies and promoting new ones—all of which, in the beginning, appeared to pay almost miraculous dividends as soon as the name of Hudson became associated with them. According to *Fraser's Magazine*, "Railway boards entered into brisk competition to have him for their chairman, and the public had faith in his measures. A hint that "Hudson" was going to "take up" such-and-such a line, would send the shares up in the market with magical buoyancy."[19] By 1845 he had become a member of Parliament, acquired country estates and a London mansion, dined with aristocracy, and was considered among the preeminent men of his age. Hudson conducted his business in the most autocratic fashion, carrying all before him at board meetings, overriding protests, silencing all doubters, and refusing to permit audits of his companies' books. As long as the shares were rising, few questioned his judgment. But the collapse of the market in railway shares proved his undoing. By 1849, Hudson had been forced to resign as chairman of several railways, and committees of investigation were formed to examine his accounts more closely. Their findings produced universal consternation. Hudson had been guilty of many irregularities: he had misappropriated huge number of shares, he had "cooked" the accounts of his companies to make them appear profitable, and the fabulous dividends of his railways turned out to have been paid out of the capital rather than out of the profits, which in many cases were nonexistent. Arraigned in Parliament and facing bankruptcy, Hudson managed to escape criminal prosecution, and lived in obscurity until 1871.[20]

Only a few years later, Hudson's exploits were rivaled by another audacious swindler, John Sadleir. Like Hudson, Sadleir had started with little and ended as the director of many railroad and joint stock companies, and as a Member of Parliament as well. With his brother, Sadleir created the Tipperary Joint Stock Bank in Ireland, and was chairman of the London and Country Bank. In 1853 he became a Junior Lord of the Treasury, and was being spoken of as future Chancellor of the Exchequer, when sinister rumors began to circulate about his enterprises. Desperately, Sadleir tried to raise money to make good certain title-deeds he had forged and fictitious shares he had manufactured, in order to avoid exposure. Failing to do so, he returned to his home in Hyde Park, ordered his tea, and wrote several letters expressing his remorse for his dishonest actions. His body was found later that evening, dead of poison, on Hampstead Heath. It was discovered shortly after that he had forged Swedish Railway shares and embezzled money from the Tipperary Bank, which eventually went bankrupt, ruining a large number of people.[21] The *Times* judged the affair to be "the greatest crash made by any individual in recent times."[22] The suicide of Sadleir occurred in February of 1856, as the first monthly parts of *Little Dorrit* were making their appearance; Dickens alluded to Sadleir in the 1857 preface as the inspiration for his swindler Merdle.

The careers of Hudson and Sadleir were the most spectacular of the mid-Victorian period, but throughout the fifties and sixties there were constant scandals in which prominent businessmen were exposed as swindlers, forgers, and thieves. The case of Joseph Windle Cole illustrated the immense danger of fraud "when fictitious credit comes largely to perform the office of capital."[23] Cole, who had set himself up in business in 1848 under the protection of a certificate of bankruptcy from his previous enterprise, managed to forge dock-warrants for fictitious merchandise in a fictitious warehouse, and was able to obtain over half a million pounds in loans from discount houses on this phony security. The case is doubly interesting because of the involvement of Overend, Gurney and Co., the largest money-discounting house in London, which seems to have learned about Cole's fraudulent warrants, but refrained from exposing him in hopes of recovering its money at the expense of his other creditors.[24]

Almost simultaneous with the scandal of John Sadleir, and also mentioned by Dickens in the preface to *Little Dorrit*, was the scandal of the Royal British Bank. Established in 1850 as a joint-stock banking company, the bank had Members of Parliament on its board, and branches all over London. The Sadleir case led directly to allegations against the Royal British Bank, and a subsequent run on the bank forced it to close its doors in September, 1856. Upon investigation, it was discovered that the directors had loaned money liberally and without security to themselves and their friends, the transactions being recorded only in a secret ledger whose key was entrusted to only a few persons. In one instance, Mr. Humphry Brown, M. P., was discovered to have become a director, opened an account of eighteen pounds, and promptly borrowed seventy thousand pounds.[25] According to the *Times*, "the directors had also a regular allowance of two thousand pounds a year among them, for what the Persians call "tooth money," for wear and tear of their teeth in masticating and swallowing what they took."[26]

The parallels with Dickens's *Little Dorrit* in this spectacle of public officials using their positions for private gain were not lost upon the *Times*, which continued, "Talk of public offices, the faimly of BARNACLES."[27] The case of the Royal British Bank was dragged through both Chancery and Bankruptcy courts, and the cost was enormous; the *Times* reported that while some shareholders were crossing the Channel, others "had been driven into Bankruptcy Court and seen their wives and children turned into the streets, not for a satisfaction of the creditors, but for the liquidation of law expenses alone."[28] The depositors of the bank had been primarily small tradesmen and the closing of the bank spelled ruin for many of them. According to the *Times:*

> It appears that there are 6,000 claims against the British Bank. What a world of misery and ruin is implied in this brief sentence! Persons in the humblest ranks of life have been swindled out of their modest deposits, and small as these may appear in the eyes of rich men, to them the loss is ruin.[29]

A very similar scandal in the following year, 1857, involved the London and Eastern Banking Corporation. Like Thackeray's Bundelcund Bank, the London and Eastern appealed to shareholders who had held high positions in India, and was milked dry by its principal directors: J. E. Stephens and his partner Colonel Waugh had within two years borrowed £245,000 with no security. Two other notorious scandals of 1857 involved large-scale forgeries. William Robson was a clerk who forged huge amounts of Crystal Palace shares, and proceeded to spend his money riotously, supporting a wife and two mistresses in extravagant style.[30] More circumspect was Leopold Redpath, a former bankrupt who became a clerk at the Great Northern Railway Co. and forged transfers of shares. Redpath lived luxuriously but quite respectably on his embezzled fortune, contributing munificent sums to charity, and serving conscientiously as a governor of Christ's Hospital before he was apprehended.[31] The exposure of Sir John Dean Paul and his partners Strahan and Bates was perhaps the most shocking of all because of the supposedly pious and respectable character of these eminent bankers.[32]

Public confidence was severely shaken by these revelations of dishonesty and corruption in mercantile life, but through the sixties, the British market continued to swarm with bills of the most speculative endeavors, a large segment of the public seemingly as unwary as ever. Railroad schemes were as prolific in the sixties as in the forties. In 1864 and 1865 an American promoter named James McHenry was immensely successful in marketing bond issues for his Atlantic and Great Western Railway. The stock was issued mainly to McHenry himself, although he had never put a cent of his own into the scheme. In spite of the fact that the railroad was insolvent, the shares sold briskly until the Panic of 1866.[33] John R. Reed has stated that

Throughout the century misgivings persisted in regard to banks, joint-stock companies and business in general. Economic crises did not end in 1866, but continued to recur, and business practices did not improve with time. Even in 1875, *The Times* (11 August 1875) expressed alarm at the extensiveness of dishonesty in private enterprise.[34]

PUBLIC OUTRAGE AT MERCANTILE CORRUPTION

To a public outraged by each new revelation of dishonesty, it must have seemed as if the emergence of corporate capitalism had unleashed a flood of corruption upon Victorian life.[35] As formerly public indignation had been heaped upon those dishonest bankrupts who used the bankruptcy law to avoid debts, scorn and anger were now directed against the entrepreneurial swindler; indeed, there was generally perceived to be a direct connection between the two. E. Welbourne has written that "Fraud itself has a posterity. Those cheats of the bankruptcy courts gave their recruits to the 'entrepreneurs' of later Victorian life."[36] And indeed it is striking how many of the swindlers of the fifties and sixties founded their enterprises under the protection of certificates of bankruptcy.

Contemporary journals and periodicals were filled with outraged exposures of stock swindles and other mercantile scandals. As early as 1845, *Blackwood's Magazine* printed a satire on the railway schemes of the day, entitled "How We Got Up The Glenmutchkin Railway, And How We Got Out Of It."[37] The article chronicles the promotion of a scheme for building a railroad in a remote part of Scotland, inhabited primarily by sheep and goats; the details of the swindle are remarkably similar to the scheme for a spurious American railroad that would be promoted by Trollope's swindler Melmotte some thirty years later in *The Way We Live Now*.

In the same year Thackeray satirized railway speculation in *Punch* and apparently coined the term "stag" to denote an individual who speculates in shares in hopes of immediate profit.[38] The fall of George Hudson was the occasion for national soul searching concerning the nature of mercantile morality. Carlyle, for one, pronounced the hero-worship of Hudson to be symptomatic of England's decadence. In one of the *Latter Day Pamphlets* (1850) entitled "Hudson's Statue," Carlyle laments that a proposed statue of Hudson was never completed:

> Why was it not set up, that the whole world might see it; that our "Religion" might be seen, mounted on some figure of a Locomotive, garnished with scrip-rolls proper; and raised aloft in some conspicuous place . . . to proclaim to the world there is still one God, you see, in England; and this is his prophet.[39]

In Carlylean terms, a people was measured by its heroes. The Victorian worshipers of Mammon, who knew no better than to elevate Quacks and

Sham heroes into deities, had elected a fitting King for their era. Carlyle's rhetoric takes on its most apocalyptic timbre as he contemplates the spectacle:

> Raise statues to the swollen Gambler as if he were great, sacrifice oblations to the King of Scrip—unfortunate mortals, you will dearly pay for it yet.[40]

> The Apotheosis of Hudson beckons to still deeper gulfs on the religious side of our affairs; into which one shudders to look down. For the eye rests only on the blackness of darkness; and, shrunk to hissing whispers, . . . come moanings of the everlasting tempest. . . .[41]

Nor was Carlyle the only spokesman who found the commercial morality of the mid-Victorian years abhorrent. Richard Burton charged England with Mammonism in *Stone Talk* (1857) and Tennyson complained in *Maud* (1855) of an age "When who but a fool would have faith in a tradesman's ware or his word? . . . When only the ledger lives, and when only not all men lie."[42] The slogan of the times, Tennyson wrote despairingly, was "Cheat and be cheated, and die. . . ."[43]

But it was not merely the poets and prophets of the Victorian age who denounced the contemporary climate of mercantile corruption and believed that it augured the worst for English society. Despair and indignation were in fact the common response to the revelations of corruption in high places. As the daily columns of the *Times* chronicled each new exposure and scandal, that worthy organ of public opinion editorialized tirelessly throughout the fifties and sixties about the sad condition of commercial morality. The fall of Hudson occasioned a cry of outrage, not only against the Railway King, but against his dupes, who were, according to the *Times*, equally guilty:

> they are dupes only now that the imposture is discovered, and its profits have vanished. Everyone knew the contents of the cauldron seething in the company's kitchen. When a 3 per cent. dividend had been declared at Midsummer, and before the half-year's accounts could be possibly be made out a dividend of 9 per cent. was declared for Christmas, everyone who had a pair of eyes in his head must have known that the last dividend was arbitrary and fraudulent.[44]

Like Carlyle, the *Times* saw Hudson as the true representative of his age ("Could there be a fitter prophet for England and the year 1845?")[45] and piously hoped that the proper lesson would be drawn from his downfall:

> There is no Royal road to wealth any more than to wisdom. If shareholders had been satisfied with 3 per cent. instead of 9, they need never have called in Mr. Hudson, and now that they have discarded him, they must return to their original notions of plain dealings and sobriety.[46]

But "plain dealings and sobriety" were clearly not to be the style of the fifties. The exposure of John Sadleir inspired the *Times* to new heights of rhetoric in its outrage against the rapacious spirit of the fifties; it registered a protest "against the fearful spirit of speculation which is the vice of our times."[47] The destiny of Sadleir is invoked in the pages of the *Times* as the inevitable fate of those who strayed from the path of plain dealing and sobriety:

> The bankrupt's despair, the felon's cell, the cold bed of the suicide on the damp moor must be reached at last, the fitting termination of a life only supported by the plunder and misery of others.[48]

Sadleir's last suicide note is quoted to grim effect ("Oh! that I had resisted the first attempt to launch me into speculation!")[49] with an ominous warning to those tempted to yield to the looser commercial morality of the day: "There are many of the English public who would do well to lay seriously to heart the dying words of John Sadleir."[50]

Other public voices were expressing alarm over the corruption that had accompanied stock-and-bond capitalism. The respected editor of *The Banker's Magazine,* David Morier Evans, published in 1859 an account of the mercantile scandals of the 1850s entitled *Facts, Failures, and Frauds* that contained "a complete record of the astounding frauds and forgeries which have of late so frequently startled the commercial community from their propriety."[51] Evans deplores the "generally diffused rage of speculation," which he claims has produced a "bad moral atmosphere that has of late pervaded the whole of the commercial world," and attributes this laxity to a growing desire for luxury and ostentation.[52]

Throughout the fifties and sixties contemporary journals were filled with outraged protests and satires aimed at the fraudulent stock schemes of the period. Dickens published several in *Household Words* and *All the Year Round;* one entitled "Starting the Rio Grande Railway" is very similar to the piece in *Blackwood's* twenty years earlier, and suggests that satire of phony railway schemes was a fairly well-established genre.[53] Anthony Trollope referred indignantly in *The Three Clerks* (1857) to the commercial immorality of the day: "the roguery of the Sadleirs and Camerons, of the Robsons and Redpaths,"[54] while in the same year the popular novelist Emily Eden declared:

> Those Pauls, and Strahans, and Redpaths, have more to answer for than the pecuniary ruin they have wrought. They have ruined all confidence, all trust; they have made dishonesty the rule, and not the exception.[55]

The sixties and seventies brought even greater concern over prominent commercial corruption. Popular novels continued to feature episodes of financial ruin through unsuccessful or dishonest speculation.[56] The eminent banking figure Thomas Baring declared in Parliament that the country's worst fears about limited liability had indeed been realized: "It was by the Limited Liability Act that they had given rise to a sort of commercial gambling which was disgraceful to the country, and . . . ruinous."[57] A similar disgust was voiced by Carlyle, who had by the sixties retreated into an embittered rage and frustration at the current scene. He denounced, in "Shooting Niagara: and After!" the contemporary phenomenon of "Cheap and Nasty" which he had come to see as the plague of the Victorian years. "Cheap and Nasty" was more than an epidemic of shoddy goods:

> Overend-Gurney Bankruptcies, Chatham-and-Dover Railway Financierings—Railway "Promoters" generally . . . all of these are diabolic short cuts towards wages; clutchings at money without just work done; all these are Cheap and Nasty in another form.[58]

No longer were Carlyle's works filled with exhortations to the Captains of Industry to do great deeds for mankind; to Carlyle and other literary observers, the development of corporate capitalism seemed to have corrupted the mercantile life of the country beyond repair, evoking the darkest prophecies for the future of industrial society.

8

Bankruptcy as Metaphor: Social Apocalypse
(*Little Dorrit, The Way We Live Now*)

With public concern over the exposure of commercial corruption grow-ing steadily, it was almost inevitable that the subject should be taken up by the novelists of the day. Indeed, it seems to have been almost expected of them as a duty. The *Times* demanded in June of 1857 after revelations concerning Stephens and Waugh and the London and Eastern Bank, "Why do not our writers of fiction, who are so desirous to present us with pictures of the social state in which we live, select for illustration such a history as that of Colonel Waugh. . . ."[1] Ironically, Dickens's *Little Dorrit* had just appeared in print. The *Times*'s editors could hardly have been unaware of it, and it may indeed have inspired their comment.

But Dickens's Mr. Merdle was not the first fictional swindler to be mod-eled after the scandalous figures from the pages of the daily newspaper. The fall of George Hudson had already inspired two previous novels, Robert Bell's *The Ladder of Gold* (1850) and Emma Robinson's *The Gold Worshippers* (1851). Both of these works concern the rise and fall of a powerful magnate. In *The Ladder of Gold,* the speculator's fall follows closely the pattern of salvation by bankruptcy that we have observed in more distinguished novels of the same period; in this case the speculator's ruin is followed by a denouement in which he earns a more modest fortune by hard work. Like other novelists writing in the late forties and early fifties, Bell in the end rewards his hero with a comfortable fortune, once it has been made "clean" by honest labor and earnest motives.[2] Although neither Bell nor Robinson succeeded in creating a memorable work, their books are evidence of the public fascination with the figure of the swindler.

Such fascination was eventually to be satisfied by the titanic conceptions of Dickens in *Little Dorrit* and Trollope in *The Way We Live Now.* Financial failure had been portrayed often enough in previous fiction, but the crimes of such characters as Dickens's Merdle and Trollope's Melmotte were something new. Bankruptcy had appeared until now to be the result of weakness—the inability of a trader such as Mr. Tulliver to master the harsh realities of economic life, or an individual moral weakness such as the pride and callow materialism of Mr.Dombey and Colonel Newcome. But Merdle and Melmotte are guilty not of weakness but of rapacity. They go bankrupt because they are greedy, dishonest thieves, and their failures, which in turn cause the failures of a large number of their followers, implicate many others besides themselves. As the *Times* editorial of 1849 had pointed out, the ruined shareholders of a burst speculation "bubble" were themselves guilty, if not of fraud or dishonesty, then at the very least of wishing to possess great sums of money that they had not earned. And in fact the downfall of the swindler tarnishes by implication large portions of the public, for Merdle and Melmotte are guilty of peculiarly modern crimes, possible only in a world corrupted by greed and illusion. As David Morier Evans shrewdly pointed out in his study of the swindles of the fifties, such crimes are conceivable only when a society accepts appearances for reality:

> Certainly at no former period of the history of this country has so much importance attached to show, and so little comparatively to substance, as at the present time. If in private life a man live in a mansion, maintain a large establishment—servants—an equipage—and all the other outward appearance of wealth, few people care much to inquire whether or not he possesses the reality—credit, almost without limit, is at his command.[3]

Robbers such as Merdle and Melmotte are thus successful in swindling millions of pounds because the public allows itself to be misled by illusions and to be manipulated by greed.

As the novel moves, then, in the mid-Victorian period, from episodes of personal bankruptcy to broader financial failures involving large numbers of the public, the metaphorical implications become ominous indeed. Only a few years earlier, bankruptcy might still be seen as leading to a personal salvation that in turn implied a certain optimism about the future of the industrial society. As the modern industrial world emerges more clearly in the late fifties, however, bankruptcy is no longer a purely personal event, but a widescale social disaster. In *Little Dorrit* and *The Way We Live Now* the bankruptcy of a character exposes not only the futility of the commercial values by which that character lives, but a corresponding bankruptcy of all social and moral values in the materialistic society around him. Once again, the model is provided by Carlyle, who in the early chapters of *The French Revolution* speaks of France on the eve of chaos, unable to pay her bills: "It is Spiritual Bankruptcy," he intones ominously, "In every man is some obscured feeling that his position . . . is a false one."[4] In Carlyle the relationship of this economic and spiritual failure to the revolution that lies ahead is clear. So too in the novels of the later Victorian period: the financial collapse of huge commercial enterprises is emblematic of a general social apocalypse that it seems to herald. Mrs. Gaskell and her generation, including the earlier Dickens, may have refused to view history apocalyptically, but for the later writers, such equanimity was perhaps no longer possible.

With the widely-publicized commercial corruption of the fifties and sixties, the scandals, swindles, panics, and failures, the sense of a hopeful new world emerging seems to have faded, and in its place a much darker vision of the capitalist society seems to haunt the pages of the later novels. The scale of Merdle's and Melmotte's bankruptcies indicates that the metaphor has progressed far beyond the scope of the earlier novels. The apocalypse of bankruptcy threatens to become general, to engulf all of society, and to bring crashing down all of the corrupt and tainted pretensions of the Victorian world. Whereas financial collapse in Carlyle's works had been a kind of harbinger of revolution, in the later novels of the Victorian period revolution seems hardly to be necessary, for bankruptcy on such a universal scale seems to be in itself sufficient apocalypse, sweeping before it all of the shams and unreality of the social structure.

In his valuable discussion of the literature of apocalypse, Frank Kermode has identified one of the recurring elements in the apocalyptic pattern as Decadence, and pointed out as well that "the mythology of Empire and of Apocalypse are very closely related."[5] The parallels between Decadence and Empire are both clearly present in Dickens and Trollope. In the Victorian years that saw the triumph of the British Empire, the paradigm of the rise and decadence and fall of the Roman Empire was never far removed from the national consciousness.[6] Merdle and Melmotte in a sense establish vast private commercial empires of their own, each in his swift rise and fall encapsulating the myth of the rise and fall of grander empires.

In addition, both Merdle and Melmotte partake of the biblical myth of the apocalypse because both swindlers, who are perceived as demi-gods by their followers, are depicted as anti-Christs, reigning in the brief decadent era that anticipates the final end. The biblical typology of *Revelation* is discernible in these works as the abortive reigns of Dickens's and Trollope's swindlers precipitate a final cataclysm that threatens to overwhelm a rotten social order. Thus the metaphor of bankruptcy has finally fulfilled the most ominous portent which has always been implicitly present in the idea of bankruptcy as a fall.

LITTLE DORRIT

The decadent society that is shaken by bankruptcy in *Little Dorrit* is guilty of all of the economic sins which Dickens had already catalogued so thoroughly in *Dombey and Son*.[7] Mr. Merdle is only the most prominent symbol of a society already contaminated by its own greed and materialism. Arthur Clennam, for example, has been blighted by a childhood made grim and dark by materialistic views: "I am the only child of parents who weighed, measured, and priced everything: for whom what could not be weighed, measured and priced had no existence" (*LD*, 1.2.20). The religion of Mrs. Clennam is hard and materialistic; her prayer is "Smite thou my debtors, Lord, wither them, crush them" (*LD*, 1.5.45). The gloom and morbidity of the Clennam home is the result of an old crime unavenged. From the beginning Arthur suspects that this old wrong must be economic in nature: "In grasping at money and in driving hard bargains . . . someone may have been grievously deceived, injured, ruined. . ." (*LD*, 1.5.47). The secret when revealed turns out to justify Clennam's fears—a small fortune has been withheld from a beneficiary who turns out to be Little Dorrit.

But the corruption has spread far beyond the Clennam house. In one memorable passage Clennam approaches his dismal house and feels the taint of its hard materialism and its old monetary crime spreading by extension over the entire city:

> It always affected his imagination as wrathful, mysterious, and sad; and his imagination was sufficiently impressible to see the whole neighborhood under some tinge of its shadow. As he went along, upon a dreary night, the dim streets by which he went seemed all depositories of oppressive secrets. The deserted counting houses, with their secrets of books and papers locked up in chests and safes; the banking-houses, with their secrets of strong rooms and walls, the keys of which were in a very few secret pockets and a very few secret breasts; the secrets of all the dispersed grinders in the vast mill, among whom there were doubtless plunderers, forgers, and trust-betrayers of many sorts, whom the light of any day that dawned might reveal; he could have fancied that these things, in hiding, imparted a heaviness to the air. The shadow, thickening as he approached its source, he thought of the secrets of the lonely church-vaults, where the people who had hoarded and secreted in iron coffers were in their turn similarly hoarded, not yet at rest from doing harm; and then of the secrets of the river, as it rolled its turbid tide between two frowning wildernesses of secrets, extending thick and dense, for many miles, and warding off the free air and the free country swept by winds and wings of birds. (*LD*, 2.10.525–26)

Behind the pervasive metaphor of prison in *Little Dorrit*, which has so often drawn critical comment,[8] seems to lie an uneasy consciousness of guilt; the preceding passage suggests that it is something like universal economic guilt. London appears to be filled with dirty financial secrets, old monetary crimes that haunt its inhabitants even to the grave. The corruption and scandals that glutted the columns of the newspapers of the fifties, the exposures of dishonest schemes, the revelations about secret ledgers with secret keys, are seen here by Dickens as converging into a kind of oppressive shadow which darkens the city; all of London has become a "wilderness of secrets" banished by the weight of its guilt from the freer air of the country.

As in *Dombey and Son,* economic corruption has spread its blight over every aspect of society. Mercenary marriage, as in all of Dickens's novels, is a major symbol of the corruption of human values; Arthur's father's marriage to Mrs. Clennam, Pet's to Henry Gowan, Fanny Dorrit's to Mrs. Merdle's son, are all poisoned by materialistic considerations.[9] The marriage of Mr. and Mrs. Merdle, which took place years before, is described as the ultimate mercantile transaction, revolving around the visual emblem of the bride's cold but ample bosom: "It was not a bosom to repose upon, but it was a capital bosom to hang jewels upon. Mr. Merdle wanted something to hang jewels upon, and he bought it for the purpose" (*LD,* 1.21.241). Having thus reduced herself synechdochically to the economic value of her most attractive part, Mrs. Merdle is well equipped to understand the rules of society. She knows "what Society's mothers were, and what Society daughters were, and what Society's matrimonial market was, and how prices ruled in it, and what scheming and counter-scheming took place for the high buyers, and what bargaining and huckstering went on . . ." (*LD,* 1.33.385).

In every walk of life sordid motives and the desire for money seem to prevail. Mr. Casby's grasping nature belies his benevolent patriarchal appearance. He is constantly exhorting his underling Pancks to squeeze the last drop of rent from his tenants, while Pancks in turn complies out of respect for the nature of economic enterprise. To work tirelessly for material profit, according to Pancks, is "the Whole Duty of Man in a commercial country" (*LD,* 1.13.154). On a more exalted level, the aristocratic family of Barnacles has encrusted the public offices of the land with the fine art of getting nothing done while drawing large public salaries. The vision of *Little Dorrit* is even darker than that of *Dombey,* for the energy of the railroad building that seems to offer hope in *Dombey* is gone; private entrepreneurs such as Daniel Doyce have been fettered by the corruption of the patronage-choked Circumlocution Office, and the energetic strivers of Staggs's Garden, such as Mr. Toodles, have been replaced by the slothful ne'er-do-wells of Bleeding Heart Yard. Society seems incapable of change or hope, and the only energy displayed originates with the swindler Merdle.

The extent to which Mr. Merdle is honored by the world around him is a measure of the corruption of that world; the eventual exposure of Merdle will in turn expose the total bankruptcy of the world he has conquered so easily. Like his real life progenitors Hudson and Sadleir, Merdle is worshiped for his success in acquiring money, and for the profit to be made in associating with him. Although no one quite knows his origins or his precise means of making money (and indeed his very name seems to suggest an association of money with filth and the gutter—*merde*—that Dickens later develops in *Our Mutual Friend*), he is nevertheless universally blessed for enhancing the reputation of British commerce. Even the most aristocratic are not exempt from Merdle-worship: "the Hampton Court Bohemians, without exception turned up their noses at Merdle as an upstart; but they turned them down again, by falling flat on their faces to worship his wealth" (*LD*, 1.33.583).The traditionally entrenched elements of society make immediate alliance with the new money of Mr. Merdle; to his dinners flock the "magnates" of the aristocracy, government, and religion, all there to see that this great new source of wealth is directed into the proper channels, mostly through their own hands. As they outdo one another in flattery and praise, the dinner guests ensure that Mr. Merdle's money is spent "to maintain the best interest of Society" (*LD*, 1.21.243). Bar suggests the purchase of an estate that involves political interest and some half-dozen church presentations, all to be manipulated "for Society's benefit." Bishop suggests that the financier "shed a little money" on missions to Africa and other church projects. The conduct of these "magnates"—the word itself is suggestive—is evidence that all of the moral and social values of society have been corrupted by the desire for material gain. The Bishop himself, supposed representative of spiritual comfort, is a most worldly figure, his dress and posture clearly signaling to onlookers "don't mind the apron; a mere form" (*LD*, 1.21.245).

But even more corrupt are the political institutions that can be bought with Mr. Merdle's money. At a second dinner party he discusses the election of his dim-witted stepson to Parliament. The young man will be returned on the orders of Mr. Merdle for "three little rotten holes in this Island, containing three little ignorant, drunken, guzzling, dirty, out of the way constituencies, that had reeled into Mr. Merdle's pocket" (*LD*, 2.12.546). Clearly the source of Merdle's political power lies in the money he has available for bribery; he has already obtained his own seat in Parliament, and there are rumors afloat of an impending peerage.

The venality of Mr. Merdle's rise to power is underscored by the vacuity of the man himself. Merdle is a perfectly ordinary, seemingly unremarkable man, ill at ease in the trappings of luxury. The hollowness of a society that worships Merdle is emphasized by the falseness of Merdle himself. Even as the evening papers are full of Mr. Merdle ("His wonderful enterprise, his wonderful wealth, his wonderful Bank") he stands abashed before his own butler, looking "far more like a man in possession of his house under a distraint, than a commercial Colossus, bestriding his own hearth-rug. . ." (*LD*, 2.12.541). The phrase, "under a distraint," is wonderfully telling; even in his moments of triumph there is a suggestion of bankruptcy, of debts unpaid and money unearned about Merdle. The reality of Merdle is hollow, there is nothing beneath the luxurious facade, and a society that cannot distinguish appearance from reality is exposed in turn as a fearful void. As J. Hillis Miller asserts, society in *Little Dorrit* is itself a fraud, "a game of false appearances, and he who puts confidence in it is absorbed into its unreality."[10]

Merdle's downfall becomes an exposure of his social world precisely because his career has been such a faithful paradigm of the values of his time. Nothing is more significant in the later Dickens canon than the interrelatedness of the social and physical world. Early in *Little Dorrit* Miss Wade envisions unknown travelers converging from distant parts to affect mysteriously one another's destinies; it is one of the great achievements of Dickens's later works that the author is so brilliantly able to make connections thus. In the words of Grahame and Angela Smith, Dickens was absorbed with the idea of human interdependence; "part of his deepening understanding of his society was to see how individuals with no apparent links between them were in fact related by the often inhuman forces of social machinery, and especially by what Carlyle called the "Cash-Nexus.""[11]

In the world of *Little Dorrit* no one is more central to this complex web of human connections than the great financier whose activities serve as both a central plot device and organizing symbol. Merdle's financial adventures touch the lives of most of the novel's characters, and his career becomes the emblem of the implacable forces that shape their lives. The parallels between Merdle's operations and the maintenance of social and political power in established society are not lost upon even so unthinking a character as Ferdinand Barnacle, the youngest representative of the family that has devoured a public office. Even in the aftermath of Merdle's terrible ruin, Barnacle cannot help but admire the speculator as a fellow practitioner of Humbug. The young man is gleefully certain that the public has learned nothing from its experience: "The next man who has as large a capacity and as genuine a taste for swindling," he says, "will succeed as well" (*LD*, 2.28.718). Merdle has recommended himself to the approval of Barnacle because they operate upon the same general principle. Each manipulates for his own private gain the willingness of the public to accept illusion for reality. The blackmailer and murderer Rigaud draws a similar moral concerning the universal greed and guilt. When accused of selling a friend, Rigaud coolly defends himself, "I sell anything that commands a price. How do your lawyers live, your politicians, your intriguers, your men of the Exchange . . . Society sells itself and sells me: and I sell Society" (*LD*, 2.28.730). In the interconnecting world that makes up *Little Dorrit*, it seems that all motives are sordid, all transactions corrupt, and that the swindler Merdle has become emblematic simply by practicing his greed with less subtlety than the others around him.

It is not quite accurate, of course, to speak of universal corruption in *Little Dorrit*, for there is a countervailing influence in the Christian goodness of Little Dorrit herself, which in some measure softens the hideous implications of the corruption of Merdle's world. The heroine is indeed the embodiment of perfect human love, and it is fascinating to reflect, as Ross Dabney has done, on how thoroughly Dickens has characterized his Christian heroine by her attitude toward money.

> She earns her keep and more; her family idles and sponges. The contrast extends beyond her family to a society dominated by parasites and confidence tricksters. Little Dorrit's attitudes towards work and money represent the most effective possible curative to a country which admires and follows Barnacles and Merdles. . . .[12]

Arthur Clennam's loss of fortune and his subsequent reunion with Little Dorrit correspond closely to the Christian pattern of salvation by bankruptcy that we have already observed in *Dombey* and other works. By succumbing to the "fever" of speculation in Merdle's shares, Clennam has in a sense been tainted with the guilt of Merdle, of Barnacle, of all of the characters who hope for gain that is unearned or out of proportion to the honest labor used to attain it. His ruin is a judgment that chastens him and awakens him to the true meaning of Little Dorrit's goodness. Like other fallen heroes, Clennam must endure a passage of death-like illness to find himself spiritually reborn. His marriage to Little Dorrit represents a moral regeneration portrayed, strangely enough, chiefly in terms of finances. As Dabney has pointed out, the negotiations before marriage are all about money, but unlike other prospective brides and grooms, Arthur and Little Dorrit must divest themselves of all wealth and give proof of their poverty before they can be united.[13] The burning of the codicil that could have proved Little Dorrit's right to the Clennam wealth is evidence that the dark economic crimes of the past will not blight the future of the hero and heroine; they begin life with no money at all, but clearly they are among the saved. The running headline that Dickens supplied for the last chapter in the 1868 edition is a fitting description of the case: "All Lost and All Gained." As the novel closes Clennam and Little Dorrit return to the world of the "roaring streets," protected by their Christian love: "They went quietly down into the roaring streets, inseparable and blessed; and as they passed along in sunshine and in shade, the noisy and the eager, and the arrogant and the froward and the vain, fretted and chafed, and made their usual uproar" (*LD*, 2.34.802).

The Christian pattern of salvation is thus unmistakably present in *Little Dorrit*. A pattern of equal, if not greater strength, however, vies with the theme of salvation, and that is the pattern of Christian satire. Mr. Merdle is seen as the locus for society's most unChristian financial ambitions. Irony is clearly intended in the description of Mr. Merdle's wonderful reputation "which it was the last new polite reading of the parable of the camel and the needle's eye to accept without inquiry" (*LD*, 1.33.386). Merdle's polite flatterer Bar praises him as "one of the greatest converters of the root of all evil into the root of all good" (*LD*, 1.21.244).

But beyond the easy satire on Merdle and his followers for their unchristian attitude toward money, is a more serious satire in which Merdle's
followers are ironically depicted as worshiping him in a perverted parody
of religion. His public is described as prostrating themselves before him
"more degradedly and less excusably than the darkest savage creeps out of
his hole in the ground to propitiate, in some log or reptile, the Deity of his
benighted soul" (*LD*, 2.11.539). Many critics have pointed out the satirical
intentions of the passage in which Mr. Merdle enters Dorrit's hotel to the
admiration of all onlookers:

> O ye son, moon, and stars, the great man! The rich man, who had in a
> manner revised the New Testament, and already entered into the king-
> dom of Heaven. The man who could have anyone he chose to dine with
> him, and who had made the money! As he went up the stairs, people
> were already posted on the lower stairs that his shadow might fall upon
> them when he came down. So were the sick brought out and laid in the
> track of the Apostle—who had not got into the good society, and had *not*
> made the money! (*LD*, 2.16.593)

There seems to be some disagreement over the exact identity of the Apos-
tle,[14] but the nature of the satire is clear. Merdle is the ironic negation of
everything implied by the sacred healing power of the saint.

Even more sharply satirical are the implied comparisons with Christ,
such as the reference to Merdle as "the shining light of the time" (*LD*,
2.7.499). This phrase was evidently a revision, the manuscript reading
originally "the shining light of the *world*" (emphasis added), and Harvey
Sucksmith has suggested that Dickens intended a topical allusion to
Holman Hunt's famous painting of Christ, *The Light of the World*, which was
exhibited at the Royal Academy in 1854 and had achieved great popularity.[15] A more explicit reference accompanies Merdle's death:

> he, the shining wonder, the new constellation to be followed by the wise
> men bringing gifts, until it stopped over certain carrion at the bottom of
> a bath and disappeared—was simply the greatest Forger and the greatest
> Thief that ever cheated the gallows. (*LD*, 2.25.691)

The irony in this reference to Christ is pointed, for "the greatest Forger
and the greatest Thief" is an inversion of every divine virtue. The frenzy of
his worshipers appears to have elevated him into a kind of arch-fiend;
Merdle is the anti-Christ whose reign and fall will shatter the world when
he is exposed at last by bankruptcy to be mere "carrion."

The vision of *Little Dorrit* has been described by John Wain as "both grand
and apocalyptic,"[16] and indeed the sweeping drama of Merdle's downfall
strikes the reader as apocalyptic because it is so spectacularly all-inclusive.
Merdle's profit-hungry career has been a poison that has contaminated all
of society. It is necessary here to recall the indignation in the editorials of

the *Times* directed not only against George Hudson and other Victorian swindlers, but against their victims as well. In the eyes of the Victorian public, these unfortunates had sinned not because they were foolish, or naive, or gullible, but because they were greedy. Speculation itself, no matter how honest, is seen in terms of traditional commercial ethics as a morally dubious attempt to get something for nothing, and the more spectacular the enterprise, the more venal the crime of the speculator's dupes. The bull market in Merdle's shares is described in book 2, chapter 13 in terms of illness: it is an "epidemic," a "moral infection," a "prevalent disease," a "fever," a "fatal mania," a "plague," a "contagion," a "virulent disorder." Its power is so great that it infects not only greedy fools like Dorrit, but even normally upright and prudent men of business like Arthur Clennam and Pancks.[17] The downfall of these otherwise virtuous and cautious men is proof of the sinister power of Merdle's enterprise, which has its origins in the natural vices of human nature: "Bred at first, as many physical diseases are, in the wickedness of men, and then disseminated in their ignorance, these epidemics, after a period, get communicated to many sufferers who are neither ignorant nor wicked" (*LD*, 2.13.566). So wildly communicable is this disease born of vice and greed, that it spreads into every corner of the social structure, infecting even the penniless rent-defaulters of Bleeding Heart Yard with admiration for the great man and his works. Merdle is elevated to a hero by a society that needs to believe in his wealth, and to worship the man for acquiring it; his bankruptcy, when it comes, thus exposes far more than his own personal failure.

The downfall of Merdle falls like a "thunderbolt" on the society that has exalted him. In his wake appear universal ruin and destruction; it is rumored that

> Numbers of men in every profession and trade would be blighted by his insolvency; old people who had been in easy circumstances all their lives would have no place of repentance for their trust in him but the workhouse; legions of women and children would have their whole future desolated by the hand of this mighty scoundrel. (*LD*, 2.25.690)

Moreover, Merdle's guilt will by extension be as universal as his ruin:

> Every partaker of his magnificent feasts would be seen to have been a sharer in the plunder of innumerable homes; every servile worshipper of riches who had helped to set him on his pedestal would have done better to worship the Devil point-blank. (*LD*, 2.25.690–91)

Images of death and destruction suggest a cataclysm of tragic proportions:

> The admired piratical ship had blown up, in the midst of a vast fleet of ships of all rates, and boats of all sizes; and on the deep was nothing but

ruin: nothing but burning hulls, bursting magazines, great guns self-exploded tearing friends and neighbors to pieces, drowning men clinging to unseaworthy spars and going down every minute, spent swimmers, floating dead, and sharks. (*LD,* 2.26.691)

The chapter in which the effects of Merdle's crash are felt is entitled "Reaping the Whirlwind"; the biblical overtone suggests that behind this particular case of bankruptcy is a much broader social apocalypse which heralds the collapse of all previous values and standards.

Miller has written that "at the center of Dickens' novels is a recognition of the bankruptcy of the relation of the individual to society."[18] As Merdle's downfall exposes the shams of the world so easily manipulated by the swindler, the social structure appears to be collapsing under the weight of its own corruption and unreality. Like the sinister crime-ridden house of the Clennams, which crashes of its own guilty weight amidst images of "thundering sound," "whirlwind," and a "storm of dust," the world that celebrated Merdle seems to collapse into a "heap of ruins" at his downfall (*LD,* 2.31.771–72). The last chapters of the last number of the novel are entitled "Going," "Going!" and "Gone." This phrase, which merges the suggestion of apocalypse with the sounds of the auctioneer's block, is of course perfectly appropriate. Like the bankruptcy proceeding that strips a ruined home of its treasured facade, the crash of Merdle has stripped the pretensions and illusions from the facade of society and exposed beneath it a void so immense that it threatens to become universal.

One of the last orders of business for the novel is the exposure of the "Patriarch" Casby, and the incident has enormous significance. Like Merdle, Casby has been a grasping, greedy swindler who has deceived the world by a false appearance. But Casby's pretensions are at once more traditional and more subtle than Merdle's, for Casby has appeared, not as a great financier, but as a benevolent Christian patriarch. For years Mr. Casby has been cultivating his venerable image in Bleeding Heart Yard while exhorting his lieutenant Pancks to squeeze the tenants for more rent. Finally disillusioned by the collapse of Mr. Merdle, and by the guilt which he feels over his own ruin and that of Arthur Clennam, Pancks resigns from the life of "Bargain and sale" he has lived with Casby, exposing him publicly as "a driver in disguise, a screwer by deputy, a wringer, and squeezer, . . . a philanthropic sneak, . . . a shabby deceiver" (*LD,* 2.32.777). With the highly symbolic act of shearing off Casby's "sacred" patriarchal locks, Pancks exposes the businessman as a sordid grubber after money, a near-relative of Merdle in more benevolent disguise. The exposure of Casby is the final gasp of the philanthropic man of business, a long line of characters, which begins with the Cheeryble brothers, and ends with the exposure of the benevolent Patriarch as a fraud. With him, perhaps, goes the last hope for individual philanthropy and Christian good will as the salvation of industrial society. The apocalypse of bankruptcy has exposed even benevolence as a fraud and pretension, and left only a void of devastation and despair for the future.

The destruction of course turns out to be not quite so universal as it first appears. Certain of the old rotten forms that sustain society will survive intact. Mrs. Merdle and Fanny Dorrit will compete as arbiters of the "interests of society," and the Circumlocution Office will continue to strangle the energy of the nation with its all-encompassing lethargy and corruption. More hopeful signs emerge as well. Arthur Clennam and Little Dorrit survive the ruin of their fortunes to unite and cultivate "a modest life of usefulness and happiness" (*LD*, 2.34.801). But Dickens has traveled very far in the decade of the fifties from the triumphant ending of *Dombey and Son*. The survivors of *Little Dorrit* are as different from the happy little community of the Wooden Midshipman as the reality of the railroad is from the fraud of Merdle's shares, or as the energy of Staggs's Garden is from the lethargic despair of Bleeding Heart Yard; as different, in fact, as one hero is from the other. Unlike Walter Gay, Arthur Clennam is not an incarnation of Dick Whittington, nor a hero of self-help; in fact, it is the swindler and scoundrel who, in this novel, is identified with Whittington. (Merdle is "all the British Merchants since the days of Whittington rolled into one, and gilded three feet deep all over" [*LD*, 2.12.540].) Unlike his predecessor, Arthur Clennam will construct no great commercial "edifice" to replace the one that has smashed. He and Little Dorrit will survive to live among the blessed, but the prophecy for the rest of society is equivocal at best. Merdle's bankruptcy has exposed a social world gone rotten at its core, and the end of the novel shows precious little activity toward a renewal or regeneration of that world. Salvation, if it is possible, must be private and inward; the "roaring streets" through which Clennam and Little Dorrit pass untouched are left, finally, to their own mad devices.

THE WAY WE LIVE NOW

While Dickens's Merdle might seem to have been the definitive portrait of the swindler in a corrupt society, public fascination with the implications of such a figure appears not to have faded for very long. The seventies saw a renewal of interest in the idea on an international scale. Zola's *La Curée* in 1871 portrayed a grasping swindler feeding upon a French society grown decadent in an orgy of speculation, and Mark Twain and Charles Dudley Warner were writing about American speculation, swindling, and corruption in *The Gilded Age* in 1873, just two years before Trollope's swindler Melmotte made his appearance in *The Way We Live Now*.[19] Trollope was thus possessed of a rich heritage of literature concerning the exploits of speculators and profiteers, although the greatest literary influence upon the creation of Mr. Melmotte, despite Trollope's denials, may well have been Dickens's Merdle.

But Trollope may just as easily have gone to the pages of his newspaper as to fiction for his models. The exploits of Hudson, Sadleir, and others in the fifties, and of the American promoter McHenry in the sixties, have already been described. The seventies happily abounded with new examples of the breed. It has been suggested that Melmotte may have been modeled after the notorious Baron Grant, a financier of Jewish ancestry who swindled a trusting public in illicit stock companies such as the Imperial Bank of China and the Central Uruguay Railway. Like Melmotte, Grant had a luxurious house in London and a seat in Parliament, although his inevitable downfall occurred only after the publication of *The Way We Live Now*.[20] Another possible candidate is the American agent of the Rothschilds, New York's own August Belmont, a financier of Jewish origins and doubtful integrity whose name, at least, suggests that of Augustus Melmotte.[21] But whatever the models available to him, it is unarguable that Trollope managed to create something unique in his portrait of the swindler. To a greater extent than any previous novelist, Trollope made the rise and fall of a businessman the sole plot device around which the novel is patterned. Even more than Dickens's Merdle in *Little Dorrit,* Melmotte stands at the center of every strand of the novel's development, wheeling and dealing, buying and selling souls, affecting the destiny of every character. The action of the novel rises and falls with Melmotte's career, and most of the novel's subplots, such as the rise and fall of the Beargarden, ironically parallel Melmotte's career.

The Way We Live Now is perhaps unequaled in its portrait of commercial venality; it is a "symptom of Trollope's bewilderment at the growing power of the world of finance and commercial speculation."[22] Michael Sadleir has called it a "fierce tremendous book":

> Trollope was angry when he wrote it, and the anger burns through its four hundred thousand words, until one fancies that the whole jerry-built society of scheming women, money-grabbing aristocrats, and blatant millionaires must needs go up in the fierce flame of the old novelist's disgusted rage.[23]

Sadleir has correctly perceived the apocalyptic quality of the novel. Like Dickens before him, Trollope uses the success and subsequent bankruptcy of a confidence man to expose the corruption and spiritual bankruptcy of a world tottering precariously upon an abyss of unreality and chaos.

The spectacular rise of Melmotte from his dubious origins to the heights of wealth, fame, and social respectability is a modern morality tale of the grimmest consequences. Like so many of his real-life progenitors, Melmotte emerges unscathed from a history of failure and bankruptcy to enjoy spectacular success; in the modern mode of commerce, where appearance is more important than reality, failure can be as much of an illusion as success. He appears full blown on the London scene, rumored to possess fabulous wealth:

> It was said that he had made a railway across Russia, that he provisioned the Southern army in the American civil war, that he had supplied Austria with arms, and had at one time bought up all the iron in England. He could make or mar any company by buying and selling stock and could make money dear or cheap as he pleased.[24]

The rumors are accepted casually for truth because Melmotte provides his audience with the appearance of wealth in his luxurious surroundings, his servants, carriage, and jewels. Brilliantly parlaying this showy facade and an apparent supply of ready money into a position of eminence in English society, Melmotte commands royal princes to attend his receptions, enters Parliament from one of the most powerful districts in England, and gives a dinner in honor of the Emperor of China.

Melmotte's wealth is a mere sham, of course, a flimsy pretense created by illusion, but his schemes succeed because the world is so willing to accept him at his word. The swindle that Melmotte and his American confederate Fisker perpetrate on the public, like that of Merdle before them, is possible only in an age when wealth is based, not on tangible property, but on the most abstract paper representations of capital. The great railway that Melmotte proposes to build from Salt Lake City to Vera Cruz is a hoax from beginning to end—it exists only in the handsome brochures put out by the speculators.

> The object of Fisker, Montague and Montague was not to make a railway to Vera Cruz, but to float a company. Paul thought that Mr. Fisker seemed to be indifferent whether the railway should ever be constructed or not. It was clearly his idea that fortunes were to be made out of the concern before a spadeful of earth had been moved. (*WWLN*, 1.9.78)

> [Fisker explains the project to Melmotte] with no reference at all to the future profits of the railway, or to the benefit such means of communication would confer upon the world at large; but applied solely to the appetite for such stocks as theirs, which might certainly be produced in the speculating world by a proper manipulation of affairs. (*WWLN*, 1.15.82)

Clearly the railroad has no other existence but in Mr. Fisker's "brilliantly printed programmes," and the job of the South Central Pacific and Mexican Railway is not to build and work a railroad, but simply to market and manipulate shares.

The same lack of substance is apparent in all of Melmotte's enterprises. Mr. Melmotte's purchase of property from the faded aristocrat Longestaffe cleverly illustrates the ability of the modern financier to manipulate money on a grand scale backed only by the illusion of great wealth. Mr. Longestaffe sells Melmotte his Pickering estate, rents his London townhouse to him, and buys Melmotte's railroad shares out of the proceeds of the sale—all without money changing hands.

> It was part of the charm of all dealings with this great man that no ready money seemed ever to be necessary for anything. Great purchases were made and great transactions apparently completed without the signing even of a cheque. [Mr. Longestaffe] . . . was partly conscious of the gradual consummation of a new era in money matters. . . . As for many years past we have exchanged paper instead of actual money for our commodities, so now it seemed that, under the new Melmotte regime, an exchange of words was to suffice. (*WWLN*, 1.14.422–23)

Economic prosperity, then, appears to be a kind of enormous, complicated super-structure, built upon a foundation of unreality. Wealth, once based upon golden coins or fertile acres, has become a thing of paper abstractions, and paper in turn has been replaced by words. The debauched young baronet Felix Carbury brings his money to the great financier and does not even receive paper for it—just Melmotte's word that he has shares. "Money was the very breath of Melmotte's nostrils, and therefore his breath was taken for money" (*WWLN*, 1.35.325). But Melmotte's breath is a false promise. His words have no substance behind them; they lead only to a void of unreality, illusion, and bankruptcy.

The nonchalant immorality of swindlers such as Melmotte and Fisker is a stunning negation of the ideal of commercial honor professed by most of the business community, and one of the most alarming aspects of such criminal enterprises is the casual attitude of the swindlers toward the moral shame of bankruptcy. Melmotte has known in the past how to protect himself by devious methods from the financial disadvantages of bankruptcy; the social disgrace appears to affect him not at all. For his American partner Fisker, bankruptcy holds even less terror. Casually, he tells Paul Montague, "there's more to be got out of the smashing up of such an affair as this, if it should smash up, than could be made by years of hard work out of such fortunes as yours and mine in the regular way of trade" (*WWLN*, 1.10.85). Sabine Nathan has observed that the modern reader can scarcely appreciate the full impact of Fisker's words for a Victorian:

> he can hardly estimate the distinct emotional reaction with which a sneer at *hard work* must have been received by readers nurtured on the cult of work. It is because Trollope shares their position, because he himself believed in the nobleness, in the Carlylean sense, of work, that he is able to penetrate to the historically true character of this new economic phenomenon.[25]

The history of the South Central Pacific and Mexican Railway is a grim fulfillment of the most ominous fears that the opponents of limited liability had expressed about the loss of commercial honor and responsibility in corporate capitalism. Melmotte chooses his Board of Directors for their aristocratic connections and their ignorance of business to ensure that no one will meddle with his running of the company. Trollope's depiction of the weekly meetings of the Board has been criticized as unrealistic,[26] but in fact, allowing for some exaggeration of his satire, Trollope's version does not differ greatly in essentials from published accounts of George Hudson's autocratic way of silencing at public meetings any question as to his methods.[27] Of all of the members of the Board, only Paul Montague takes a traditionally ethical view of his personal responsibility in an enterprise in which he has invested money and accepted a position of eminence. He protests to Melmotte, "That as we sit here as directors and will be held responsible as such by the public, we ought to know what is being done" (*WWLN*, 1.37.346). But Paul is powerless to take effective control of events. Under the new rules of stock-and-bond financing, the capitalist appears to be unable to maintain direct control of his capital. A managerial apparatus has replaced the old concept of the honorable "man of business" and individual responsibility is no longer possible or even desirable.

That this economic immorality has gained widespread currency is emphasized by the way in which Melmotte's entrepreneurial adventures are parodied in the parallel plot of the gambling in the aristocratic Beargarden club. Here Trollope harks back to the old eighteenth-century concept of "ruin"—the image of the imprudent young rake who gambles himself into debt—to underscore the modern image of bankruptcy. The debauched young "swells" of the Beargarden are affected by the same casual notions of financial morality that motivate Melmotte's speculations: "even into the Beargarden there had filtered . . . a feeling that people were not bound to be so punctilious in the paying of money as they were a few years since" (*WWLN*, 2.74.229). The huge gambling debts that Felix Carbury and the other young men owe to one another bear no more relationship to reality than do Mr. Melmotte's railway shares, and the paper IOU's with which they pay their debts circulate wildly among them, never to be collected. It is quite appropriate that several members of the Beargarden serve as directors of Mr. Melmotte's great railway. The parallel between the world of the rakes in the gambling den and the gambling of Melmotte in the City is recognized explicitly by other characters. Roger Carbury, the conservative country squire, contemptuously calls Melmotte a "card sharper," but others are more tolerant. Poor Lady Carbury, Felix's long-suffering mother, wonders, "Why, with such a preceptor [Melmotte] to help him, should not Felix learn to do his gambling on the Exchange, or among the brokers?" (*WWLN*, 1.12.112).

The explicitly drawn connection between the disparate worlds of the City and the Beargarden confirms the idea that the rise, fall, and bankruptcy of Melmotte function as a broad social metaphor in *The Way We Live Now*. The social and spiritual bankruptcy of an entire age is implied in the unthinking adulation of Melmotte by a worshipful public. Like Carlyle, Trollope measures the spirit of the nation by the qualities of its heroes; it is his ironic insight in *The Way We Live Now* that in an age of economic speculation and profligacy, all of society is implicated in the crimes of the swindler. The complicity of the victims lies in their own greed and in their *need* to believe in Melmotte as their economic savior. The same theme was to be pictured in brilliant detail by William Powell Frith a few years after the publication of Trollope's novel in the first painting of his *Race for Wealth* series (1880), "The Spider's Office." In this painting (see drawing on page 53) scores of eager victims swarm about the crowded city office of the financier, bowing and cringing before him. Among them is the clergyman who will be shown in a later painting to suffer the terrible consequences of bankruptcy; in this first painting, however, he is as eager as the others to press his savings upon the swindler in the hope that this man will be the making of his fortune. It is clear from the painting that it is the greed of the victims, and their desire to make money quickly and painlessly, that makes them vulnerable. So, too, in Trollope's novel, the Longestaffes and the others who are fleeced by Melmotte lose their money precisely because they are attempting to regain their fortunes without making any effort. In one of his most openly scornful passages, Trollope states that

> There are men—and old men too—who ought to know the world—who think that if they can only find the proper Medea to boil the cauldron for them they can have their ruined fortunes so cooked that they shall come out of the pot fresh and new and unembarrassed. No greater Medea than Mr. Melmotte had ever been potent in money matters. (*WWLN*, 1.114–15)

With his reputation for magical powers, Melmotte quickly becomes all things to all people. To the Longestaffes he is the financial genius who can save their fortunes; to Lady Carbury he is the benevolent power who will be the making of her son. Both political parties want Melmotte's political and financial support, and both the Anglican and Catholic churches advance claims on his spiritual belief and his money. For the public at large, there is a great hunger for such a philanthropic hero: "It seemed that there was but one virtue in the world, commercial enterprise,—and that Melmotte was its prophet" (*WWLN*, 1.44.411). For the struggling and envious mortals who make up his worshiping public, Melmotte is the fulcrum of their own financial hopes, the image of their own aspirations.

It is clear, then, that Melmotte in his swollen degeneracy is simply reflecting the values of the bankrupt society around him. In the world of

The Way We Live Now, the rules that once governed social relationships have been broken or abandoned outright, and the world has been corrupted at every turn by materialism and folly. The young Lord Nidderdale decides to marry Melmotte's daughter for her fortune in spite of the fact that she has just attempted to elope with Sir Felix: "He had an idea that a few years ago a man could not have done such a thing . . . but that now it did not much matter what a man did,—if only he were successful" (*WWLN*, 2.53.27).

Among the other objects of his scorn, Trollope is indicting an exhausted upper class bereft of money, morals, or energy. The novel ironically surveys a social world in which old nobility and established wealth are sinking listlessly beneath the onslaughts of the nouveaux riches, and have adopted the venal new standards as their own. Mr. Melmotte's grand reception is attended by the old aristocracy who make it clear that they are willing to sell him social respectability for cash. There is even a hint that, like Dickens's Merdle, Melmotte may eventually be able to purchase a title. The Duchess of Stevenage attends his reception because her brother, Lord Grendall, has been bailed out of financial difficulties. A "prince of the royal blood" is there because the jewels of a certain lady have been restored from the pawnbroker. The necessity for flexibility in lowering one's standards is explained casually by Lady Monogram as she justifies herself for attending Melmotte's reception: "there's the butcher . . . or the man who comes to do my hair. I don't at all think of asking them to my house. But if they were suddenly to turn out to be wonderful men, and go everywhere, no doubt I shall be glad to have them here. That's the way we live . . ." (*WWLN*, 2.60.90). Mr. Melmotte's grand dinner for the Emperor of China is not only *attended* by aristocracy; there is a fierce competition for the honor of being present. Mr. Melmotte has obtained the distinction of entertaining the Emperor by the simple expedient of promising to spend ten thousand pounds on the dinner—in return for which he is invited to a reception for the Emperor at Windsor Palace. Clearly even royalty itself is willing to risk the taint of contamination by the newly rich for a high enough price.

The most blatant example of fallen nobility is Sir Felix Carbury. Like the wastrel sons painted by Frith in *The Road to Ruin* and Martineau in *The Last Day in the Old Home,* Sir Felix has gambled away the property left to him by his father and is now draining his mother's income, helplessly in debt, and oblivious to the fact that he is ruining his mother and sister as well as himself. Sir Felix's story perfectly encapsulates the themes that Frith and Martineau suggest, the ruin of the established old families, and the innocent role of women as victims of their men's financial irresponsibility. Trollope's wry description of Sir Felix might well serve as the caption for Martineau's painting of the young man toasting the future as the auctioneers dismantle his home: "It seemed that he lacked sufficient imagination to realise future misery" (*WWLN*, 1.2.17). Admitting that "I never could see the end of anything" (*WWLN*, 1.3.22), Felix lives by carpe diem, borrowing money when he loses at cards, and spending it freely when he wins. In fact, all of Felix's elegant young companions at the Beargarden represent the same mentality; their presence as directors on the Board of the railway company is a further indication of the degeneracy of the old order. Caring nothing about the workings of the company, they allow their aristocratic old names to be used as window dressing for Melmotte's financial schemes in the hopes of realizing a great profit at the cost of no great labor to themselves.

But the aristocratic characters of *The Way We Live Now* are no match for the cunning of the swindler, who uses them all for his own ends. Hoping that by grasping onto the coattails of the great man their ruined fortunes will somehow miraculously revive, Lord Grendall and his son quickly find themselves functioning as hired flunkeys to the vulgar and low-born speculator. The Longestaffes entertain Melmotte in the country, rent him their townhouse and sell him their estate, only to find that although they have not been paid, Melmotte has already realized a profit by mortgaging the estate for cash. The old aristocratic family estates totter on the verge of bankruptcy, as little by little Melmotte annexes their property.

The loss of old homes and valued possessions is the most constant image of bankruptcy in the painting and fiction of the nineteenth century, and it is underscored in *The Way We Live Now* by the way in which Melmotte swallows property whole and then destroys it. He purchases Pickering and then mortgages it, sending workmen down to "renovate" it before it has been paid for; he rents Mr. Longestaffe's townhouse and proceeds to pick the lock of the drawer of Longestaffe's desk; he dismantles his own recently purchased townhouse for the reception of the Emperor of China. To accommodate the large number of guests at the Emperor's reception, walls must be thrown down, the house stripped and cluttered with planks, ladders, and mortar. Trollope describes the scene after dinner: "Within the hall the pilasters and trophies, the wreaths and the banners, which three or four days since had been built up with so much trouble, were now being pulled down and hauled away. And amidst the ruins Melmotte himself was standing" (*WWLN*, 2.68.164).

The image of Melmotte among the elegant debris of the old way of life is poignant, for Melmotte is the spoiler who hastens the break-up of the old social order. His energy and daring function as foils for the lethargy and helplessness of the exhausted old establishment, and vulgar and immoral as he is, he takes on almost heroic proportions compared to the enfeebled remnants of the aristocracy around him, bankrupt in character and energy as well as in wealth. Although Melmotte commits suicide in the end rather than face prison, he has a kind of arrogant courage that enables him to face the voters of Westminster in spite of the rumors of forgery, and to appear in Parliament in spite of his impending arrest. He acknowledges to himself that his own ambition and arrogance have tripped him up; in aiming too high, running for Parliament, entertaining the Emperor, treating powerful lords as flunkeys, he has brought ruin upon himself. Nevertheless, he attains a kind of stature in his last moments that is not lessened even by his drunken scene in Parliament: "He told himself over and over again that the fault had been not in circumstances—not in that which men call Fortune,—but in his own incapacity to bear his position" (*WWLN*, 2.81. 295). Sir Felix Carbury has no comparable moment of self-knowledge—he staggers instead to his ruin mired in self-pity and stupidity.

The Way We Live Now is Trollope's most bitterly satirical novel, and like most satirists, Trollope perceives his fictitious world from a deeply conservative point of view. He deplores the passing of the old traditional social order in which one's "place" was defined by unmistakable indexes of birth and tradition, and he clearly considers the rise of a class of people, like Melmotte, "without origins," as a sign of the degeneracy of the times. Despite the vitality of the nouveaux riches who replace the attenuated old aristocracy, Trollope clearly regards their ascendancy as ominous. Mr. Melmotte is the worst of such newcomers, a creature of the gutter, aping the manners and social customs of a "better" class of people, although he does not perfectly comprehend them. His air of wealth and high position are obviously fraudulent, and his habitual forgeries indicate a lifetime of role-playing in false identities. The comedy of his befuddled first appearance in Parliament is a measure of his ignorance and vulgarity, and a contemptuous indictment as well of the corruption of a society that can elevate such a man to high office. Melmotte, however, is merely the most daring of a whole race of sleazy new businessmen who have risen out of the debacle of the old social order, and who have become rich feeding upon the ruins of the old established fortunes. The bailiffs and auctioneers who take over old homes and dismantle their possessions in so many paintings, dramas, and novels of the Victorian period—the unlicensed brokers who crowd the office of the "Spider" in Frith's *Race for Wealth* series; the grasping middlemen, like the club steward in *The Way We Live Now*, Herr Vossner, who fleeces the Beargarden so professionally; the unscrupulous new breed of lawyers like Dolly Longestaffe's Squercum who profit by inciting heirs to squeeze money out of hard-pressed parents—such are the hordes of vermin who fatten and flourish in the new society.

Among their many objectionable characteristics is the strong implication that many of these successful manipulators of the new methods of finance are "of the Hebrew persuasion." Trollope, like Dickens and Thackeray before him, was capable of appealing to his audience's deeply conservative distrust of "new" or "foreign" elements to strengthen his case against modern industrial society. Thus, while Mr. Melmotte's ancestry is never fully explained, his wife is explicitly styled as a "Bohemian Jewess" and her appearance is correspondingly unappetizing. Mr. Alf, "a rising character," who manipulates the power of the press to his own advantage, is suspected of being born a German Jew. Lady Monogram refuses to invite to her home Mr. Brehgert (the banker and associate of Melmotte whom Georgiana Longestaffe has decided in desperation to marry) because he is fat and greasy and his eyes are "set too near together in his face for the general delight of Christians" (*WWLN*, 2.9.91). And Georgiana's father steadfastly believes that his own economic problems and all the evils of the present time stem from allowing Jews into Parliament. The extent to which the old established order is rapidly disintegrating is discernible in the number of Jews who have been able to infiltrate the best society. Inexorably the barriers seem to be falling; Lady Julia is reported to have run off with a man named Goldsheiner who is received everywhere, and even Lord Nidderdale declares himself perfectly willing to marry a Goldsheiner daughter if the remuneration is attractive enough. Georgiana reflects upon the altered times: "though she hardly knew how to explain the matter even to herself, she was sure that there was at present a general heaving-up of society on this matter, and a change was in progress which would soon make it a matter of indifference whether anybody was Jew or Christian" (*WWLN*, 2.6.92).

The ease with which the scruples of the old order are being eroded by a rising tide of "new people" is just one element of what Trollope calls with contempt "the way we live now," a total corruption of the traditional social values. Among other social customs, marriage has been degraded into a monetary transaction. The marriage of convenience, of course, has a long history dating back well before the Victorian era of high finance, and has long been one of the traditional concerns of the novel. Even in *The Way We Live Now*, such marriages are certainly nothing new; Lady Carbury, for example, married her husband only for position and security. Marriage is the traditional path by which the nouveau riche buys his way into the established order. As Trollope puts it, "Rank squanders money; trade makes it;—and then trade purchases rank by re-gilding its splendour" (*WWLN*, 2.57.59). The negotiations of marriage in *The Way We Live Now*, however, are particularly venal. Mr. Melmotte offers his daughter Marie, along with "half a million down" as bait for a titled son-in-law, to insure his own respectability. As he rises in prestige and power, he can afford to drive a harder bargain, however, and he lowers her dowry correspondingly. Clearly there is a price tag on Marie as visible as the green ticket that Ethel Newcome flaunts in *The Newcomes* and even more degrading; "Each [of Marie's suitors] treated the girl as an encumbrance he was to undertake—at a very great price" (*WWLN*, 1.4.33). Her father's manipulating have the effect of reducing Marie to a chattel.

Trollope sees nineteenth-century life as everywhere bankrupt, not just in its relationships between people, but in all of its established institutions. Literary life is a sham, based upon the same principles of opportunism as Melmotte's financial deals. Lady Carbury's system of achieving literary fame by flattering, bribing, and pleading with editors for good reviews Trollope scorns as "absolutely and abominably foul." A wretchedly inept writer, Lady Carbury cajoles the editor Mr. Broune into noticing her book favorably, and bribes the reviewer Mr. Booker by writing a favorable notice of his own scholarly work. Mr. Booker, being a poor man, unfortunately needs a favorable review and he therefore writes a pleasant one for Lady Carbury although he does not force himself to the extreme of reading her book. As Roger Slakey has observed, Lady Carbury's literary activities are a perversion of language in the same way that Melmotte's promises are a perversion. "Words used as these editors and Lady Carbury use them pretend to represent the facts they ignore . . . they do not represent a substantial reality,"[28] The same grim void of unreality lies behind the glib books of Lady Carbury and the polite reviews of her editorial friends, as behind the railway shares of Melmotte and the IOU's of the Beargarden; literary life has become as much of a sham and a fraud as the stock market or the card table.

Even Christianity appears to have failed as a refuge from the growing abyss of unreality and illusion. The Longestaffe women go to church faithfully as an example to the parish, sitting through the sermon "without the slightest sign either of weariness or of attention" (*WWLN*, 1.21.194). Lady Carbury always goes to church in the country because "it was one of those moral habits, like early dinner and long walks, which suited country life" (*WWLN*, 1.17.158). Georgiana Longestaffe hopes to induce her Jewish fiancé *not* to go to church "so that she might be able to pass him off as a Christian" (*WWLN*, 2.9.93). And the bishop is a good, moral, amiable man who does immense good in his diocese and never talks about his faith.

But of all the bankrupt institutions of Victorian England, none is in so sad a state as political life. Both Conservative and Liberal parties are eager to sponsor Mr. Melmotte for Parliament, regardless of his political principles, which fortunately are nonexistent, and both parties are apparently equally willing to admire him in the interests of winning elections. When he becomes the candidate of the Conservative cause, Melmotte is triumphantly elected in spite of the rumors of his being a swindler and a forger; indeed, the rumors appear to have helped him among the working classes, who support him gleefully because his crimes have injured only the rich. Political life, then, is as corrupt as other aspects of society, and Mr. Melmotte falling drunkenly into the lap of another gentleman on the floor of Parliament is a fitting symbol of the kind of leader the democratic electoral reforms will produce when the "new people" are allowed into political life as well as into respectable drawing rooms.

As bad as these abuses are, the greatest corruptions of the age are located not in Victorian England at all, but in the young country that epitomizes all of the worst aspects of the materialistic and "democratic" era. Trollope deliberately has the scheme for a railway originate in America. Hamilton

Fisker, who "had sprung out of some California gully" (*WWLN*, 1.35.324), explains to Mr. Melmotte's inquiry about capital, "We take care, sir, in the West, not to cripple commerce too closely with old-fashioned bandages" (*WWLN*, 1.9.83). The American values are expressed bluntly by that alarming manifestation of American womanhood, Mrs. Hurtle, who states coolly that "wealth is power, and power is good" (*WWLN*, 1.26.246). She fervently admires the great Melmotte and his railway scheme, and more than once she expresses the desire to be a man, that she might do something similar. Further, it is hardly an accident that when Marie Melmotte turns out to be "her father's own daughter," it is toward America that she turns. Marie's development is an interesting one; originally merely a pawn in her father's schemes, her individuality begins to assert itself as she applies the lessons learned in the Melmotte household and decides to rob her father to elope with Felix. The departure for New York of Mr. Fisker, Marie Melmotte, Mme. Melmotte, and Mrs. Hurtle at the end of the novel leaves the reader with the distinct impression that America is the proper place for adventurers and swindlers.

In the new world dominated by the speculators Melmotte and Fisker, and their greedy corrupted victims like Sir Felix, the Longestaffes, and the Grendalls, there is not much left of the old traditional values, but what little tradition remains is represented in the novel by the country gentleman Roger Carbury. Roger represents all of the old virtues: he owes no money to tradesmen, lives on his land himself, refuses to borrow or to live beyond his means—in short, he upholds the old-fashioned gentlemanly traditions of commercial honor so antithetical to Mr. Melmotte, who, whatever else he is, is clearly *not* a "gentleman." Roger's conservative values are strongly linked to the land and to Carbury Manor. The Carburys have never had anything but land, but in the modern world, land, once the foundation of all wealth, is simply a drain on income. "Land is a luxury, and of all luxuries is the most costly" (*WWLN*, 1.6.48). Roger's pride in his old Tudor home, which has been in the Carbury family for centuries, is an inconvenience to him, for the manor is more picturesque than comfortable. Nevertheless, it symbolizes all of the older values; the surrounding estates, while larger and grander, are also newer and "savor of trade"—they are owned by people who a generation or so back have been "in trade," whereas the Carburys, although not a powerful family, have always been the Caburys of Carbury Manor.

Roger believes that he occupies Carbury Manor in trust for future generations, and his strong belief in heritage and tradition makes him scornful of the new financial trends of speculation; he views Melmotte's railway scheme as "building a house upon sand" (*WWLN*, 1.14.133). Like the ideal country squire celebrated in the novels of Fielding and Smollett, Carbury is the parental protector of his tenants. He takes it upon himself to follow Ruby Ruggles, the flighty granddaughter of his tenant, to London, and to persuade her to forget the attentions of the rakish Sir Felix. Swayed by the prudent advice of Roger Carbury, Ruby returns to the country at last to do her duty by marrying the honest laborer John Crumb.

Indeed, *The Way We Live Now* ends like so many eighteenth-century novels—back in the country, with a renewal of social harmony symbolized by a series of weddings—Ruby to John Crumb, and Hetta to Paul Montague. As the adventurers have all been packed off to America, so the prudent characters have all settled in the country to live out a well-regulated life of order and traditional values. The disposition of Carbury Manor is of crucial importance to this resolution. In an age when other old family estates are being lost in the growing tide of speculation, debt, and bankruptcy, Roger considers the question carefully: "The disposition of a family property is . . . a matter which a man should not make in accordance with his own caprices. . . . He owes a duty to those who live on his land, and he owes a duty to his country. And . . . I think he owes a duty to those who have been before him. . ." (*WWLN*, 2.100.472–73). His decision to reject Sir Felix as his heir and to settle Carbury manor on Hetta's children instead is absolutely crucial to a final vision of traditional harmony, because it protects the estate from a reign of recklessness and profligacy, and insures that at least temporarily the conservative values of prudence and respect for tradition will be honored. Roger's last words are a benediction to this effect: "he spoke much of the land and of the tenants and the labourers, of his own farm, of the amount of income, and of the necessity of so living that the income might always be more than sufficient for the wants of the household" (*WWLN*, 2.100.473). Thus Trollope closes with a vision of a prudent, conservative way of life still possible in a quiet corner of the country. It is his ideal vision, but it is also a wistful one; in his heart Trollope knows that bankruptcy, rather than prudence, is the way we live now.

And, indeed, it is bankruptcy, rather than quiet prosperity, which is the final impression of the novel. Nor is Melmotte alone in his downfall. So ascendant is the swindler that his ruin must necessarily bring widespread financial suffering throughout society. Earlier in the novel, Lord Albert Grendall had predicted that should Melmotte ever fail, "it would be the bursting up of half London" (*WWLN*, 1.44.420); indeed, the shock waves are felt throughout society when Melmotte is known to be a forger, a thief, and finally a suicide. As though Melmotte's crash were the signal for a general universal collapse, the aristocratic Beargarden club comes tumbling down at exactly the same time as the financier. The club's steward Herr Vossner is in a small way the parallel figure to the swindler Melmotte; like Melmotte, he has pandered to the greed and folly of his clients by offering them the illusion of financial solidity. The ruin that arrives in the wake of these thieves dissipates the old sham and imposes a harsh reality of its own. The downfall of the club, coinciding with the crash of the greater swindler, signifies, in a sense, the end of a certain way of life among the

members of the Beargarden. At least two of them, Sir Felix and Miles
Grendall, find themselves condemned to a penniless exile on the Continent, and all of them see in the ruin of Melmotte the collapse of their own
fondest hopes and illusions.

The final cataclysm of Melmotte's downfall will, of course, hardly take
the reader by surprise. From the very beginning there has been a forebod-
ing sense of apocalypse hanging over his adventures. One of the most
ominous elements of Melmotte's reign has been the suggestion of the rise of
a far-flung empire, and the implicit comparison with the fall of Rome.

Clearly Mr. Melmotte has achieved imperial status, for he seems to have
possessed the power to re-make the face of the globe. People speak of
wealth so immense that he will open up new worlds, and renew exhausted
old ones. Melmotte is supposed to be negotiating for a fleet of ships to carry
hordes of emigrants out of overpopulated countries such as Ireland, and
into new lands ripe for nation-building. He is constructing one railway
across America, another across Russia, and laying a cable around the Cape
of Good Hope to keep England in communication with India. He is pur-
chasing the liberty of Arabian fellahs from the Khedive of Egypt and
receiving the compensation of African territory four times larger than
England. He dines on terms of equality with the Emperor of China, the
Brother of the Sun. All of this frenzied activity, or the rumors of such
activity, contribute to the public conception of Melmotte as the founder of a
new commercial empire. But of course such a conception is founded upon
illusion. In actuality Melmotte's "empire" insofar as it exists at all is seething
with corruption and hypocrisy. Such decadence implicitly suggests a comparison with Rome on the verge of collapse, and the comparison is made
explicit by that crusty moralist, Roger Carbury, who mutters, "in Rome, they
were worshipping just such men as this Melmotte" (*WWLN*, 2.55.46).

Moreover, the apocalyptic overtones are echoed strongly in the image of
Melmotte as a kind of anti-Christ. Like Dickens's Merdle before him,
Trollope's confidence man constantly evokes ironic comparisons to divinity.
Lady Carbury, for instance, wants to flatter Melmotte that he is a god, and
construe for him "that passage about the divinity of joining ocean to ocean"
(*WWLN*, 1.30.278). But as often as he is called a "prophet" and a "divinity,"
Mr. Melmotte is also seen as a devil. "As he was a demi-god to some, so was
he a fiend to others" (*WWLN*, 1.44.411). To his followers he is a great
"commercial Jove," to his opponents a "Satan of speculation" (*WWLN*,
1.44.413). Like Dickens's Merdle, Melmotte is both god and devil, savior and
demon, and his reign announces a cataclysmic downfall of the old rotten
social order. *The Way We Live Now* is a despondent jeremiad that prophesies
the sad ravages which time and change and a new kind of economy will
wreak upon a decadent world.

In *The Sense of an Ending*, Kermode has discussed the union of the myth
of apocalypse with the myth of tragedy as they occur in a great work such as

King Lear: "The end is now a matter of immanence; tragedy assumes the figurations of apocalypse, of death and judgment, heaven and hell; but the world goes forward in the hands of exhausted survivors."[29] There is some relationship here to the endings of *Little Dorrit* and *The Way We Live Now,* and yet "tragedy" certainly does not seem to be the appropriate mode. The ruin and death of the financiers Merdle and Melmotte partake more of irony than of tragedy. Their downfalls are a kind of apocalypse that shatters a corrupt and foolish world, and yet, surprisingly, nothing really changes in these novels. In spite of dire predictions of catastrophe, even the financial ruin turns out, when all the final calculations are made, to be not nearly so widespread as feared, and the world continues intact, as foolish and as corrupt as ever. The "exhausted survivors" may have reached a salvation of their own, but they neither possess nor desire the power of the survivors in *King Lear* to remake the world in a better image. The Carburys retreat to Carbury manor in the country, and Little Dorrit and Clennam can somehow hold themselves separate from the "roaring streets" around them. Clearly they are among the blessed, but just as clearly such salvation is necessarily private and domestic, and can be achieved only by turning one's back on the degenerate world and abandoning it to its own grim fate.

In these novels, then, Dickens and Trollope have brought the metaphor of bankruptcy to its ultimate conclusion, an apocalyptic vision of a world ironically poised, unknowing and uncaring, upon the brink of destruction. Once such destruction has become inevitable, however, once the old verities have been shattered forever, the metaphor of bankruptcy loses its force and its drama; we would hardly expect, therefore, that the modern age would produce novels in which bankruptcy functions as both structure and organizing metaphor for the vision of the author. In considering the question of why there are scarcely any modern novels of bankruptcy, it is instructive to examine a work from the period of transition between the Victorian era and our own; *Tono-Bungay* (1931) by H. G. Wells might indeed be considered the last "novel of bankruptcy" ever written.

On the surface, the hero of *Tono-Bungay* appears to bear a striking resemblance to the confidence men of Dickens and Trollope. Wells's hero emerges from an earlier history of bankruptcy and failure to embark on a spectacular career of high finance. Like Merdle and Melmotte before him, Ponderevo is a builder of empires ("The Napoleon of domestic conveniences") whose career ironically suggests divine powers. ("Astraddle on Tono-Bungay, he flashed athwart the empty heavens—like a comet.")[30] And like his predecessors, Ponderevo ends in ruin, exposed as a forger and a bankrupt. Wells, like Trollope before him, portrays his financier aping the pretensions of an older gentry, annexing and despoiling their aristocratic old home and leaving it in the aftermath of his downfall "a colossal litter of bricks and mortar." Moreover, Wells is quite as bitter as Trollope about the influence of the "new people" in society: "they have nothing new about them . . . [but] a disorderly instinct of acquisition; and the prevalance

of them and their kind is but a phase in the broad slow decay of the great
social organism of England" (*TB*, 71–72).

But the vision of Wells is far darker than that of Trollope, and closer to
that of our own time. Wells is remarkably prescient, for example, about the
power of advertising to remake the world according to the illusions desired
by the public. Tono-Bungay is an innocuous elixer that promises health,
strength, and beauty—"bottling rubbish for the consumption of foolish,
credulous and depressed people" (*TB*, 158). Like the false advertising of
this bogus product, the modern world appears to be increasingly grounded
in illusions and corruption. Ponderevo's nephew George, the troubled
narrator of the novel, notes

> The whole of this modern investing civilisation is indeed such stuff as
> dreams are made of. A mass of people swelters and toils, great railway
> systems grow, cities arise to the skies . . . . Yet it seems to me indeed at
> times that all this present commercial civilisation is no more than my poor
> uncle's career writ large, a swelling, thinning bubble of assurances . . .
> that it all drifts on perhaps to some tremendous parallel to his individual
> disaster . . . and beneath it all, you know . . . nothing but fictitious values
> as evanescent as rainbow gold. (*TB*, 258–59)

Wells also seems to anticipate the dangers of commercial exploitation of
radioactive material in our own age. The remarkable chapters that deal
with the expedition to hunt for radioactive "quap-heaps" have perhaps
more in common with Conrad's *Heart of Darkness* than with Trollope's *The
Way We Live Now*, as George leads a piratical expedition into a remote and
primitive territory and ends by murdering a native in his own pursuit of the
valuable material. The strange "cancerous" properties of quap (which produces sores on the hands of men who touch it, and eventually rots away the
ship that carries it) cause all natural life to shrivel and decay around it. The
ominous vision of Wells's novel suggests by extension a world threatened
with similar decay:

> [Quap] is in matter exactly what the decay of our old culture is in society,
> a loss of traditions and distinctions and assured reactions. . . . I am
> haunted by a grotesque fancy of the ultimate eating away and dry-rotting
> and dispersal of all our world. So that while man still struggles and
> dreams his very substance will change and crumble from beneath him
> . . . . Suppose, indeed, that is to be the end of our planet; no splendid
> climax and finale, no towering accumulations of achievements, but just—
> atomic decay! (*TB*, 386–87)

Such an apocalyptic vision seems to forewarn of the stark realities of our
own time. Moreover, capitalism in *Tono-Bungay* has lost whatever ame-
liorative prospects it once possessed; George Ponderevo is haunted by the
sight of processions of unemployed men shambling through the streets of
London, "the gutter waste of competitive civilisation." Nor is there any

saving vision in Wells of a privileged few who are blessed and live apart from the unreality and decay of their society; unlike earlier heroes who retreat into a private domestic salvation, George Ponderevo ends his career rather ambiguously serving the corrupt society of the novel by building destroyers.

Increasingly, then, illusion and decay appear to be the givens of modern life. Bankruptcy can hardly be a potent dramatic event in a doomed world where economic life is seen more in terms of impersonal and sinister forces than in terms of individual social and moral struggle. Moreover, crisis seems to have become a permanent feature of the modern landscape; when apocalypse is always present, the economic downfall of a single individual can scarcely retain the mythic resonance it once held. Losing our money is no longer the most fearsome hell we can imagine for ourselves; we have now more ominous nightmares that haunt our imagination.

Nevertheless, the later Victorian novels were a harrowing portrait in their own time of an age of transition in which the old certainties were still fiercely valued even as they were inexorably losing their force. In a sense our modern era may be said to have begun with the crisis created by the Victorian recognition that industrial capitalism had transformed the collective social life beyond the power of the individual to control his own fate or to affect the destiny of his community, and the recognition, still unhappily with us, that our lives must necessarily be shaped by forces against which there are no appeals. For those writers who were experiencing the uneasiness of life in a period of transition, bankruptcy emerged as a natural metaphor for the spiritual crisis which had been produced by economic change; economic ruin was, in fact, the perfect apocalypse for a crisis that had its origins in materialism. The Victorian novels of bankruptcy remain with us as testimony to an age not unlike our own in which transition and mutability seem to have become the permanent condition of human life.

Appendix
The Trouble with Bankruptcy Statistics

Although the history of the industrial revolution has been endlessly chronicled, surprisingly little has been written by economic historians about the way in which Englishmen of the period succeeded or failed. One explanation for this may lie in the great difficulty of organizing meaningful statistics about bankruptcy. Until well into the middle of the nineteenth century, statistics were not regarded as being of great scientific importance. In his 1831 pamphlet addressed to Earl Grey, Thomas Foster cites figures for bankruptcy that appear to be wildly inflated, and then admits with disarming candor, "calculations have been made without any reference to public estimates or documents any farther than the recollections they left upon my mind at the time they were laid before the public, and principally from my own knowledge of the matters involved and from reckonings upon their relative proportions to each other."[1] Even when Parliamentary commissions on bankruptcy began to demand more accurate figures, the process of bankruptcy is such a complicated and technical one that confusion abounded. To cite just one problem of bankruptcy statistics, very often a bankruptcy fiat (or after 1831, a bankruptcy commission) would be filed, but for various reasons the case might never be adjudicated. (The creditors might fail to prove either the debt or the act of bankruptcy, or creditors and debtor might decide to arrange the case privately, outside the Bankruptcy Court.) Thus there is often confusion about what a bankruptcy statistic represents—the number of cases filed, or the number eventually adjudicated.

There are other pitfalls as well. Ian Duffy presents two sets of bankruptcy statistics from two highly respected economic historians, T. S. Ashton and N. J. Silberling, both allegedly based on the figures of the *London Gazette*. The statistics differ, sometimes to a significant degree, mainly because of the difficulty of eliminating from the lists of the *Gazette* those commissions that were abandoned, or those that had to be repeated.[2]

176

Nor are primary sources always to be relied upon. Statistics in the Parliamentary Papers are often both confusing and contradictory: sometimes one set of papers will be based upon petitions filed, while another set will be based upon bankruptcies actually adjudicated; some years have been calculated from 30 November to 30 November, and some from 31 December to 31 December; and sometimes figures are simply incorrect (numbers added incorrectly, e.g.). For many other sources it is simply not possible to ascertain the origin of their figures. For example, the *British Almanac,* from 1830 to 1850, gives statistics of annual bankruptcy; the figures have no resemblance to the figures given in either the *Gazette* or in the Parliamentary Papers for the same years.

Moreover, the statistics themselves are meaningless unless accompanied by a thorough understanding of the very complex history of English bankruptcy law, for quite often the figures change drastically—not in response to changing economic conditions, but rather to the passing of new laws governing bankruptcy. Thus an apparent quantum leap in the numbers of bankruptcies from 1861 to 1862 (see Tables 5 and 6) may be explained by the passage of the Bankruptcy Act of 1861. This new law permitted all debtors, including those who formerly would have been considered Insolvent Debtors, to absolve themselves from their liabilities by becoming bankrupt voluntarily. Similarly, the number of bankrupts declined precipitously between 1869 and 1870 (see Tables 6 and 7) because of the passage of a much more stringent bankruptcy law.

In addition, it must be kept in mind that the official statistics represent most likely only a small percentage of the actual cases of bankruptcy. Little provision was made before 1861 for recording such private arrangements as liquidations, compositions, and assignments, and yet a glance at such figures as are available (Table 4) shows that such private arrangements far outnumber the official bankruptcies. Moreover, even after 1861, when such arrangements were regulated by the Court and officially recorded, it is certain that in many bankruptcies there were simply not enough assets involved to make a bankruptcy proceeding worth the creditor's time and effort, and therefore many, indeed perhaps most, cases of failure were never officially recorded as bankruptcies. Thus the statistics of Victorian bankruptcy can never be more than a highly imprecise approximation of a truly appalling problem.

In examining the statistics of bankruptcy, then, it is necessary to keep in mind their limitations. In constructing the following tables, I have relied, whenever possible, on information given in the parliamentary returns, on the theory that, while the parliamentary numbers are not necessarily more accurate than any one else's, they represent the "official" estimation by Victorians of their bankruptcy problems, and would probably have been the set of figures that most contemporary authorities would have trusted. (When William Hawes testified before a parliamentary commission in 1848 that bankruptcy in England amounted to £50,000,000 yearly, that figure was accepted, and appeared often thereafter in parliamentary debates and in contemporary newspaper and magazine articles.) Once again, it is important to stress that my major concern has been to establish how the Victorians themselves estimated this problem, and in what way their perceptions are reflected in their literature.

TABLE 1
Average Annual Bankruptcies, 1732–1826

Years	Average Annual Bankruptcies
1732–39	208
1740–49	202
1750–59	227
1760–69	254
1770–79	456
1780–89	496
1790–99	764
1800–09	938
1810–19	1,664
1820–26	1,357

Source: Duffy, p. 165.

TABLE 2
Number of Bankrupts and Insolvents
Before the Reforms of 1831

Year	Bankruptcy Commissions	Insolvent Debtors
1813	1,945	1,447
1814	1,598	2,464
1815	2,271	3,344
1816	2,701	4,060
1817	1,917	3,970
1818	1,241	3,909
1819	2,043	3,919
1820	1,685	5,183
1821	1,572	5,611
1822	1,412	5,587
1823	1,238	4,738
1824	1,231	4,503
1825	1,469	4,399
1826	3,301	4,490
1827	1,680	5,665
1828	1,512	4,571
1829	2,161	5,117
1830	1,716	5,186
1831	1,918	5,261

Source: Based on data in B.P.P., Return of the Bankrupts and Insolvent Debtors in Each Year Between 1801 and 1819, and 1820 and 1846 (1847–1848) 51, no. 120, p. 171.

TABLE 3
Number of Bankrupts and Insolvent Debtors
After the Reforms of 1831 and 1842

Year	Bankruptcy Fiats	Insolvent Debtors
1832	1,734	5,535
1833	1,294	5,086
1834	1,370	5,116
1835	1,309	4,624
1836	1,189	4,757
1837	1,954	5,206
1838	1,086	5,254
1839	1,468	3,676
1840	1,887	4,667
1841	1,837	5,103
1842	1,655	5,352
1843	1,259	4,461
1844	1,099	2,905
1845	1,160	1,292
1846	1,532	1,461

Source: Based on data in B.P.P., Return of the Bankrupts and Insolvent Debtors in Each Year Between 1801 and 1819, and 1820 and 1846 (1847–1848) 51, no. 120, p. 171.

TABLE 4
Bankruptcies, Compositions, and Assignments, 1846–1853

Year	Bankruptcies	Compositions	Assignments
1846	1,533	6,960	1,391
1847	1,599	9,860	1,589
1848	2,181	8,932	1,331
1849	1,550	7,192	915
1850	938	6,972	1,388
1851	959	6,032	1,063
1852	982	6,032	1,182
1853	799	6,264	952

Source: Based on data in B.P.P., Report of Her Majesty's Commissioners appointed to inquire into Fee, Funds and Establishments of the Court of Bankruptcy, and the Operation of the Bankrupt Law Consolidation Act, 1849 (1854) 23, no. 1770., pp. 1, 500.

TABLE 5
Number of Bankruptcies, 1854–1861

Year	Bankruptcies
1854	1,073
1855	1,444
1856	1,146
1857	1,255
1858	1,343
1859	1,054
1860	1,430
1861	1,034

Sources: Based on data in B.P.P.:
Returns from the Accountant in Bankruptcy (1857–1858) 47 no. 189., p. 1.
Court of Bankruptcy Proceedings of the London and District Courts, in the Year 1858 (1859) 26, p. 545.
Report from the Select Committee to inquire into the workings of the New Bankruptcy Act (1864) 5, no. 512, p. xi.
Proceedings of the Court of Bankruptcy, 1861 (1862) 56, p. 685.

TABLE 6
Failures Registered with Bankruptcy Court, 1862–1869

Year	Bankruptcies	Total number of persons taking the benefit of the Bankruptcy Act*
1862	9,663	12,314
1863	8,470	11,486
1864	7,224	10,868
1865	8,305	13,509
1866	8,126	13,585
1867	8,994	15,905
1868	9,195	17,240
1869	10,396	15,064

*Includes private arrangements, such as liquidation, composition, and inspectorship.

Sources: Based on data in B.P.P.:
General Returns by the Chief Registrar of the Court of Bankruptcy, 1862, 1863 (1864) 48, p. 303.
General Return for the year 1864 of All Matters Judicial and Financial within the Bankruptcy Act, 1861 (1865) 65, p. 1.
Proceedings of the Court of Bankruptcy for 1865 (1866) 68, p. 681.
General Return for the year 1866 by the Chief Registrar of the Court of Bankruptcy (1867) 57 p. 33.
General Return for the year 1867 by the Chief Registrar of the Court of Bankruptcy (1867–1868) 57, p. 1.
General Return for the year 1868 by the Chief Registrar of the Court of Bankruptcy (1868–1869) 51, p. 89.
General Return for the year 1869 by the Chief Registrar of the Court of Bankruptcy (1870) 57, p. 5.

TABLE 7
Failures Registered with Bankruptcy Court, 1870–1876

Year	Bankruptcies	Liquidations by Arrangement	Compositions with Creditors	Total number of persons taking the benefit of the Bankruptcy Act
1870	1,351	2,035	1,616	5,002
1871	1,238	2,872	2,170	6,280
1872	933	3,694	2,208	6,835
1873	915	4,152	2,422	7,489
1874	930	4,440	2,549	7,919
1875	965	4,233	2,691	7,889
1876	976	4,968	3,287	9,249

Source: Based on data in B.P.P.: General Reports by the Comptroller in Bankruptcy
For the year 1870 (1871) 58, no. 210., p. 1.
For the year 1871 (1872) 50, no. 237, p. 1.
For the year 1872 (1873) 54, no. 251., p. 1.
For the year 1873 (1874) 54, no. 68., p. 1.
For the year 1874 (1875) 61, no. 272., p. 17.
For the year 1875 (1876) 61, no. 210., p. 7.
For the year 1876 (1877) 69, no. 314., p. 23.

Notes

Chapter 1. Introduction

1. Thomas Carlyle, *Past and Present* (London: Oxford University Press, 1960), 70.

2. The exact details of John Dickens's failure are still disputed. See Lawrence J. Clipper, "The Blacking Warehouse Experience Again: Another View," *Dickens Studies Newsletter* 12 (September 1981): 77–80, and David Paroissien, "Release from the Marshalsea and Warren's: A Rejoinder," *Dickens Studies Newsletter* 13 (September 1982): 71–74 for a review of what is known about this incident and about Charles Dickens's early familiarity with the Insolvent Debtors Act.

3. John Vernon, *Money and Fiction: Literary Realism in the Nineteenth and Early Twentieth Centuries* (Ithaca: Cornell University Press, 1984), 172.

4. George Eliot, *The Mill on the Floss*, ed. Gordon S. Haight, Riverside Editions (Boston: Houghton Mifflin, 1961), bk. 3, chap. 7, p. 216.

5. John Butt and Kathleen Tillotson, *Dickens at Work* (London: Methuen, 1957), 93.

6. Robert Nisbet, *Sociology as an Art Form* (London: Oxford University Press, 1976), 61.

7. Quoted (from *Manifesto of the Communist Party*) in John Kenneth Turner, *Challenge to Karl Marx* (New York: Reynal and Hitchcock, 1941), 160.

8. Nisbet, *Art Form*, 40.

9. Quoted in Anthony Giddens, *Capitalism and Modern Social Theory: An Analysis of the Writings of Marx, Durkheim, and Max Weber* (London: Cambridge University Press, 1971), 86.

10. From *Suicide*, quoted in Robert Nisbet, *The Sociology of Emile Durkheim* (New York: Oxford University Press, 1974), 233.

11. Quoted (from *The Division of Labor in Society*) in Giddens, 79–84.

12. From *Suicide*, quoted in Nisbet, *Emile Durkheim*, 265.

Chapter 2. The Reality of Bankruptcy

1. Peter Mathias, *The First Industrial Nation* (London: Methuen, 1969), 236.

2. David S. Landes, *The Unbound Prometheus* (Cambridge: Cambridge University Press, 1969), 10.

3. H. Heaton, "Financing the Industrial Revolution," *Bulletin of the Business Historical Society* 11 (February 1937): 6.

4. E. J. Hobsbawm, *Industry and Empire: The Making of Modern English Society*, vol. 2, *1750 to the Present Day* (New York: Random House, 1968), 166–67.

5. Arthur D. Gayer, W. W. Rostow, and H. J. Schwartz, *The Growth and Fluctuation of the British Economy, 1790–1850*, vol. 2 (Oxford: Clarendon Press, 1953), 885, 887.

6. T. S. Ashton, *Economic Fluctuation in England, 1700–1800* (Oxford: Clarendon Press, 1959), 114.

7. Landes, *Unbound Prometheus,* 42–43.

8. Charles Dickens, *Sketches by Boz,* New Oxford Illustrated Dickens (London: Oxford University Press, 1957), 182–83.

9. Leland H. Jenks, *The Migration of British Capital to 1875* (New York: Thomas Nelson and Sons, 1927), 151.

10. Quoted in David Morier Evans, *The Commercial Crisis, 1847–1848* (1848; reprint, New York: Burt Franklin, 1970), 72–73.

11. Landes, *Unbound Prometheus,* 75.

12. Leland Jenks, 246.

13. Ian Duffy, "Bankruptcy and Insolvency in London in the Late Eighteenth and Early Nineteenth Centuries" (Diss., Oxford University, 1973), 229.

14. Leland Jenks, 246.

15. Duffy, 232.

16. In 1730 the population of England was somewhere between 5.5 million and 6 million; a century and a half later, at the end of the 1870s, it was 29.7 million, close to five times greater. (From M. W. Flinn, *An Economic and Social History of Britain, 1066–1939* [London: MacMillan, 1964], p. 332.) The rise in bankruptcy, however, was even more dramatic. In the 1730s there were approximately 200 official bankruptcies reported annually, while at the end of the 1870s there were close to 10,000 officially reported bankruptcies, approximately fifty times more. It should be noted that it is difficult to establish reliable statistics of bankruptcy from official records, and in fact the actual instances of bankruptcy were probably far more numerous than the official figures indicated (see appendix).

17. "Report from the Select Committee on the Law of Partnerships," *British Parliamentary Papers* 18 (1851): 135.

18. "Observations on Credit," *Pamphleteer* 13 (1819): 360.

19. (London: Bentley, 1831), 3–4. For a discussion of Foster's statistics, see Appendix, "The Trouble with Bankruptcy Statistics."

20. Foster, 11.

21. "Bankruptcy and Insolvency," *Westminster Review* 46 (1846): 514.

22. "Bankruptcy Law Reform," *Banker's Magazine and Journal of the Money Market* 9 (June 1849): 325.

23. *Times,* 21 May 1849, p. 4.

24. *Hansard's Parliamentary Debates,* 3d ser., vol. 174 (1864), col. 680.

25. "Bankruptcy Laws and Mercantile Corruption," *Fraser's Magazine* 99 (April 1879): 431.

26. Jerome Hamilton Buckley, *The Victorian Temper: A Study in Literary Culture* (Cambridge: Harvard University Press, 1951), 2.

27. Christopher Hill, "Protestantism and the Rise of Capitalism," in *The Rise of Capitalism,* ed. David S. Landes (New York: Macmillan, 1966), 42. Max Weber's theories concerning the influence of the Calvinist ethos on the development of capitalism are still being debated after almost three quarters of a century. For a general overview of the positions of Weber and critics of his position such as Tawney and Samuelson, as well as a discussion of the Marxist critique of Weber, see Robert W. Green, *Protestantism, Capitalism, and Social Science: The Weber Thesis Controversy* (Lexington, Mass.: D. C. Heath, 1973). Some more recent attempts to assess the issue are contained in Jacob Viner, *Religious Thought and Economic Society,* ed. Jacques Melitz and Donald Winch (Durham, N.C.: Duke University Press, 1978), and Gordon Marshall, *In Search of the Spirit of Capitalism: An Essay on Max Weber's Protestant Ethic Thesis* (New York: Columbia University Press, 1982). Anthony Giddens's *Capitalism and Modern Social Theory: An Analysis of the Writings of Marx, Durkheim, and Max Weber* (London: Cambridge University Press, 1971) is particularly deft at putting into perspective the divergences between Marxist theory and Weber's position.

28. Mathias, 208.

29. J. R. Harvey, *Victorian Novelists and Their Illustrators* (New York: New York University Press, 1971), 51–52.

30. Ibid., 53.

31. Thomas Carlyle, *Past and Present* (London: Oxford University Press, 1960), 138.

32. Aina Rubinius, *The Woman Question in Mrs. Gaskell's Life and Works* (Cambridge: Harvard University Press, 1950), 221.

33. Mathias, 208–9.

34. Asa Briggs, Introduction to Samuel Smiles, *Self-Help* (1859; reprint, London: John Murray, 1969), 9.

35. Samuel Smiles, *Thrift* (New York: Harper, 1875), 14.

36. Smiles, *Self-Help*, 34.

37. Ibid., 266.

38. Ibid., 279.

39. Quoted in Ivan Melada, *The Captain of Industry in English Fiction, 1821–1871* (Albuquerque: University of New Mexico Press, 1970), 44.

40. *The Economist*, 1 February 1851, quoted in E. Royston Pike, *Golden Times: Human Documents of the Victorian Age* (New York: Frederick A. Praeger, 1967), 43.

41. Smiles, *Thrift*, 301.

42. Ibid., 302.

43. Pauline Gregg, *A Social and Economic History of Britain, 1760–1970*, 6th ed. (London: George G. Harrap, 1971), 204–5.

44. H. A. Shannon, "The Coming of General Limited Liability," *Economic History* 2 (January 1931): 285.

45. *Hansard's Parliamentary Debates*, 3d ser., vol. 134 (1854), cols. 752–800.

46. *Parl. Deb.*, 3d ser., vol. 114 (1851), col. 842.

47. "The Law of Bankruptcy," *Westminster Review* 52 (1849): 431.

48. "Bankruptcy and Insolvency," *Westminster Review* 46 (1846): 501.

49. Ibid., 507.

50. *Parl. Deb.*, 3d ser., vol. 187 (1867), col. 1765.

51. *Times*, 27 October 1840, p. 4.

52. Ibid.

53. *The Collected Works*, vol. 3, *Principles of Political Economy* (Toronto: University of Toronto Press, 1965), 909–10.

54. *Times*, 23 November 1840, p. 4.

55. *Parl. Deb.*, 3d ser., vol. 187 (1867), col. 1765.

56. *Parl. Deb.*, 3d ser., vol. 157 (1860), col. 649.

57. *Parl. Deb.*, (Commons), 3d ser., vol. 161 (1861), col. 719.

58. "Minutes of Evidence Taken Before the Select Committee of the House of Lords, Appointed to Consider of the Bankruptcy Bill," *British Parliamentary Papers* 22 (1852–53): 1.

59. "Report of the Commissioners for Inquiring into Bankruptcy and Insolvency," *British Parliamentary Papers* 16 (1840): 74.

60. Ibid., p. 113.

61. Edward Jenks, *A Short History of the English Law* (London: Methuen, 1912), 382.

62. W. S. Holdsworth, *A History of English Law*, vol. 3 (London: Methuen, 1903), 229–45.

63. Duffy, 9–10.

64. *Parl. Deb.*, 3d ser., vol. 75 (1844), col. 1175.

65. *Parl. Deb.*, 3d ser., vol. 159 (1860), col. 1995.

66. *Parl. Deb.*, 3d ser., vol. 161 (1861), col. 719.

67. *Times*, 7 June 1861, p. 8.

68. Foster, 72.

69. *Parl. Deb.*, new ser., vol. 24 (1830), col. 227; 3d ser., vol. 75 (1844), col. 1175; and 3d ser., vol. 76 (1844), col. 1398.

70. *British Parliamentary Papers* 16 (1840).

71. Mill, 907–8.

72. "The Law of Bankruptcy," *Westminster Review* 52 (1849): 420.

73. *Parl. Deb.*, 3d ser., vol. 196 (1869), col. 1402.

74. Ibid.

75. "The Urgent Need for Amending Our Bankruptcy Legislation," *The Fortnightly Review* 31 (1 March 1879): 485.

76. "The Bankruptcy Laws and Mercantile Corruption," *Fraser's Magazine* 99 (April 1879): 436.

77. *Parl. Deb.*, 3d ser., vol. 161 (1861), col. 719.

78. *Parl. Deb.*, 3d ser., vol. 185 (1867), col. 1867.

79. Herbert T. Round, "First Prize Essay," in *Prize Essays: Bankruptcy Legislation and Defaulters in the Legal Profession* (London: Joseph Causton, 1879), 9.

80. *Parl. Deb.*, vol. 39 (1819), col. 1380; and new ser., vol. 8 (1831), col. 654.

81. *Parl. Deb.*, 3d ser., vol. 195 (1869), col. 142.

82. *British Almanac of the Society for the Diffusion of Useful Knowledge* (London: Charles Knight, 1847), 259.

83. *Times*, 4 January 1831; 6 June 1849; and 16 August 1858.

84. "Report of Her Majesty's Commissioners Appointed to Inquire into Fees, Funds, and Establishments of the Court of Bankruptcy, and Appointed to Inquire into the Operation of the Bankrupt Law Consolidation Act, 1849," *British Parliamentary Papers* 23 (1854): 201.

85. *The Gazette of Bankruptcy*, vol. 1 (London: Chief Office, Lincoln's Inn, W.C., 1862).

86. *Parl. Deb.*, 3d ser., vol. 162 (1861), col. 623.

87. Duffy, 145–48.

88. Edward Stanley Roscoe, *The Growth of English Law: Being Studies in the Evolution of Law and Procedure in England* (London: Stevens, 1911).

89. *Parl. Deb.*, vol. 28 (1814), col. 797.

90. *Times*, 15 July 1847, p. 4.

91. *Times*, 6 April 1869, p. 9.

92. *Parl. Deb.*, 3d ser., vol. 187 (1867), col. 1765.

93. Edward Jenks, 382–83.

94. Holdsworth, 385.

95. E. Welbourne, "Bankruptcy Before the Era of Victorian Reform," *The Cambridge Historical Journal* 4 (1932): 51–62.

96. *Parl. Deb*, vol. 38 (1818), col. 981.

97. Edward Jenks, 384.

98. Duffy, 27–33.

99. *Parl. Deb.*, vol. 38 (1818), col. 981.

100. *Parl. Deb.*, 3 ser., vol. 7 (1831), col. 901.

101. *Parl. Deb.*, 3 ser., vol. 162 (1861), col. 623.

102. Holdsworth, 385.

103. Duffy, 57, 103–5.

104. *Parl. Deb.*, 3 scr., vol. 100 (1848), col. 565.

105. "House of Commons: Report from the Select Committee on the Bankruptcy Law Consolidation Bill," *British Parliamentary Papers* 8 (1849): 60.

106. *British Parliamentary Papers* 16 (1840).

107. William Makepeace Thackeray, *The Newcomes: Memoirs of a Most Respectable Family, edited by Arthur Pendennis, Esq.* The Biographical Edition in 13 vols., vol. 8 (New York: Harper, 1899), bk. 2, chap. 33. p. 759.

108. *British Parliamentary Papers* 22 (1852–53) and 23 (1854).

109. *British Parliamentary Papers* 22 (1852–53): 51.

110. *Parl. Deb.*, 3d ser., vol. 164 (1861), col. 1590.

111. *British Parliamentary Papers* 22 (1852–53): 9.

112. *Parl. Deb.*, 3d ser., vol. 157 (1860), col. 649.

113. *Parl. Deb.*, 3d ser., vol. 161 (1861), col. 719.

114. *British Parliamentary Papers* 23 (1854): 331.

115. Edward Jenks, 386.

116. "Report from the Select Committee to Inquire into the Working of the New Bankruptcy Act," *British Parliamentary Papers* 5 (1864).

117. Ibid., xi.

118. Ibid.

119. Edward Jenks, 386.

120. "The Bankruptcy Laws and Mercantile Corruption," *Fraser's Magazine* 99 (April 1879): 429.

CHAPTER 3. THE SPECTER OF BANKRUPTCY IN POPULAR ART

1. Maurice Wilson Disher, *Blood and Thunder: Mid-Victorian Melodrama and Its Origins* (London: Frederick Muller, 1949), 12.

2. "In Difficulties. Three Stages," *All The Year Round* 18 (20 July 1867): 92; 18 (27 July 1867): 105; and 18 (3 August 1867): 136.

3. "Rich and Poor Bankrupts," *All The Year Round* 19 (16 May 1868): 540.

4. Graham Reynolds, *Painters of the Victorian Scene* (London: B. T. Batesford, 1953), 2.

5. Raymond Lister, *Victorian Narrative Paintings* (London: Museum Press, 1966), 10.

6. Ibid., 54–59.

7. "George Cruikshank," catalogue (London: Victoria and Albert, 1974), 56.

8. Graham Reynolds, *Victorian Painting* (London: Studio Vista, 1966), 95.

9. William Bayne, *Sir David Wilkie, R.A.* (New York: Charles Scribner's Sons, 1903), 70–71.

10. Lister, 62.

11. Ibid., plates 16–20, pp. 62–71.

12. Aubrey Noakes, *William Frith, Extraordinary Victorian Painter: A Biographical and Critical Essay* (London: Jupiter, 1978), 122.

13. John Baldwin Buckstone, *Luke the Labourer*, in *British Plays of the Nineteenth Century*, ed. J. O. Bailey (New York: Odyssey Press, 1966).

14. Douglas Jerrold, *The Rent Day*, in *British Plays*, ed. Bailey.

15. Gilbert B. Cross, *Next Week—East Lynn: Domestic Drama in Performance, 1820–1874* (Lewisburg, Pa.: Bucknell University Press, 1977), 205.

16. Ibid., 182.

17. Dion Boucicault, *London Assurance*, in *Representative British Dramas*, ed. Montrose J. Moses (Boston: Little, Brown, 1931).

18. Jerome K. Jerome, *Stage-Land*, 65–66, quoted in Michael R. Booth, *English Melodrama* (London: Herbert Jenkins, 1965), 127n.

19. Booth, *English Melodrama*, 152.

20. Dion Boucicault, *Mercy Dodd; or Presumptive Evidence*, in *Forbidden Fruit and Other Plays*, ed. Allardyce Nicoll and F. Theodore Cloak (Princeton: Princeton University Press, 1940).

21. Douglas Jerrold, *Black Ey'd Susan*, in *Nineteenth Century Plays*, ed. George Rowell (London: Oxford University Press, 1953).

22. Tom Taylor, *Our American Cousin*, in *British Plays of the Nineteenth Century*, ed. Bailey.

23. Boucicault, *The Colleen Bawn*, in *Nineteenth Century Plays*, ed. Rowell.

24. W. S. Foote, *Bitter Cold*, in Booth, *English Melodrama*.

25. Boucicault, *Mercy Dodd*, in *Forbidden Fruit and Other Plays*, ed. Nicoll and Cloak.

26. George Coleman, *John Bull, or The Englishman's Fireside*, in *The Magistrate and Other Nineteenth Century Plays*, ed. Michael R. Booth (London: Oxford University Press, 1974).

27. Isaac Pocock, *The Miller and His Men*, in *The Magistrate*, ed. Booth.

28. Hilda Laura Norman, *Swindlers and Rogues in French Drama* (Chicago: University of Chicago Press, 1928).

29. Michael Booth, introduction to *The Magistrate*, ix.

30. Boucicault, *The School for Scheming*, in *Forbidden Fruit and Other Plays*, ed. Nicoll and Cloak.

31. Slingsby Lawrence [George Henry Lewes], *The Game of Speculation* in *Lacy's Acting Edition of Plays, Dramas, Farces, and Extravagances*, vol. 5, ed. Thomas Hailes Lacy (London: 1848–1904).

32. Michael R. Booth, "The Metropolis on Stage," in *The Victorian City: Images and Realities*, ed. H. J. Dyos and Michael Wolff, vol. 1 (London: Routledge and Kegan Paul, 1973), 223–24.

33. Tom Taylor, *Still Waters Run Deep* (Chicago and New York: The Dramatic Publishing Co., n.d.).

34. Tom Taylor, *Payable on Demand*, in *Lacy's Acting Edition*, vol. 41.

35. Tom Taylor, *The Settling Day*, in *Lacy's Acting Edition*, vol. 76.

36. Richard D. Altick, *The English Common Reader: A Social History of the Mass Reading Public, 1800–1900* (Chicago: University of Chicago Press, 1957), 26.

37. John R. Reed in his chapter on "Swindles" in *Victorian Conventions* notes that "Financial failure was a major theme in Victorian literature," and that "personal bankruptcy was a familiar convention in nineteenth century literature" (Ohio: Ohio University Press, 1975), 176–77.

38. Margaret Dalziel, *Popular Fiction, 100 Years Ago: An Unexplored Tract of Literary History* (London: Cohen and West, 1957), 32.

39. Robert Bell's *The Ladder of Gold* (1850) and Emma Robinson's *The Gold Worshippers* (1851) were both modeled on the career of railway speculator George Hudson. (See chapter 8 for a discussion of the origins of Dickens's Mr. Merdle and Trollope's Mr. Melmotte.)

40. J. M. S. Tomkins, *The Popular Novel in England, 1770–1800* (London: Constable and Co., 1932), 68–69.

41. British Museum, Add MSS 46, 656, quoted in Guinevere L. Griest, *Mudie's Circulating Library and the Victorian Novel* (Bloomington: Indiana University Press, 1970), 126.

42. Tomkins, 79–80.

43. Dalziel, 29.

44. Ibid., 88.

45. Tomkins, 129.

Chapter 4. The Major Novelists' View of Bankruptcy

1. George Eliot, *The Mill on the Floss*, ed. Gordon S. Haight, Riverside Editions (Boston: Houghton Mifflin, 1961), bk.2, chap. 2, p. 138. Further references will appear in the text as *MF*.

2. Charles Dickens, *Little Dorrit*, ed. Harvey Peter Sucksmith, The Clarendon Dickens (Oxford: The Clarendon Press, 1979), bk. 1, chap. 6, p. 99. Further references will appear in the text as *LD*.

3. William Makepeace Thackeray, *The Newcomes: Memoirs of A Most Respectable Family, edited by Arthur Pendennis, Esq.* The Biographical Edition in 13 vols., vol. 8 (New York: Harper, 1899), chap. 49, pp. 705–6. Further references will appear in the text as *N*.

4. Elizabeth Gaskell, *North and South*, ed. Angus Easson, Oxford English Novels (London: Oxford University Press, 1973), bk. 2, chap. 25, p. 423. Further references will appear in the text as *NS*.

5. William Makepeace Thackeray, *Vanity Fair: A Novel Without A Hero*, ed. Geoffrey and Kathleen Tillotson, Riverside Editions (Boston: Houghton Mifflin, 1963), chap. 18, p. 170. Further references will appear in the text as *VF*.

6. Charles Dickens, *Dombey and Son*, ed. Alan Horsman, The Clarendon Dickens (Oxford: Clarendon Press, 1974), chap. 58, p. 773. Further references will appear in the text as *DS*.

7. George Eliot, *Middlemarch*, ed. Gordon S. Haight, Riverside Editions (Boston: Houghton Mifflin, 1956), bk. 3, chap. 24, p. 183. Further references will appear in the text as *M*.

8. Charlotte Brontë, *Shirley*, ed. Andrew Hook and Judith Hook (Harmondsworth: Penguin Books, 1975), chap. 2, p. 60. Further references will appear in the text as *S*.

9. Most critics have taken Dickens at his word in the matter of Little Dorrit's stain; only F. R. Leavis has argued strongly that the author is being ironic. For a good review of both sides of the argument, see Graham Mott, "Was There a Stain Upon Little Dorrit?" *The Dickensian* 796 (Spring 1980): 31–36.

10. Joseph Kestner attests to the achievement of women writers of the "condition of England" novels and their insight, particularly Gaskell's, into the male industrialist in "Men in Female Condition of England Novels," in *Men by Women*, ed. Janet Todd, *Women and Literature*, vol. 2 (new series), (New York: Holmes and Meier, 1982).

11. Winifred Gerin, *Charlotte Brontë: The Evolution of Genius* (London: Oxford University Press, 1967), 390.

12. Arnold Shapiro has discussed the way in which the public and private themes of *Shirley* are merged in Robert's conversion. See "Public Themes and Private Lives: Social Criticism in *Shirley*," *Papers on Language and Literature* 5 (Winter 1968): 74–84.

13. John R. Reed has discussed extensively the appearance of bankruptcy in the Victorian novel as a "convention" that could be used as a test of moral worth or as an indication of Victorian distrust of materialistic values. Reed, however, for the most part denies any "symolic or emblematic" function of bankruptcy, with the exception of Dickens's *Little Dorrit*. See *Victorian Conventions* (Athens: Ohio University Press, 1975), 172–92.

14. Alfred Tennyson, "Maud," *The Poems of Tennyson*, ed. Christopher Ricks, Annotated English Poets (London: Longman, 1969), 1049.

15. Thomas Carlyle, *The French Revolution: A History*, *The Works of Thomas Carlyle*, vol. 2, Centenary Edition (London: Chapman and Hall, 1898), vol. 1, bk. 3, chap. 1, p. 53.

16. Ibid., vol. 1, bk. 3, chap. 1, p. 66.

17. Ibid.

CHAPTER 5. BANKRUPTCY AS METAPHOR: THE THREATENED SELF

1. N. N. Feltes, "Community and the Limits of Liability in Two Mid-Victorian Novels," *Victorian Studies* 17 (June 1974): 356.

2. Steven Marcus, *The Other Victorians: A Study of Sexuality and Pornography in Mid-Nineteenth Century England* (New York: Basic Books, 1964), 21–22.

3. Ibid., 22, 26, 22.

4. Ibid., 159.

5. M. A. Blom, "Charlotte Brontë, Feminist Manquée," *Bucknell Review* 21 (Spring 1973): 87.

6. F. A. C. Wilson, "The Primrose Wreath: The Heroes of the Brontë Novels," *Nineteenth Century Fiction* 29 (June 1974): 41.

7. Blom, 101.

8. Wilson, 45.

9. Blom, 91.

10. Shapiro, 75–77.

11. Robert Heilman, "Charlotte Brontë's 'New' Gothic," *The Victorian Novel: Modern Essays in Criticism*, ed. Ian Watt (London: Oxford University Press, 1971), 473.

12. The inner dynamics of such situations were later described by the social thinker Georg

Simmel: "Women consider it embarrassing and degrading to take money from their lovers. . . . On the contrary, women find pleasure and satisfaction in giving money to their lovers. . . . The superiority of whoever gives money over whoever takes money . . . gives to the woman in these contrary instances the satisfaction of imposing dependency upon those whom she would otherwise consider her superiors." The observation, appropriately enough, occurs within the context of a discussion of prostitution. In Georg Simmel, *Philosophie des Geldes* (1907; reprint, trans. Tom Bottomore and David Frisby, London: Routledge and Kegan Paul, 1978), 379.

13. John Pikoulis, *"North and South:* Varieties of Love and Power," *Yearbook of English Studies* 6 (1976): 176.

14. Ibid.

15. Ibid., 185.

16. Alexander Welsh, *The City of Dickens* (Oxford: Clarendon Press, 1971). The loss of spiritual harmony in the architecture of the modern city had been pointed out by A. W. N. Pugin in his celebrated work, *Contrasts* (1836; reprint, New York: Humanities Press, 1969).

17. Welsh, 194.

18. Ibid., 160.

19. Mario Praz, *The Hero in Eclipse in Victorian Fiction,* trans. Angus Davidson (London: Oxford University Press, 1956), 416.

20. Welsh, 160.

21. J. Hillis Miller, *Charles Dickens: The World of His Novels* (Cambridge: Harvard University Press, 1958), 267.

22. Henri Talon, *"Dombey and Son:* A Closer Look at the Text," *Dickens Studies Annual* 1 (1970): 150.

23. Ibid., 149.

24. Deborah A. Thomas discusses the "mercenary feast" in *Dombey and Son, Little Dorrit,* and *Our Mutual Friend* in "Dickens and Indigestion: The Deadly Dinners of the Rich," *Dickens Studies Newsletter* 14 (March 1983): 7–12.

25. Talon, 149.

26. *British Parliamentary Papers* 23 (1854), examination of Edward Lawrence, solicitor, 29 November 1853, p. 37.

27. Richard Altick believes that for Dickens's and Thackeray's readers this scene would have "typified a traumatic event in the experience of many early Victorian families," setting off a conditioned response rooted in the "deep-seated Victorian dread of losing one's money" ("*Dombey and Son* and Its Readers," *The Yearbook in English Studies* 10 (1980): 88). John Vernon also comments that "the seizure and sale of a character's possessions to satisfy creditors" occurs so often in the realistic novel "that we may recognize in it one of the collective nightmares of the middle class in the nineteenth century" (*Money and Fiction*, 69).

28. At least one commentator, John P. Bushnell, feels that the ending, "with its emphasis on energy and hope and life," leaves Maggie triumphant, rather than the self-sacrificing martyr her critics usually assume her to be. See "Maggie Tulliver's 'Stored-up Force': A Rereading of *The Mill on the Floss,*" *Studies in the Novel* 16 (Winter 1984): 380.

CHAPTER 6. BANKRUPTCY AS METAPHOR: MORAL AND SPIRITUAL REBIRTH

1. The tradition of economic downfall as a fortunate fall may be traced at least as far back as Goldsmith's *The Vicar of Wakefield* (1766) in which Parson Primrose emerges from his time in debtor's prison greatly ennobled by his sufferings.

2. Thomas Carlyle, *Chartism, Thomas Carlyle's Works,* vol. 8, The Ashburton Edition, *Critical and Miscellaneous Essays,* vol. 3, (London: Chapman and Hall, 1883), 303.

3. Ibid., 323.

4. *Past and Present,* 198.

5. Ibid., 201.

6. Shapiro, 83.

7. Pikoulis, 182.

8. Ibid., 189.

9. John Lucas, "Mrs. Gaskell and Brotherhood," in *Tradition and Tolerance in Nineteenth Century Fiction: Critical Essays on Some English and American Novels,* ed. David Howard, John Lucas, and John Goode (London: Routledge and Kegan Paul, 1966), 200.

10. Ibid., 199, 201.

11. Stephen Gill, "Price's Patent Candles: New Light on *North and South,*" *Review of English Studies* 27 (1976): 315–16.

12. Gill, 313–16.

13. Ian Campbell, like Gill, is content with the ending of *North and South.* He praises Gaskell for working out "in a credible plot some of the difficulties of applying the Carlylean analysis to his times." See Ian Campbell, "Mrs. Gaskell's *North and South* and the Art of the Possible," *Dickens Studies Annual* 8 (1980): 231–50. Catherine Gallagher, on the other hand, in "*Hard Times* and *North and South:* The Family and Society in Two Industrial Novels," believes that the successful ending of the novel depends rather upon the author's belief in an ideal feminine influence that could benefit men in their public enterprises. See *The Arizona Quarterly* 36 (Spring 1980): 70–96.

14. Lawrence Lerner, "Literature and Money," in *Essays and Studies* 28, ed. Robert Ellradt, The English Association (London: John Murray, 1975), 106.

15. Ross H. Dabney, *Love and Property in the Novels of Dickens* (Berkeley and Los Angeles: University of California Press, 1967), 22.

16. Welsh, *The City of Dickens,* 66.

17. Ibid., 67.

18. J. Hillis Miller, 148.

19. Edgar Johnson has been one of many critics to point this out. See Edgar Johnson, *Charles Dickens: His Tragedy and His Triumph,* vol. 2 (New York: Simon and Schuster, 1952), 630.

20. Dabney, 120.

21. Welsh, *The City of Dickens,* 72.

22. Talon, 157.

23. Chesterton, 87.

24. John Lucas, "Dickens and *Dombey and Son:* Past and Present Imperfect," in *Tradition and Tolerance in Nineteenth Century Fiction,* 99.

25. Steven Marcus, *Dickens: From Pickwick to Dombey* (New York: Simon and Schuster, 1965), 313.

26. Talon, 155.

27. Chesterton, 87.

28. Talon, 159.

29. Quoted in Lucas, "Dickens and *Dombey and Son,*" 131.

30. Quoted in Gordon Ray, *Thackeray: The Age of Wisdom, 1847–63* (New York: McGraw-Hill, 1958), 470.

31. Ibid., 470 n.5.

32. See Martin Meisel, "The Ending of *Great Expectations,*" *Essays in Criticism* 15 (July 1965): 326–31.

33. Angus Wilson, "The Heroes and Heroines of Dickens," in *Dickens and The Twentieth Century,* ed. John Gross and Gabriel Pearson (Toronto: University of Toronto Press, 1962), 4.

34. Julian Moynahan, "Dealings with the Firm of Dombey and Son: Firmness Versus Wetness," in *Dickens and the Twentieth Century,* 128.

35. Ibid., 124–29.

36. Michael Steig, "Structure and the Grotesque in Dickens: *Dombey and Son; Bleak House,*" *The Centennial Review* 14 (1970): 316, 321.

37. John Lucas, "Dickens and *Dombey and Son,*" 131.

38. Moynahan, 129–30.

39. Robin Gilmour, "Dickens and the Self-Help Idea," in *The Victorians and Social Progress,* ed. J. Butt and J. F. Clarke (London: David and Charles, 1973), 88.

40. Kathleen Tillotson has pointed out the pervasiveness of this pattern in *Novels of the Eighteen Forties* (1954; reprint, Oxford: Oxford University Press, 1961). See also William F. Axton, *Circle of Fire: Dickens' Vision and Style and the Popular Victorian Theater* (Lexington: University of Kentucky Press, 1966), 184–86.

41. Pikoulis, 188.

42. Jean Sudrann, "The Philosopher's Property: Thackeray and the Use of Time," *Victorian Studies* 10 (June 1967): 359–88.

43. Ibid., 359–60.

44. Ray, *Thackeray: The Age of Wisdom,* 247.

45. Alexander Welsh, Introduction to *Thackeray: A Collection of Critical Essays* (Englewood Cliffs, N.J.: Prentice-Hall, 1968), 13.

46. Juliet MacMasters, *Thackeray: The Major Novels* (Toronto: University of Toronto Press, 1971), 155–56.

47. Barbara Hardy, *The Exposure of Luxury: Radical Themes in Thackeray* (London: Peter Owen, 1972), 152.

48. MacMasters, 130.

49. Sudrann, 362, 384.

50. MacMasters, 168.

51. Chesterton, 83.

52. Sudrann, 363.

53. Ina Ferris discusses Thackeray's "continuing struggle with the problem of ending and its conventions" in "Realism and the Discord of Ending: The Example of Thackeray," *Nineteenth Century Fiction* 38 (December 1983): 289–303.

54. Sudrann, 379.

55. MacMasters, 171.

56. Sudrann, 379–80.

57. MacMasters, 172.

CHAPTER 7. THE DEVELOPMENT OF CORPORATE CAPITALISM

1. Pikoulis, 193.

2. Landes, *The Rise of Capitalism,* 102.

3. John Stuart Mill, for example, advocated limited liability as a means to the "improvement and elevation of the working classes." Mill looked forward optimistically to an "association of the operatives as virtual partners with the capitalist" when complete freedom in the conditions of partnership was permitted (Mill, 903). Limited liability, however, was not a major issue in the work of Mill or other classical economists and received surprisingly little attention in their writing. See Christine E. Amsler, Robin Bartlett, and Craig J. Bolton, "Thoughts of Some British Economists on Early Limited Liability and Corporate Legislation," *History of Political Economy* 13 (Winter 1981): 774–93.

4. *Parl. Deb.,* 3d ser., vol. 139 (1855), col. 1378.

5. Ibid.

6. Shannon, 287.

7. Leland Jenks, 233–34.

8. Ibid., 234.

9. Ibid., 234, 237–38.

10. David Thompson, *England in the Nineteenth Century, 1815–1914* (Harmondsworth: Penguin Books, 1959), 140, as cited by Sabine Nathan in "Anthony Trollope's Perception of The Way We Live Now," *Zeitschrift für Anglistik und Amerikanistik* 10 (1962): 261.

11. Leland Jenks, 240.

12. Landes, *The Rise of Capitalism*, 104.

13. R. A. Church in *The Great Victorian Boom, 1850–1873* states that "the joint-stock limited liability legislation of 1855–62 did not prove to be a stabilising influence in business during its early years of operation" (London: Macmillan, 1971), 54.

14. David Morier Evans, *The Commercial Crisis, 1847–1848* (1848; reprint, New York: Burt Franklin, 1970), 19.

15. Leland Jenks, 191.

16. Ibid., 261.

17. G. P. Pool and A. G. Pool speak of the "abuses which the *laissez-faire* spirit of the joint-stock acts almost invited," and attribute some of the corruption to the credulity of a general public not prepared by training or education to read and comprehend prospectuses, balance sheets, and the financial press. *A Hundred Years of Economic Development in Great Britain* (London: Gerald Duckworth, 1940), 134–35.

18. Although some of the scandals to be discussed in this chapter actually occurred before the passage of limited liability, they are representative of the kind of corporate structure that would later become common.

19. "Mr. Hudson," *Fraser's Magazine* 36 (August 1847): 219.

20. David Morier Evans, *Facts, Failures, and Frauds: Revelations, Financial, Mercantile, Criminal* (London: Groombridge and Sons, 1859), 6–73; and Robert Lee Wolff, "The Way Things Were," *Harvard Magazine* 77 (March 1975): 48.

21. Evans, *Facts, Failures, and Frauds*, 226–27.

22. *Times*, 26 February 1856, p. 9.

23. Evans, *Facts, Failures, and Frauds*, 156.

24. Ibid., 154–225.

25. Ibid., 268–390.

26. *Times*, 23 September 1856, p. 6.

27. Ibid.

28. *Times*, 6 March 1857, p. 7.

29. *Times*, 8 October 1856, p. 6.

30. Evans, *Facts, Failures, and Frauds*, 391–431.

31. Ibid., 432–83.

32. Ibid., 106–53; *Times*, 29 October 1859, 6.

33. Leland Jenks, 255–59.

34. Reed, 176.

35. Whether in actual fact there was more commercial corruption in the late 1850s than in previous times is a complicated issue. Most standard economic histories hardly address the question of commercial dishonesty, but there seems to be some evidence to suggest that in its earliest years the law of limited liability did indeed lead to much instability and fraud (see Church, 54 and Pool and Pool, 134–35). What is essential for the purposes of this study, however, is not to establish the exact extent of corruption in the 1850s, but to note the extraordinary amount of publicity and public discussion accorded to prominent examples of such corruption.

36. Welbourne, 62.

37. W. E. Aytoun, "How We Got Up The Glenmutchkin Railway, And How We Got Out Of It," *Blackwoods Magazine* 58 (October 1845), 453–66.

38. Michael Steig, "*Dombey and Son* and the Railway Panic of 1845," *The Dickensian* 67 (September 1971): 145–48. Steig suggests that this term, which gained widespread usage, suggested the name of Staggs's Garden to Dickens in *Dombey and Son*. Steig also argues that the image of a menacing runaway train, which appears in Browne's frontispiece, is inspired by the common symbol of the Railway Panic of 1845, which appears in the work of Cruikshank and in *Punch* cartoons as a runaway train.

39. *Latter Day Pamphlets, Works,* vol. 20, Centenary Edition, (London: Chapman and Hall, 1898), 255–56.

40. Ibid., 287.

41. Ibid., 276.

42. Tennyson, 1042.

43. Ibid.

44. *Times,* 1 May 1849, p. 4.

45. Ibid.

46. *Times,* 10 May 1849, p. 5.

47. *Times,* 26 February 1856, 9.

48. Ibid.

49. Ibid.

50. Ibid.

51. Evans, *Facts, Failures, and Frauds,* iv. Evans's work is an invaluable source of information concerning the scandals of the fifties.

52. Ibid., 3, 5.

53. Monroe Engel, *The Maturity of Dickens* (Cambridge: Harvard University Press, 1959), 66.

54. Anthony Trollope, *The Three Clerks* (New York: Dover Publications, 1981), 314.

55. Emily Eden, *The Semi-Attached Couple* and *The Semi-Detached House* (New York: Dial Press, 1979), 135–36.

56. Reed mentions Meredith's *Evan Harrington* (1860), Miss Bradon's *Birds of Prey* (1867), Charles Reade's *Put Yourself In His Place* (1870), and Mrs. Oliphant's *At His Gates* (1872) in *Victorian Conventions,* 188.

57. *Parl. Deb.,* (Commons), 3rd ser., vol. 196 (1869), col. 1402.

58. Thomas Carlyle, "Shooting Niagara: and After!" *Critical and Miscellaneous Essays,* vol. 3, *Thomas Carlyle's Works,* vol. 17, Ashburton Edition (London: Chapman and Hall, 1883), 616.

CHAPTER 8. BANKRUPTCY AS METAPHOR: SOCIAL APOCALYPSE

1. *Times,* 22 July 1857, p. 9.

2. Grahame Smith and Angela Smith, "Dickens as a Popular Artist," *The Dickensian* 67 (September 1971): 134–35.

3. Evans, *Facts, Failures, and Frauds,* 74.

4. Carlyle, *The French Revolution,* vol. 1, p. 79.

5. Frank Kermode, *The Sense of an Ending* (New York: Oxford University Press, 1967), 9.

6. See, for example, J. Hillis Miller, *Charles Dickens: The World of His Novels,* on the use of Gibbon's *Decline and Fall of the Roman Empire* in *Our Mutual Friend.* Miller states, "It is clear that, for Dickens, nineteenth-century England is repeating the fall of Rome . . ." (p. 296).

7. Reed has discussed Dickens's use in *Little Dorrit* of "a broad perspective of bankruptcy as the inevitable outbreak of the lingering disease that he had described earlier in *Dombey and Son.*" He states perceptively that "financial ruin was the most forceful metaphor Dickens could find to indicate to his society that they had misplaced their values . . ." (pp. 185–86).

8. See, for example, Edgar Johnson, *Charles Dickens: His Tragedy and His Triumph,* 883–903; and Lionel Trilling, *"Little Dorrit," Kenyon Review* 15 (1953): 579.

9. Dabney, 115.

10. Miller, 226.

11. Smith, 142.

12. Dabney, 114.

13. Ibid., 122.

14. He is identified as Saint Peter in Grahame Smith and Angela Smith, 138; and as Saint

Paul in Alexander Welsh, *The City of Dickens*, 66.

15. Harvey Peter Sucksmith, "Dickens and the Pre-Raphaelites: Mr. Merdle and Holman Hunt's 'The Light of the World,'" *The Dickensian* 72 (September 1976): 159.

16. John Wain, *"Little Dorrit,"* in *Dickens and the Twentieth Century*, ed. John Gross and Gabriel Pearson (Toronto: University of Toronto Press, 1962), 186.

17. Dabney, 121.

18. Miller, 277.

19. Robert Lee Wolff, "The Way Things Were," *Harvard Magazine* 77 (March 1975): 47.

20. Ibid., 48.

21. Ibid.

22. J. A. Banks, "The Way They Lived Then: Anthony Trollope and the 1870's," *Victorian Studies* 12 (December 1968): 183.

23. Michael Sadleir, *Trollope: A Commentary* (London: Constable and Co., 1945), 399.

24. Anthony Trollope, *The Way We Live Now*, The World's Classics (London: Oxford University Press, 1941), vol. 1, p. 31. Further references will appear in the text as *WWLN*.

25. Nathan, 265.

26. Banks, 184–85.

27. "Mr. Hudson," *Fraser's Magazine*, 215.

28. Roger L. Slakey, "Melmotte's Death: A Prism of Meaning in *The Way We Live Now*," *ELH* 34 (1967): 250.

29. Kermode, 82.

30. H. G. Wells, *Tono-Bungay*, (New York: Modern Library, 1931), 5. Further references will appear in the text as *TB*.

Appendix

1. Foster, 13.

2. Duffy, 330–31. For further discussion of the problems of interpreting bankruptcy statistics, and a description of the bankruptcy records stored in the Public Records Office, see Sheila Marriner, "English Bankruptcy Records and Statistics before 1850," *The Economic History Review* 33, series 2 (August 1980): 351–66.

Bibliography

PARLIAMENTARY SOURCES

British Parliamentary Papers

Report of the Commissioners for Inquiring into Bankruptcy and Insolvency. (1840) 16, no. 274.

Return of the Bankrupts and Insolvent Debtors in each Year between 1801 and 1819, and 1820 and 1846. (1847–48) 51, no. 120.

Report from the Lord's Select Committee on the Bankruptcy Consolidation Bill. (1849) 8, no. 372.

House of Commons: Report from the Select Committee on the Bankruptcy Law Consolidation Bill. (1849) 8, no. 551.

Report from the Select Committee on the Law of Partnerships. (1851) 18, no. 509.

Minutes of Evidence Taken Before the Select Committee of The House of Lords, Appointed to Consider of the Bankruptcy Bill. (1852–53) 22, no. 659.

Report of Her Majesty's Commissioners Appointed to Inquire into Fees, Funds, and Establishments of the Court of Bankruptcy, and the Operation of the Bankrupt Law Consolidation Act, 1849. (1854) 23, no. 1770.

Returns from the Accountant in Bankruptcy. (1857–58) 47, no. 189.

A Return of the Number of Applications for Bankrupts Certificates Heard Before Each Commissioner during each of the last Five Years. (1859) 22, no. 52.

Court of Bankruptcy Proceedings of the London and District Court, in the year 1858. (1859) 26, p. 545.

Proceedings of the Court of Bankruptcy, 1861. (1862) 56, p. 685.

Report from the Select Committee to Inquire into the Working of the New Bankruptcy Act. (1864) 5. no. 512.

General Returns by the Chief Registrar of the Court of Bankruptcy, 1862 and 1863. (1864) 48, p. 303.

General Return for the Year 1864 of All Matters Judicial and Financial within the Bankruptcy Act, 1861. (1865) 65, p. 1.

Proceedings for the Court of Bankruptcy for 1865. (1866) 68, p. 681.

General Return for the Year 1866 by the Chief Registrar of the Court of Bankruptcy. (1867) 57, p. 33.

General Return for the Year 1867 by the Chief Registrar of the Court of Bankruptcy. (1867–68) 57, p. 1.

General Return for the Year 1868 by the Chief Registrar of the Court of Bankruptcy. (1868–69) 51, p. 89.

General Return for the Year 1869 by the Chief Registrar of the Court of Bankruptcy. (1870) 57, p. 5.

General Report by the Comptroller in Bankruptcy for the Year 1870. (1871) 58, no. 210.

General Report by the Comptroller in Bankruptcy for the Year 1871. (1872) 50, no. 237.

General Report by the Comptroller in Bankruptcy for the Year 1872. (1873) 54, no. 251.

General Report by the Comptroller in Bankruptcy for the Year 1873. (1874) 54, no. 68.

General Report by the Comptroller in Bankruptcy for the Year 1874. (1875) 61, no. 272.

General Report by the Comptroller in Bankruptcy for the Year 1875. (1876) 61, no. 210.

Report to the Lord Chancellor of a Committee appointed to consider the working of the Bankruptcy Act, 1869. (1877) 69, no. 152.

General Report by the Comptroller in Bankruptcy for the Year 1876. (1877) 69, no. 314.

Hansard's Parliamentary Debates

Commons, vol. 7 (1806), col. 839; Commons, vol. 12 (1809), cols. 832 and 1141; Lords, vol. 28 (1814), col. 797; Commons, vol. 36 (1817), col. 820; Commons, vol. 38 (1818), col. 981; Commons, vol. 39 (1819), col. 1380; *New Series:* Commons, vol. 10 (1824), col. 213; Commons, vol. 24 (1830), col. 227; *Third Series:* Lords, vol. 7 (1831), col. 495; Commons, vol. 7, (1831), cols. 654, 725, 781, and 901; Commons, vol. 56, (1841), col. 481; Lords, vol. 75 (1844), col. 1175; Lords, vol. 76 (1844), col. 1398; Commons, vol. 76 (1844), col. 1706; Commons, vol. 88 (1846), col. 345; Lords, vol. 92 (1847), col. 256; Lords, vol. 100 (1848), col 565; Commons, vol. 100 (1848), col. 1270; Lords, vol. 105 (1849), col. 1139; Commons, vol. 107 (1849), 995; Commons, vol. 114 (1851), col. 842; Lords, vol. 118 (1851), col. 129; Commons, vol. 119 (1852), col. 172; Commons, vol. 134 (1854), col. 752; Commons, vol. 139 (1855), col. 1378; Lords, vol. 147 (1857), col. 333; Lords, col. 148 (1858), col. 1592; Lords, vol. 151 (1858), cols. 220 and 2295; Commons, vol. 157 (1860), col. 649; Commons, vol. 159 (1860), cols. 1995 and 2156; Commons, vol. 161 (1861), col. 719; Lords, vol. 162 (1861), col. 623; Commons, vol. 164 (1861), col. 1590; Commons, vol. 174 (1864), vol. 680; Commons, vol. 177 (1865), cols. 93 and 120; Commons, vol. 183 (1866), col. 673; Commons, vol. 185 (1867), col. 1867; Commons, vol. 187 (1867), cols. 1556 and 1765; Lords, col. 191 (1868), col. 1; Commons, vol. 191 (1868), col. 265; Commons, vol. 194 (1869), col. 776; Commons, vol. 195 (1869), col. 142; and Commons, vol. 196 (1869), cols. 1211, 1402, and 1897.

PRIMARY SOURCES AND CRITICISM

Altick, Richard D. "*Dombey and Son* and Its Readers." *The Yearbook in English Studies* 10 (1980): 70–94.

———. *The English Common Reader: A Social History of the Mass Reading Public, 1860–1900.* Chicago: University of Chicago Press, 1957.

Amsler, Christine E., Robin Bartlett, and Craig J. Bolton. "Thoughts of Some British Economists on Early Limited Liability and Corporate Legislation." *History of Political Economy* 13 (Winter 1981): 774–93.

"Anomalies of the Bankruptcy System." *The Banker's Magazine* 13 (September 1853): 609–15.

Ashton, T. S. *Economic Fluctuation in England, 1700–1800.* Oxford, Clarendon Press, 1959.

———. *An Economic History of England: The Eighteenth Century.* London: Methuen and Co., 1955.

Auerbach, Nina. "Old Maids and The Wish for Wings." In *Perspectives on Nineteenth-Century Heroism,* edited by David C. Leonard. Essays from the 1981 Conference of the Southeastern Nineteenth-Century Studies Association. Madrid: Porrua Turanzas, 1982.

Axton, William F. *Circle of Fire: Dickens' Vision and Style and the Popular Victorian Theater.* Lexington: University of Kentucky Press, 1966.

Aytoun, W. E. "How We Got Up the Glenmutchkin Railway, and How We Got Out Of It." *Blackwood's Magazine* 58 (October 1845): 453–66.

Bailey, J. O., ed. *British Plays of the Nineteenth Century.* New York: Odyssey Press, 1966.

"Bankruptcy Administration." *The Banker's Magazine* 14 (October 1854): 541–45.

"Bankruptcy Analysis." *British Almanac of the Society for the Diffusion of Useful Knowledge.* London: Charles Knight, 1831–50.

"Bankruptcy and Insolvency." *Westminster Review* 46 (1846): 500–16.

"Bankruptcy Bill, The." *The Banker's Magazine* 38 (June 1878): 457–64.

"Bankruptcy Law Reform." *Banker's Magazine and Journal of the Money Market* 9 (June 1849): 322–26.

"Bankruptcy Laws and Mercantile Corruption, The" *Fraser's Magazine* 99 (April 1879): 428–37.

"Bankruptcy Reform." *The Banker's Magazine* 14 (June 1854): 289–96.

Banks, J. A. "The Way They Lived Then: Anthony Trollope and the 1870's." *Victorian Studies* 12 (December 1968): 177–200.

Bayne, William. *Sir David Wilkie, R.A.* New York: Charles Scribner's Sons, 1903.

Blom, J. M. "The English 'Social Problem' Novel: Fruitful Concept or Critical Evasion?" *English Studies* 62 (April 1981): 120–27.

Blom, M. A. "Charlotte Brontë, Feminist Manquée." *Bucknell Review* 21 (Spring 1973): 87–102.

Booth, Michael R. *English Melodrama*. London: Herbert Jenkins, 1965.

———. "The Metropolis on Stage." In *The Victorian City: Images and Realities,* edited by H. J. Dyos and Michael Wolff, vol. 1. London: Routledge and Kegan Paul, 1973.

Booth, Michael R., ed. *The Magistrate and Other Nineteenth Century Plays.* London: Oxford University Press, 1974.

Boucicault, Dion. *The Colleen Bawn.* In *Nineteenth Century Plays,* edited by George Rowell. London: Oxford University Press, 1953.

———. *London Assurance.* In *Representative British Drama,* edited by Montrose J. Moses. Boston: Little, Brown and Co., 1931.

———. *Mercy Dodd; or Presumptive Evidence.* In *Forbidden Fruit and Other Plays,* edited by Allardyce Nicoll and F. Theodore Cloak. Princeton: Princeton University Press, 1940.

———. *The School for Scheming.* In *Forbidden Fruit and Other Plays,* edited by Allardyce Nicoll and F. Theodore Cloak. Princeton: Princeton University Press, 1940.

Brontë, Charlotte. *Shirley.* Edited by Andrew Hook and Judith Hook. Harmondsworth: Penguin Books, 1975.

Buckley, Jerome Hamilton. *The Victorian Temper: A Study in Literary Culture.* Cambridge: Harvard University Press, 1951.

Buckstone, John Baldwin. *Luke the Labourer.* In *British Plays of the Nineteenth Century,* edited by J. O. Bailey. New York: Odyssey Press, 1966.

Bushnell, John P. "Maggie Tulliver's 'Stored-Up Force': A Re-reading of *The Mill on the Floss.*" *Studies in the Novel* 16 (Winter 1984): 378–95.

Butt, John and Kathleen Tillotson. *Dickens at Work.* London: Methuen and Co., 1957.

Campbell, Ian. "Mrs. Gaskell's *North and South* and the Art of the Possible." *Dickens Studies Annual* 8:231–50.

Carlyle, Thomas. *Chartism.* In *Critical and Miscellaneous Essays.* Vol. 17, *Thomas Carlyle's Works.* The Ashburton Edition. London: Chapman and Hall, 1883.

———. *The French Revolution: A History.* Vol. 2, *The Works of Thomas Carlyle.* Centenary Edition. London: Chapman and Hall, 1898.

———. "Hudson's Statue." In *Latter Day Pamphlets.* Vol. 20, *The Works of Thomas Carlyle.* Centenary Edition. London: Chapman and Hall, 1898.

———. *Past and Present.* London: Oxford University Press, 1960.

———. "Shooting Niagara: and After!" In *Critical and Miscellaneous Essays.* Vol. 17, *Thomas Carlyle's Works.* Ashburton Edition. London: Chapman and Hall, 1883.

Catalogue. Paris: Galerie Sedelmyer, 12–14 June, 1907: 80–84.

Century of Law Reform, A: Twelve Lectures on the Changes in the Law of England During the Nineteenth Century. London: 1901. Reprint. South Hackensack, N.J.: Rothman Reprints, 1972.

Chesterton, G. K. *Charles Dickens: A Critical Study.* 1906. Reprint. New York: Dodd Mead, 1951.

Church, R. A. *The Great Victorian Boom, 1850–1873.* London: Macmillan, 1971.

Clipper, Lawrence J. "The Blacking Warehouse Experience Again: Another View." *Dickens Studies Newsletter* 12 (September 1981): 77–80.

Coleman, George. *John Bull, or The Englishman's Fireside.* In *The Magistrate and Other Nineteenth Century Plays,* edited by Michael R. Booth. London: Oxford University Press, 1974.

Cross, Gilbert B. *Next Week—East Lynne: Domestic Drama in Performance, 1820–1874.* Lewisburg, Pa.: Bucknell University Press, 1977.

Dabney, Ross. *Love and Property in the Novels of Dickens.* Berkeley and Los Angeles: University of California Press, 1967.

Dalziel, Margaret. *Popular Fiction, 100 Years Ago: An Unexplored Tract of Literary History.* London: Cohen and West, 1957.

Dickens, Charles. *Dombey and Son.* Edited by Alan Horsman, The Clarendon Dickens. Oxford: The Clarendon Press, 1974.

———. *Little Dorrit.* Edited by Harvey Peter Sucksmith, The Clarendon Dickens. Oxford: The Clarendon Press, 1979.

———. *Sketches by Boz.* New Oxford Illustrated Dickens. London: Oxford University Press, 1957.

Disher, Maurice Wilson. *Blood and Thunder: Mid-Victorian Melodrama and Its Origins.* London: Frederick Muller, 1949.

Duffy, Ian. "Bankruptcy and Insolvency in London in the Late Eighteenth and Early Nineteenth Century." Diss., Oxford University, 1973.

Eden, Emily. *The Semi-Attached Couple* and *The Semi-Detached House.* New York: Dial Press, 1979.

Eliot, George. *Middlemarch.* Edited by Gordon S. Haight, Riverside Editions. Boston: Houghton Mifflin, 1956.

———. *The Mill on the Floss.* Edited by Gordon S. Haight, Riverside Editions. Boston: Houghton Mifflin, 1961.

Engel, Monroe. *The Maturity of Dickens.* Cambridge: Harvard University Press, 1959.

Evans, David Morier. *The Commercial Crisis, 1847–1848.* 1848. Reprint. New York: Burt Franklin, 1970.

———. *Facts, Failures, and Frauds: Revelations, Financial, Mercantile, Criminal.* London: Groombridge and Sons, 1859.

Feltes, N. N. "Community and the Limits of Liability in Two Mid-Victorian Novels." *Victorian Studies* 17 (June 1974): 355–69.

Ferris, Ina. "Realism and the Discord of Ending: The Example of Thackeray." *Nineteenth Century Fiction* 38 (December 1983): 289–303.

Foster, Thomas. *A Letter Addressed to the Right Hon. The Earl Gray, First Lord of His Majesty's Treasury on the Subject of Our Commercial Laws In So Far As They Relate to Bankrupts and Insolvents.* London: Bentley, 1831.

Frith, William Powell. *My Autobiography and Reminiscences.* London: Richard Bentley and Sons, 1887.

Gallagher, Catherine. "*Hard Times* and *North and South:* The Family and Society in Two Industrial Novels." *The Arizona Quarterly* 36 (Spring 1980): 70–96.

Gaskell, Elizabeth. *North and South.* Edited by Angus Easson, Oxford English Novels. London: Oxford University Press, 1973.

Gayer, Arthur D., W. W. Rostow, and H. J. Schwartz. *The Growth and Fluctuation of the British Economy, 1790–1850,* vol. 2. Oxford: Clarendon Press, 1953.

Gazette of Bankruptcy, The, vol. 1. London: Chief Office, Lincoln's Inn, W. C., 1862.

"George Cruikshank." Catalogue. London: Victoria and Albert, 1974.

Gerin, Winifred. *Charlotte Brontë: The Evolution of Genius.* London: Oxford University Press, 1967.

Giddens, Anthony. *Capitalism and Modern Social Theory: An Analysis of the Writings of Marx, Durkheim, and Weber.* London: Cambridge University Press, 1971.

Gill, Stephen. "Price's Patent Candles: New Light on *North and South.*" *Review of English Studies* 27 (1976): 313–21.

Gilmour, Robin. "Dickens and the Self-Help Idea." In *The Victorians and Social Progress,* edited by J. Butt and J. F. Clarke. London: David and Charles, 1973.

Green, Robert W. *Protestantism, Capitalism, and Social Science: The Weber Thesis Controversy.* Lexington, Mass.: D. C. Heath, 1973.

Gregg, Pauline. *A Social and Economic History of Britain, 1760–1970,* 6th ed. London: George G. Harrap, 1971.

Griest, Guinevere L. *Mudie's Circulating Library and the Victorian Novel.* Bloomington: Indiana University Press, 1970.

Hardy, Barbara. *The Exposure of Luxury: Radical Themes in Thackeray.* London: Peter Owen, 1972.

Harrison, J. F. C. "The Victorian Gospel of Success." *Victorian Studies* 1 (December 1957): 155–64.

Harvey, J. R. *Victorian Novelists and Their Illustrators.* New York: New York University Press, 1971.

Heaton, H. "Financing the Industrial Revolution." *Bulletin of the Business Historical Society* 11 (February 1937): 1–10.

Heilman, Robert. "Charlotte Brontë's 'New' Gothic." In *The Victorian Novel: Modern Essays in Criticism,* edited by Ian Watt. London: Oxford University Press, 1971.

Hill, Christopher. "Protestantism and the Rise of Capitalism." In *The Rise of Capitalism,* edited by David S. Landes. New York: Macmillan, 1966.

Hobsbawm, E. J. *Industry and Empire: The Making of Modern English Society,* vol. 2, 1750 to the Present Day. New York: Random House, 1968.

Holdsworth, W. S. *A History of English Law,* vol. 3. London: Methuen and Co., 1903.

"In Difficulties, Three Stages." *All The Year Round* 18 (20 July 1867); 18 (27 July 1867); and 18 (3 August 1867).

Jenks, Edward. *A Short History of the English Law.* London: Methuen, 1912.

Jenks, Leland H. *The Migration of British Capital to 1875.* New York: Thomas Nelson and Sons, 1927.

Jerrold, Douglas. *Black-Ey'd Susan.* In *Nineteenth Century Plays,* edited by George Rowell. London: Oxford University Press, 1953.

————. *The Rent Day.* In *British Plays of the Nineteenth Century,* edited by J. O. Bailey. New York: Odyssey Press, 1966.

Johnson, Edgar. *Charles Dickens: His Tragedy and His Triumph.* 2 vols. New York: Simon and Schuster, 1952.

Kermode, Frank. *The Sense of an Ending.* London: Oxford University Press, 1967.

Kestner, Joseph. "Men in Female Condition of England Novels." In *Men by Women,* edited by Janet Todd. *Women and Literature* 2, new series (New York: Holmes and Meier, 1982): 77–99.

Landes, David S., ed. *The Rise of Capitalism.* New York: Macmillan, 1966.

————. *The Unbound Prometheus.* Cambridge: Cambridge University Press, 1969.

"Law of Bankruptcy, The." *Westminster Review* 52 (1849): 419–35.

Lawrence, Slingsby, pseud. [George Henry Lewes] *The Game of Speculation.* In *Lacy's Acting Edition of Plays, Dramas, Farces, and Extravagances,* vol 5, edited by Thomas Hailes Lacy. London: 1848–1904.

Lerner, Lawrence. "Literature and Money." *Essays and Studies* 28 London: John Murray, 1975.

"Limited Liability." *Chamber's Journal* 24 (1855): 196–99.

Lister, Raymond. *Victorian Narrative Paintings.* London: Museum Press, 1966.

Lucas, John. "Dickens and *Dombey and Son:* Past and Present Imperfect." In *Tradition and Tolerance in Nineteenth Century Fiction: Critical Essays on Some English and American Novels,* edited by David Howard, John Lucas, and John Goode. London: Routledge and Kegan Paul, 1966.

————. "Mrs. Gaskell and Brotherhood." In *Tradition and Tolerance in Nineteenth Century Fiction: Critical Essays on Some English and American Novels,* edited by David Howard, John Lucas, and John Goode. London: Routledge and Kegan Paul, 1966.

Maas, Jeremy. *Victorian Paintings.* New York: G. P. Putnam's Sons, 1969.

MacMasters, Juliet. *Thackeray: The Major Novels.* Toronto: University of Toronto Press, 1971.

Marcus, Steven. *Dickens: from Pickwick to Dombey.* New York: Simon and Schuster, 1965.

————. *The Other Victorians: A Study of Sexuality and Pornography in Mid-Nineteenth Century England.* New York: Basic Books, 1964.

Marriner, Sheila. "English Bankruptcy Records and Statistics Before 1850." *The Economic History Review* (series 2) 33 (August 1980): 351–66.

Marshall, Gordon. *In Search of the Spirit of Capitalism: An Essay on Max Weber's Protestant Ethic Theory.* New York: Columbia University Press, 1982.

Martin, Carol A. "Gaskell, Darwin, and *North and South.*" *Studies in the Novel* 15 (Summer 1983): 91–107.

————. "No Angel in The House: Victorian Mothers and Daughters in George Eliot and Elizabeth Gaskell." *Midwest Quarterly* 24 (Spring 1983): 297–314.

Mathias, Peter. *The First Industrial Nation.* London: Methuen and Co., 1969.

Meisel, Martin. "The Ending of *Great Expectations.*" *Essays in Criticism* 15 (July 1965): 326–31.

Melada, Ivan. *The Captain of Industry in English Fiction, 1821–1871.* Albuquerque: University of New Mexico Press, 1970.

Mill, John Stuart. *Principles of Political Economy.* Vol. 3, *The Collected Works.* Toronto: University of Toronto Press, 1965.

Miller, J. Hillis. *Charles Dickens: The World of His Novels.* Cambridge: Harvard University Press, 1958.

"Mr. Hudson." *Fraser's Magazine* 36 (August 1847): 215–22.

Moses, Montrose J., ed. *Representative British Dramas.* Boston: Little, Brown, 1931.

Mott, Graham. "Was There a Stain Upon Little Dorrit?" *The Dickensian* 76 (Spring 1980): 31–36.

Moynahan, Julian. "Dealings with the Firm of Dombey and Son: Firmness versus Wetness." In *Dickens and the Twentieth Century,* edited by John Gross and Gabriel Pearson. Toronto: University of Toronto Press, 1962.

Muir, Edwin. *The Structure of the Novel.* New York: Harcourt, Brace and Ward, 1969.

Nathan, Sabine. "Anthony Trollope's Perception of The Way We Live Now." *Zeitschrift für Anglistik und Amerikanistik* 10 (Jahrung 1962): 259–78.

"New Bankruptcy Bill, The." *The Banker's Magazine* 37 (June 1877): 445–51.

Nisbet, Robert A. *Sociology as an Art Form.* London: Oxford University Press, 1976.

————. *The Sociology of Emile Durkheim.* London: Oxford University Press, 1974.

Noakes, Aubrey. *William Frith, Extraordinary Victorian Painter: A Biographical and Critical Essay.* London: Jupiter, 1978.

Norman, Hilde Laura. *Swindlers and Rogues in French Drama.* Chicago: University of Chicago Press, 1928.

"Observations on Credit." *Pamphleteer* 13 (1819): 359–67.

Paroissien, David. "Release from the Marshalsea and Warren's: A Rejoinder." *Dickens Studies Newsletter* 13 (September 1982): 71–74.

Pike, E. Royston. *Golden Times: Human Documents of the Victorian Age.* New York: Frederick A. Praeger, 1967.

Pikoulis, John. "*North and South:* Varieties of Love and Power." *Yearbook of English Studies* 6 (1976): 176–93.

Pocock, Isaac. *The Miller and His Men.* In *The Magistrate and Other Nineteenth*

Century Plays, edited by Michael R. Booth. London: Oxford University Press, 1974.

Pool, G. P. and A. G. Pool. *A Hundred Years of Economic Development in Great Britain.* London: Gerald Ducksworth, 1940.

Praz, Mario. *The Hero in Eclipse in Victorian Fiction.* Translated by Angus Davidson. London: Oxford University Press, 1956.

Prize Essays: Bankruptcy Legislation and Defaulters in the Legal Profession. London: Joseph Causton and Sons, 1879.

Pugin, A. W. N. *Contrasts.* 1836. Reprint. New York: Humanities Press, 1969.

Ray, Gordon. *Thackeray: The Age of Wisdom, 1847–63.* New York: McGraw-Hill, 1958.

———. *Thackeray: The Uses of Adversity, 1811–1846.* New York: McGraw-Hill, 1955.

Reed, John R. *Victorian Conventions.* Athens: Ohio University Press, 1975.

"Report of the Comptroller in Bankruptcy, The." *The Banker's Magazine* 37 (July 1877): 537–44.

Reynolds, Graham. *Painters of the Victorian Scene.* London: B. T. Batesford, 1953.

———. *Victorian Painting.* London: Studio Vista, 1966.

"Rich and Poor Bankrupts." *All The Year Round* 19 (May 16, 1868).

Roscoe, Edward Stanley. *The Growth of English Law: Being Studies in the Evolution of Law and Procedure in England.* London: Stevens, 1911.

Round, Herbert T. "First Prize Essay." *Prize Essays: Bankruptcy Legislation and Defaulters in the Legal Profession.* London: Joseph Causton, 1879.

Rowell, George, ed. *Nineteenth Century Plays.* London: Oxford University Press, 1953.

Rubinius, Aina. *The Woman Question in Mrs. Gaskell's Life and Works.* Cambridge: Harvard University Press, 1950.

Sadleir, Michael. *Trollope: A Commentary.* London: Constable and Co., 1945.

Shannon, H. A. "The Coming of General Limited Liability." *Economic History* 2 (January 1931): 267–91.

Shapiro, Arnold. "Public Themes and Private Lives: Social Criticism in *Shirley.*" *Papers on Language and Literature* 5 (Winter 1968): 74–84.

Simmel, Georg. *Philosophie des Geldes.* 1907. Reprint. *The Philosophy of Money.* Translated by Tom Bottomore and David Frisby. London: Routledge and Kegan Paul, 1978.

Slakey, Roger L. "Melmotte's Death: A Prism of Meaning in *The Way We Live Now.*" *English Literary History* 34 (1967): 248–59.

Smiles, Samuel. *Self-Help.* 1859. Reprint. Introduction by Asa Briggs. London: John Murray, 1969.

———. *Thrift.* New York: Harper Brothers, 1875.

Smith, Grahame and Angela Smith. "Dickens as a Popular Artist." *The Dickensian* 67 (September 1971): 131–44.

"Statistics of Failures in the United Kingdom." *The Banker's Magazine* 38 (February 1878): 106–8.

Steig, Michael. "*Dombey and Son* and the Railway Panic of 1845." *The Dickensian* 67 (September 1971): 145–48.

―――. "Structure and the Grotesque in Dickens: *Dombey and Son; Bleak House*." *The Centennial Review* 14 (1970): 313–25.

Sucksmith, Harvey Peter. "Dickens and the Pre-Raphaelites: Mr. Merdle and Holman Hunt's 'The Light of The World.' " *The Dickensian* 27 (September 1976): 159–63.

Sudrann, Jean. "The Philosopher's Property: Thackeray and The Use of Time." *Victorian Studies* 10 (June 1967): 359–88.

Sutherland, John A. "Trollope at Work on *The Way We Live Now*." *Nineteenth Century Fiction* 37 (December 1982): 472–93.

Talon, Henri. "*Dombey and Son:* A Closer Look at the Text." *Dickens Studies Annual* 1 (1970): 147–60.

Taylor, Tom. *Our American Cousin*. In *British Plays of the Nineteenth Century*, edited by J. O. Bailey. New York: Odyssey Press, 1966.

―――. *Payable on Demand*. In *Lacy's Acting Edition of Plays, Dramas, Farces, and Extravagances*, vol. 41, edited by Thomas Hailes Lacy. London: 1848–1904.

―――. *The Settling Day*. In *Lacy's Acting Edition of Plays, Dramas, Farces, and Extravagances*, vol. 76, edited by Thomas Hailes Lacy. London: 1848–1904.

―――. *Still Waters Run Deep*. Chicago: The Dramatic Publishing Co., n.d.

Tennyson, Alfred Lord. *The Poems of Tennyson*. Edited by Christopher Ricks. Annotated English Poets. London: Longman, 1969.

Thackeray, William Makepeace. *The Newcomes: Memoirs of a Most Respectable Family, edited by Arthur Pendennis, Esq.* Vol. 8 of 13 vols., The Biographical Edition. New York: Harper, 1899.

―――. *Vanity Fair: A Novel Without a Hero*. Edited by Geoffrey Tillotson and Kathleen Tillotson. Riverside Editions. Boston: Houghton Mifflin, 1963.

Thomas, Deborah A. "Dickens and Indigestion: The Deadly Dinners of the Rich." *Dickens Studies Newsletter* 14 (March 1983): 7–12.

Thompson, J. H. *The Principles of Bankruptcy Law*. London: H. F. L. Publishers, 1967.

Tillotson, Kathleen. *Novels of the Eighteen Forties*. 1954. Reprint. Oxford: Oxford University Press, 1961.

Times (London). Bankruptcy Notices (5 Jan. 1831): 2; (6 June 1849): 2; and (18 Aug. 1858):6.

Times (London). Untitled articles (27 Sept. 1831): 2; (27 Oct. 1840): 4; (2 Nov. 1840): 4; (17 Nov. 1840): 4; (20 Nov. 1840): 4; (23 Nov. 1840): 4; (28 Nov. 1840): 4; (3 Dec. 1840): 4; (10 Aug. 1842): 4; (15 July 1847): 4; (10 Apr. 1849): 5; (1 May 1849): 4; (10 May 1849): 5; (21 May 1849): 4; (7 July 1849): 5; (29 Oct. 1855): 6; (18 Feb. 1856): 12; (26 Feb. 1856): 9; (25 July 1856): 8; (18 Sept. 1856): 8; (23 Sept. 1856): 6; (24 Sept. 1856): 6; (6 Oct. 1856): 8; (8 Oct. 1856): 6; (16 Feb. 1857): 6; (6 Mar. 1857): 7; (13 Mar. 1857): 9; (16 Mar. 1857): 7; (22 July 1857): 9; (15 Dec. 1857): 9; (1 Mar. 1858): 8; (20 Jan. 1859): 8; (16 Feb. 1859): 8; (17 Feb. 1859): 8; (24 Nov. 1859): 8; (22 Mar. 1861): 8; (7 June 1861): 8; (20 June 1861): 8; (11 Jan.

1865): 8; (12 May 1866): 9; (16 Mar. 1867): 9; (5 June 1867): 8; (10 June 1867): 8; and (6 Apr. 1869): 9.

Tomkins, J. M. S. *The Popular Novel in England, 1770–1800.* London: Constable and Co., 1932.

Trilling, Lionel. *"Little Dorrit." Kenyon Review* 15 (1953): 577–90.

Trollope, Anthony. *The Three Clerks.* New York: Dover, 1981.

———. *The Way We Live Now.* The World's Classics. London: Oxford University Press, 1941.

Turner, John Kenneth. *Challenge to Karl Marx.* New York: Reynal and Hitchcock, 1941.

"Urgent Need for Amending Our Bankruptcy Legislation, The." *The Fortnightly Review* 31 (March 1879): 469–85.

Vernon, John. *Money and Fiction: Literary Realism in the Nineteenth and Early Twentieth Centuries.* Ithaca: Cornell University Press, 1984.

Viner, Jacob. *Religious Thought and Economic Society.* Edited by Jacques Melitz and Donald Winch. Durham, N.C.: Duke University Press, 1978.

Wain, John. *"Little Dorrit."* In *Dickens and the Twentieth Century,* edited by John Gross and Gabriel Pearson. Toronto: University of Toronto Press, 1962.

Wasserman, Renata R. Maunter. "Narrative Logic and the Form of Tradition in *The Mill on the Floss." Studies in the Novel* 14 (Fall 1982): 266–79.

Welbourne, E. "Bankruptcy Before the Era of Victorian Reform." *The Cambridge Historical Journal* 4 (1932): 51–62.

Wells, H. G. *Tono-Bungay.* New York: Modern Library, 1931.

Welsh, Alexander. *The City of Dickens.* Oxford: The Clarendon Press, 1971.

———. Introduction to *Thackeray: A Collection of Critical Essays.* Englewood Cliffs, N.J.: Prentice-Hall, 1968.

Wilson, Angus. "The Heroes and Heroines of Dickens." In *Dickens and the Twentieth Century,* edited by John Gross and Gabriel Pearson. Toronto: University of Toronto Press, 1962.

Wilson, F. A. C. "The Primrose Wreath: The Heroes of the Brontë Novels." *Nineteenth Century Fiction* 29 (June 1974): 40–57.

Wilson, Sir Roland Knyvet. *History of Modern English Law.* London: Rivingtons, 1875.

Wolff, Robert Lee. "The Way Things Were." *Harvard Magazine* 77 (March 1975): 44–50.

Index

Barbara Weiss received her doctorate in English literature from Columbia University in 1981. She has taught literature and writing courses at Fairleigh Dickinson University, Columbia University, and Manhattanville College and has written articles on the economic issues in Victorian literature. She has also written about the treatment of women in the Victorian novel and about female Victorian novelists. She is currently working for a publishing firm.